WALT DISNEY WORLD®

with Kids

2004

KIM WRIGHT WILEY

Fourteenth Edition

Fodor's

To my children,
Leigh and Jordan,
the best ride-testers in the business.

Published by Fodor's Travel Publications, a unit of Fodors LLC
Fodor's is a registered trademark of Random House, Inc.
www.fodors.com

Every effort has been made to make this book complete and accurate as of the date of publication. In a time of rapid change, however, it is difficult to ensure that all information is entirely up-to-date. Although the publisher and authors cannot be liable for any inaccuracies or omissions in this book, they are always grateful for corrections and suggestions for improvement.

All products mentioned in this book are trademarks of their respective companies.

Previously published by Prima Publishing.

Fourteenth Edition

ISBN 0-7615-2628-5
ISSN 1083-2424

Printed in the United States of America
10 9 8 7 6 5 4 3 2 1

Contents

Chapter 3 Once You Get There 87

Chapter 4 Touring Tips and Plans 115

Chapter 5 The Magic Kingdom 139

Chapter 6 Epcot   183

HELPFUL PHONE NUMBERS

All Orlando numbers have a 407 area code. Be sure to make all resort reservations through the W-DISNEY (934-7639) number and use the resort's direct line only to call Guest Services, to call the child-care centers, or to reach a registered guest.

General Disney World Information	824-4321
Florida Relay Service	TDD/TDY 800-955-8771
Voice	800-955-8770
General Accommodation Information	W-DISNEY (934-7639)
Priority Seating	WDW-DINE (939-3463)
ABC Mothers	857-7447
Alamo Car Rental	800-462-5266
All-Star Movies Resort	939-7000
All-Star Music Resort	939-6000
All-Star Sports Resort	939-5000
American Airlines	800-321-2121
Animal Kingdom Lodge	938-3000
Avis Car Rental	800-331-1212
Beach Club Resort	934-8000
Beach Club Villas	934-2175
BoardWalk Resort	939-5100
BoardWalk Villas	939-5100
Camp Sea World	800-406-2244/363-2380
Caribbean Beach Resort	934-3400
Contemporary Resort	824-1000
Coronado Springs Resort	939-1000
Delta Airlines	800-872-7786
Delta Orlando Resort	800-776-3358/351-3340
Discovery Cove	351-3600
Disney Club Reservations	824-2600
Disney Cruise Line	800-951-3532
Disney Travel Company	800-828-0228
Dollar Car Rental	800-800-4000
Dolphin Resort	934-4000
Embassy Suites	800-EMBASSY (362-2779)
Fort Wilderness Campground	824-2900

Gatorland	800-393-JAWS/855-5496
Golf Information	WDW-GOLF (939-4653)
Grand Floridian Resort	824-3000
Hertz Car Rental	800-654-3131
Hilton Disney Village	800-782-4414/827-4000
Holiday Inn Sunspree	800-HOLIDAY/239-4500
Hyatt Grand Cypress	800-233-1234/239-1234
Islands of Adventure	363-8000
Kennedy Space Center	321-452-2121
Kids' Night Out	827-5444
Mears Shuttle Service	423-5566
National Car Rental	800-227-7368
Old Key West Resort	827-7700
Orlando Science Center	896-7151
Orlando Visitor's Bureau	800-255-5786
Pleasure Island	934-7781
Polynesian Resort	824-2000
Port Orleans Resort	934-5000/6000
River Country	824-2760
Sea World Information	351-3600
Sports Information	824-2621
Super Sitters	382-2558
Swan Resort	934-3000
Tennis Information	WDW-PLAY (939-7529)
TicketMaster	839-3900
Tour Information	939-TOUR (939-8687)
Typhoon Lagoon	560-4141
Universal Studios	888-U ESCAPE (837-2273)
USAir	800-455-0123
Wet 'n Wild	800-992-WILD/351-9453
Wide World of Sports	828-3267
Wilderness Lodge	938-4300
Wilderness Lodge Villas	824-3200
Yacht Club	934-7000

HELPFUL WEB SITES

LIST OF MAPS

LIST OF QUICK GUIDE REFERENCE TABLES

ABBREVIATIONS, TERMS, AND ICONS

Abbreviations and Terms

AK	Animal Kingdom
Downtown Disney	A shopping, dining, and entertainment complex composed of Pleasure Island, the Marketplace, and the West Side
MGM	The Disney-MGM Studios Theme Park
MK	Magic Kingdom
Minor parks	Typhoon Lagoon, River Country, Pleasure Island, and Blizzard Beach
Major parks	The Magic Kingdom, Epcot, Disney-MGM Studios, and Animal Kingdom
Off-season	The less crowded times of the year—specifically those weeks between September and May that do not flank major holidays
On-season	The most crowded times of the year—specifically summers, holidays, and spring break
Off-site	Any resort or hotel not owned by Disney
On-site	A Disney-owned resort
TTC	Ticket and Transportation Center: The monorail version of a train station, where riders can transfer to monorails bound for Epcot, the Magic Kingdom, or monorail-line hotels. You can also catch buses at the TTC bound for the parks, the on-site hotels, and Downtown Disney.
WDW	Walt Disney World

Icons

 Helpful Hint

 Hidden Mickey

 Insider's Secret

 Money-Saving Tip

 Scare Factor

 Time-Saving Tip

Preface

How Has Walt Disney World Changed?

The simple answer is, it's gotten bigger. And they're still building.

In the 14 years since I began researching the first version of this guide, Disney has added one major park, three minor ones, six hotels, a cruise line, and more attractions and eateries than I can count. It was once possible for a fleet-footed and well-prepared family to see most of Walt Disney World in a four- or five-day stay. But this is no longer true. As the Disney complex expands, it is more vital than ever that you target in advance what you most want to see, work these priorities into your schedule, and then relax. Anything beyond that is pure gravy.

Many tourists treat Orlando as if it were a kiddie version of Vegas—you go there to play the numbers, and a family that hits 24 attractions a day must, by definition, be having four times as much fun as a family that sees six. Not so. You'll find a lot of crying kids and exasperated parents by midafternoon, largely because everyone is frantic with the idea that, because this trip is so expensive, you'd darn well better squeeze the most out of every minute.

Insider's Secret

Sometimes I'm asked if the prevalence of travel guides renders them less useful to their readers. After all, if everyone knows the "secret tip," is it still a secret?

Good question, but actually a very small percentage of WDW visitors do make advance preparations or read travel guides. The vast majority of people still show up late and wander around aimlessly. So anyone with a touring plan is automatically a step ahead of the crowd.

With this in mind, I've replaced my touring plans with advice on how you can customize a general touring plan for your own family. I've made these changes because, although it's nice to be able to shave 22 seconds off your morning dash to Splash Mountain by ducking through the restroom tunnel in Adventureland, the most successful plan seems to boil down to a few simple guidelines. You'll have twice as much fun with half as much stress if you follow these five tips:

1. Plan your trip for times of the year when the parks are less crowded. When people write to me about having bad experiences at Walt Disney World, it seems that about 90 percent of the disasters occur in July.

2. Order maps and tickets and arrange all reservations or priority seating well in advance. Every phone call you make from home is a line you won't have to stand in later.

3. Read up on attractions and let each family member choose the two or three things per park that are absolute must-sees. An amazing number of parents plan this trip for the kids, but neglect to ask them what they want to do.

4. Accept your differences and be willing to split up occasionally. Forcing a 14-year-old to endure It's a Small World or strapping a 6-year-old into Alien Encounter in

the interest of family togetherness will guarantee at least one tantrum per hour.

5. Arrive at the parks very early, go back to your hotel for a nap or swim in the afternoon, and return to the parks at night. Walt Disney World can be exhausting, and regular rest stops are key.

What hasn't changed is my belief that Walt Disney World is the best family travel destination on the planet. There is truly something for everyone within these gates, and the spectacular, awe-inspiring rides are counterbalanced with sweet, small moments of joy that often linger in the mind for years.

When you check into your hotel the first night and find you can see the IllumiNations fireworks from your balcony . . . when Merlin picks your 5-year-old to pull the sword from the stone and be declared ruler of all England . . . when they re-lease the doves at the end of the Beauty and the Beast show . . . or when your 13-year-old actually smiles—then, trust me, you'll remember why you came to Disney.

CHAPTER

1

Before You Leave Home

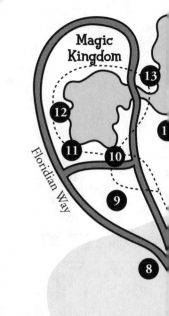

1. Coronado Springs Resort
2. Wide World of Sports
3. Swan Resort
4. Dolphin Resort
5. Yacht & Beach Club Resorts
6. Disney's BoardWalk, BoardWalk Inn & Villas
7. Magic Kingdom Main Entrance
8. Car Care Center
9. Transportation & Ticket Center Parking
10. Transportation & Ticket Center
11. Polynesian Resort
12. The Grand Floridian
13. Contemporary Resort
14. Wilderness Lodge
15. Fort Wilderness Campground
16. Dixie Landings Resort
17. Port Orleans Resort
18. Old Key West Resort
19. Lake Buena Vista Golf Course
20. Disney Institute
21. Disney Institute Villas
22. Disney's West Side
23. Pleasure Island
24. Caribbean Beach Resort

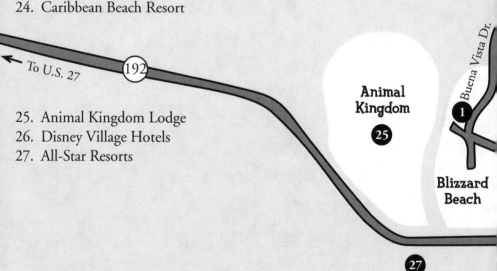

25. Animal Kingdom Lodge
26. Disney Village Hotels
27. All-Star Resorts

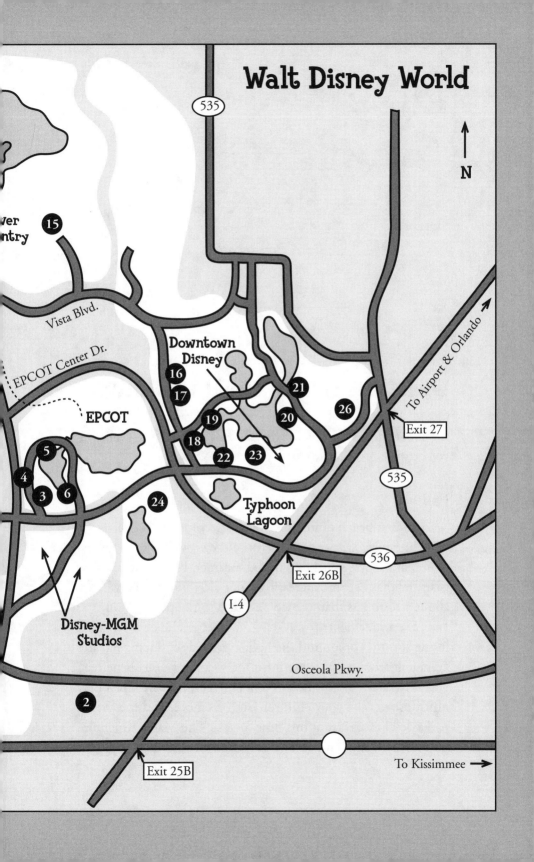

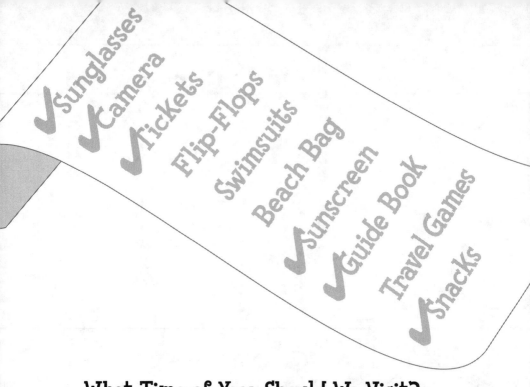

✓Sunglasses ✓Camera ✓Tickets Flip-Flops Swimsuits Beach Bag ✓Sunscreen ✓Guide Book Travel Games ✓Snacks

What Time of Year Should We Visit?

Crowd levels at Walt Disney World vary seasonally, so one of the most important decisions you will make while planning your trip is deciding when to go.

Fall

When I first began doing this guide, I recommended fall as the best time for a Disney visit, because the crowds then were less than half the size you'd find in the summer. But in the past few years, fall has become increasingly popular; now the crowds are about a third less than those you'd find in the peak season.

Even so, a fall trip is still a much better choice than going in the summer or around the holidays. And with temperatures averaging around 70° Fahrenheit, the weather is usually perfect.

There are disadvantages to a fall visit, however. You may not want to take your children out of school, and the theme parks do close earlier at this time of year. The Magic Kingdom, the Animal Kingdom, and MGM often close as early as 6 P.M., although Epcot generally remains open until 9 P.M. These earlier closings mean that some of the special evening presentations, such as the evening parade in the Magic Kingdom, are either suspended during the off-season or are scheduled only on weekends.

Fall is also hurricane season in Florida, so there is some risk you'll schedule your trip for the exact week that Hurricane Laluna pounds the coast. (In terms of tropical storms, September and October are riskier than November.) Fortunately, Orlando is an hour inland, which means that even the worst coastal storms usually yield only rain at Disney World. Furthermore, there are more rainy days in the summer months than there are in the fall, so in general the advantages of autumn touring far outweigh the disadvantages.

Spring

Spring is a great time to visit. With the exceptions of the holiday weeks around Presidents' Day in February, spring break, and Easter, springtime crowds average around 40,000 a day—not as sparse as in fall but still far better than in summer. And the weather is sublime, with highs in the 70s, lows in the 60s, and less rainfall than in any other season.

Disney maintains longer park hours in spring than in fall, but schedules vary widely in the weeks between January and May. To check projected hours of operation, call 407-824-4321 before you leave home.

Helpful Hint

Don't underestimate the effect holidays can have on crowds. The weeks flanking Easter and Christmas are obviously swamped, but any holiday where kids are out of school— such as Martin Luther King Day weekend or Presidents' Day weekend—will draw larger-than-average crowds.

Summer

The good news about summer is that everything is open and operational, and the parks run very long hours. The bad news is that it is hot and crowded—so crowded that the wait for many rides can be as long as 90 minutes.

Helpful Hint
If your children are preschoolers or younger, avoid summers like the plague.

If your children's school schedule dictates that you must visit in summer, the first two weeks of June and the last two weeks of August are your best bet. Check out "Special Tips for Extra-Crowded Times" in chapter 3.

Winter

Winter is a mixed bag. The absolute worst times are holidays. Christmas and New Year's can pull in 80,000 visitors per day, and even extended hours can't compensate for crowds of this size. Although special parades and shows are always worth seeing, you're better off at home watching them on TV.

Helpful Hint
Special holiday packages, which include price breaks on lodging, a party with the characters, and access to the Christmas parades and shows, run from the end of November to mid-December.

But if you avoid the holiday weeks, winter can be an ideal time for touring. January and February are pleasantly cool, and Disney World is relatively uncrowded then, although the water parks are sometimes closed during this period, and the parks run the same shortened schedule as in fall.

The first two weeks of December are another good option. Disney World's fetching Christmas decorations go up just after Thanksgiving. So if you make an early December visit, you'll have all the trees and wreaths and carolers you could wish for—as well as a nearly deserted theme park.

Insider's Secret

Winter can be a great time to visit Walt Disney World, but water babies take note: pools may be closed for refurbishing during January and February. Only one water park is generally operative and even it may be closed if the temperature dips below 60 degrees.

How Long Should We Stay?

It will take at least five days for a family with young kids to tour the Magic Kingdom, Epcot, the Animal Kingdom, and MGM. Park Hopper Plus passes—which admit holders to Pleasure Island, Typhoon Lagoon, Blizzard Beach, and River Country, as well as the major theme parks—are the best buy, if you plan to visit a water park. If not, then just get a Park Hopper Pass.

If you plan to spend a lot of time at the minor theme parks, especially the water parks, schedule six days. Six days are also necessary for families who enjoy boating, tennis, swimming, or golf—or those who would like to tour at a more leisurely pace.

If you wish to visit other area attractions such as Sea World or Universal Orlando, allow no less than a week.

Should We Take the Kids Out of School?

Even if you're sold on the advantages of fall and spring touring, you may be reluctant to take your children out of school for a week. There are ways to highlight the educational aspects of a trip to Disney World; let's look at a few.

Insider's Secret

If you're considering a trip that will require an absence of more than two school days, make your kid's teacher your partner.

Work together with the teacher to create a plan so that your child can avoid falling behind. Ideally, half of the makeup work should be done before you leave— the post-trip blues are bad enough without facing three hours of homework each night of the first week you're back. Also, timing is everything. Don't plan your trip for the week the school is administering exams or standardized testing. Check with the teacher to see if there are better times for your child to be absent.

To make up for being absent on school days, have your child do a project related to the trip. Some suggestions are listed on the following page.

Your child might also want to make a scrapbook or collection display. The mother of one preschooler helped him create an "ABC" book before he left home, and he then spent his week at Disney World collecting souvenirs for each page— Goofy's autograph on the "G" page, a postcard of a Japanese pagoda on the "P" page, and so on. An older child might gather fallen leaves from the various trees and bushes imported from the countries represented in the World Showcase. Or a young photographer could demonstrate her proficiency with various lighting techniques by photographing the Cinderella Castle in early morning, at noon, at sunset, and after dark. You can even work on math if you give your kids a set amount of mythical money to spend (such as $1,000). Then let them keep track of expenses, deducting them from their starting total and making decisions about what they can and cannot afford on their budget.

Epcot Projects

• The greenhouse tour in the Land pavilion is full of information on space-age farming.

• Marine biology is the theme of the Living Seas pavilion.

• Missing health class? The Wonders of Life pavilion is devoted to that greatest of all machines, the human body.

• Interested in geography? Some students have done reports on the cultures of countries represented in the World Showcase.

• Innoventions, although often described as the world's hippest arcade, is also a preview of future technology.

Animal Kingdom Projects

• Cretaceous Trail—a path filled with plants and animals that have survived from the Cretaceous period— is an excellent intro to botanical evolution.

• Rafiki's Planet Watch is the park's research and education hub, where kids can tour veterinary labs, use the Eco-web to find the conservation organization closest to their home, and watch interactive videos about endangered animals.

• Younger kids might like to simply do a report on one of the animals they see on Kilimanjaro Safaris.

Other Orlando Educational Programs

Disney World isn't the only place in Orlando that can be educational. Consider one of the following:

Sea World

Sea World offers daily tours and classes, as well as weeklong and overnight programs during summer and holidays. Call 407-351-3600 or log on to www.seaworld.org for more information.

Orlando Science Center

This impressive facility has oodles of hands-on exhibits, one-day programs for kids of all ages, and evening planetarium shows. If you request the brochure, you'll find something is happening all the time and the prices are reasonable. All programs must be booked in advance.

Admission to the center is $13, $12 for seniors, and $10.50 for kids ages 3 to 11. Classes are individually priced. Call 407-514-2000 or log on to www.osc.org for more information.

Kennedy Space Center

Orlando is only about an hour from Kennedy Space Center, so it's an easy day trip. Kids will enjoy the Rocket Garden, which holds eight rockets from the Mercury through Gemini programs, and the new Apollo/Saturn V Center, where you can see Saturn V, the most powerful rocket ever built. The films, projected on the five-story-high screen in the IMAX theater, are also a highlight. Call the center before you leave home to see if a launch is scheduled while you'll be in Florida. If so, plan your trip for that day. The crowds will be heavier, but your kids will experience a rare thrill.

Crew passes, which include a shuttle tour of the Space Center as well as the IMAX film, are $33 and $23 for kids ages 3 to 11. Call 321-452-2121.

Should We Buy a Package?

This is a toughie. There are advantages to package trips, most notably that it is possible to save a good deal of money. It's also helpful to know up front what your vacation will cost. Packages often require hefty prepayments, which are painful at the time—but at least you don't return home with your credit card utterly maxed out.

Package trips can have drawbacks, however. Like buying a fully loaded car off a dealer's lot, you may find yourself paying for options you don't want and don't need. Packages are often padded with perks such as reduced golf greens fees, which interest only a few families, or rental cars, which you may not need if you're staying on site. At the other end of the spectrum are deeply discounted packages that place you in rundown or out-of-the-way hotels.

Money-Saving Tip

Don't automatically assume that a package will save you big bucks. Unless you're sure you need every feature that the package includes, you may actually end up losing money on the deal.

Disney Package Vacations

Disney's standard vacation package is called a Dream Maker Package, and includes on-site lodging and Ultimate Park Hopper passes. These packages start as low as $349 per adult for a three-night package at a value resort. The three-night rate for a child aged 10 to 17 is $222 and for a child aged 3 to 9 it's $177. Obviously if you want to add more days or upgrade to a midpriced resort, the package price rises accordingly.

For many families the basic plan is enough, but needless to say, Disney doesn't stop with the basics. They also offer the Silver Plan, which allows you to add on a character breakfast or dinner and some meals at an additional $67 per night for adults and kids 10 to 17 and $54 per night for kids 3 to 9. You can also choose from a menu of recreational options such as golf, parasailing, or theme parks tours. The next step up, the Gold Plan, adds three meals a day including character meals, unlimited on-site child care, tickets to the Cirque du Soleil, unlimited recreational activities, selected spa treatments, and unlimited tours for an additional $139 per night for adults and kids 10 to 17 and $94 for kids 3 to 9. In other words, the Silver Plan offers you plenty of dining and recreational options, but you're limited to two selections from the features menu per person per day. On the Gold Plan you get lots more of the same, in the sense that all meals are included and your recreational choices are basically unlimited.

The Platinum Plan has a $199 add-on per night for adults and kids 10 to 17 and a $119 add-on for kids 3 to 9 and is obviously the top of the line. You get everything in the Gold Plan, plus more. You're housed in a luxury resort, and perks include dinner at Victoria and Albert's, a fireworks cruise, in-room child care, and a personalized itinerary. Somehow I suspect that if you have the money to pay for this sort of thing, you're not reading this book.

So who needs what? First-time visitors will have enough to handle just seeing the parks and probably don't need anything beyond the basic package.

The Silver and Gold add-ons are a good deal only for families who have done Disney a couple of times before and are ready to branch out into other areas of entertainment such as sports, behind-the-scenes tours, and Cirque du Soleil. Does the inclusion of meals offset the increase in price? Only if you know you'll really want three full meals a day. Readers who have in the past purchased packages that include dining report that while unlimited dining appeals to adults, families may feel like they're spending all day going from restaurant to restaurant just to make sure they're getting their money's worth. (After all, you may feel funny using a dining option to grab a burger from a counter-service stand when you know that the same dining option qualifies you for a three-course meal at a spiffy restaurant.)

And while adults or teens may eat enough to justify the increase in cost, it's unlikely that a child will.

A good rule of thumb is this: If you're a family who has been to Disney before and are looking to expand your experience by trying a few nice restaurants, some sporting options, and perhaps a behind-the-scenes tour or two, consider the Silver Plan. If you've been to Disney several times, your children are old enough to appreciate (and happily sit through) a variety of restaurant meals and you really want to "do it right" this time, consider the Gold Plan. But don't think that just because they're packages, they're automatically saving you big bucks. When you do the math, you'll likely find that they're not. The primary advantage of Disney packages is convenience and the fact that they prod you to try things such as pedicures and parasailing that you might otherwise skip.

Airline Packages

If you're flying, check out the airline's own packages, which include airfare, theme park tickets for Disney and other Orlando attractions, car rental, and lodging at either on-site or off-site hotels. Again, there's a huge range of amenities—you can have valet parking and use of a camcorder if you're willing to pay for them. And again, the packages can be fine-tuned to meet your needs. If you'll be flying Delta, call 800-872-7786 for a brochure; the number for USAir is 800-455-0123; American Airlines is 800-321-2121.

Insider's Secret
The airlines control a limited number of on-site hotel rooms, so call at least six months in advance if you have your heart set on a particular Disney resort.

Money-Saving Tip

While Disney's current economic woes have led to some cutbacks within the parks, there are some advantages for consumers. With empty hotel rooms to fill, Disney has been offering more price breaks on their on-site resorts. Needless to say, these deals are most likely to be available during the off-season.

• For the first time in several years, travel agents and AAA are offering genuine discounts on Disney hotels. If you have a travel agent you regularly use at home or are a AAA member, check with them for prices and then call Disney directly to compare.

• Prefer to book online? Go to Disney's own Web page, www.disneyworld.com, and click on "Vacation Savings." Or check out www.expedia.com. Online discounts average about 20 percent.

• If you find yourself in Orlando without a room (or if you're staying at an off-site hotel and decide you'd like to move to a Disney property), call the Ocala Disney Information Center at 352-845-0770 and see if any rooms are available. The center works on a walk-in basis and is designed to fill rooms for that very night, so you can't make any advance reservations and it's by nature a hit-or-miss type deal. Some families have received whopping 50 percent discounts, so if you're willing to take a chance, this is an option.

• If using Disney's direct line (407-W-DISNEY) to book rooms, remember to always ask if any special offers are available.

Money-Saving Tip

If you're planning to stay off-site, travel agents are often aware of Orlando hotels that offer packages, and they are a good source of comparative-rate shopping. Large travel agencies sometimes put together their own packages, which include airfare, lodging at an off-site hotel, and a rental car. If you need all three of these components, it'll probably come out cheaper to buy a package through your local agent than to book all three separately.

Cruise Packages

The Walt Disney Company's cruise ships, *Disney Magic* and *Disney Wonder*, offer families the chance to combine a cruise with a Disney World vacation.

Families may opt to spend either three or four nights at sea and the remainder of the week in Orlando. Park admissions are included in the packages, as is airfare, a rental car, and your meals while aboard ship. During the cruise segment of the week, you'll find a staggeringly full program for children, including dawn-to-dusk kids' clubs, special menus, parties and mixers geared for teens and preteens, and the Disney characters. Seven-day cruises are also available, with a variety of itineraries.

Check out the Web page at www.DisneyCruise.com. You can book the cruises through your travel agent or by calling 800-511-1333. See chapter 12 for more information.

Cheapie Deals

You frequently see ads in the travel sections of major newspapers offering Disney World at extremely low rates. But proceed with caution. The hotels are sometimes as far as 50 miles away

Money-Saving Tip
Be doubly wary of the very cheap packages offered in Sunday papers. If a deal sounds too good to be true, it probably is.

from the Disney gates. (With a rental car and an alarm clock, even this obstacle can be overcome— but you should know what you're up against.) Other pitfalls include tickets that are good only at certain times of the year or extremely inflexible touring arrangements that require you to ride from attraction to attraction in slow-moving, overloaded buses.

Another drawback is that the hotels featured may not be in a very desirable area of town. Unless either you or your travel agent is familiar with the area where the hotel is located, be wary. A family interested in saving money is far better off driving and camping at Fort Wilderness or trying the All-Star Resorts than signing up for one of these packages.

Helpful Hint
We're sorry to announce that the Disney Club, which was a great source of savings, will close as of December 31, 2003. Current members will continue to receive benefits through that date, but Disney is no longer accepting membership applications.

What Kind of Tickets Do We Need?

This decision, believe it or not, needs to be made long before you get to the theme park gates. First of all, prepare yourself for the news that, at least in the eyes of the Disney accountants, your 10-year-old is an adult. Then consider how many days you'll need the tickets, whether you'd like to visit the minor parks, and if you plan to visit more than one park in a single day. (Most of the tips and touring plans in this book assume that you will.)

As we go to press, the following ticket options are available, and the prices quoted are before tax. (Florida tax is 6 percent.) Disney "adjusts"—that is, raises—prices on a regular basis, so you should always confirm prices and ticket options by calling 407-824-4321 or go online at www.DisneyWorld.com.

Seven-Day Park Hopper Plus

Admits holders to the four major parks, plus four visits to the minor ones. Children under age 3 are admitted free.

- Adult (and children over 9): $319
- Child (ages 3 to 9): $256

Six-Day Park Hopper Plus

Admits holders to the four major parks, plus three visits to the minor ones. Children under age 3 are admitted free.

- Adult (and children over 9): $289
- Child (ages 3 to 9): $232

Five-Day Park Hopper Plus

Admits holders to the four major parks, plus two visits to the minor ones. Children under age 3 are admitted free.

- Adult (and children over 9): $259
- Child (ages 3 to 9): $208

Five-Day Park Hopper Pass

Admits holder to the four major parks. Children under age 3 are admitted free.

- Adult (and children over 9): $229
- Child (ages 3 to 9): $184

Four-Day Park Hopper Pass

Admits holder to the four major parks. Children under age 3 are admitted free.

- Adult (and children over 9): $199
- Child (ages 3 to 9): $159

One-Day Ticket

Admits holder to one park only. Children under age 3 are admitted free.

- Adult (and children over 9): $50
- Child (ages 3 to 9): $40

Money-Saving Tip

The multiday Park Hopper Plus is enough for most families, but if you have older kids who'd like to make a visit to the mega-arcade called Disney-Quest, consider the Ultimate Park Hopper, the only ticket that throws in admission to DisneyQuest.

Money-Saving Tip

Guests at the on-site hotels should consider the Ultimate Park Hopper Pass, which can be purchased for any length of stay from two days on up. The pass offers unlimited access to both the major and minor parks during the time you're staying at a Disney hotel, and although the price is obviously tied to how long you stay, the pass is the only way to get park hopper privileges for stays of less than four days.

It's also worth noting that the Park Hopper passes do not have to be used on consecutive days and, in fact, never expire. Assuming that your kids don't move from the child to the adult category in the meantime, you can return in five years and the unused days will still be valid. Even though Disney no longer issues the Four-Day Value Pass, it still honors the pass, along with any other multiday passes that the company no longer issues.

Helpful Hint

One word of caution about buying tickets: The Guest Services desk at off-site hotels may be run not by your hotel at all but by a separate company that exists solely to sell tickets and bus fares to tourists. These companies offer their own version of the multiday passes, which they hawk aggressively, usually by telling you that it is much cheaper than the Disney ticket. It isn't.

Time-Saving Tip

In the off-season, when the Magic Kingdom closes early, Disney sometimes offers a special "E ticket" to on-site guests. To be used in conjunction with a Park Hopper pass, the E ticket allows you into the Magic Kingdom on a night when it is closed to the general public. About 10 attractions are open, and only 5,000 E tickets are generally sold, meaning very short lines. The open rides include Space Mountain, Splash Mountain, and other big-name attractions, so the E ticket is most appealing to families with older kids. Few Fantasyland attractions are open. The price is $12 per adult, and $10 for kids 3 to 9.

Helpful Hint

Theme park tickets demagnetize easily, so keep them in a separate pouch or pocket, away from your credit cards. If your passport does become de-magnetized and won't swipe at the turnstile entrance to one of the theme parks, Disney will gladly replace it. But that involves a trip to Guest Services, and it's maddening to have to make this detour when you're itching to get to the rides.

Money-Saving Tip

Another rip-off to look out for: overpriced shuttle tickets at off-site hotels. The agents hawking these tickets may tell you that you'll save the "horren-dous" cost of Disney parking by taking their shut-tle, but the truth is that it costs $7 to park no matter how many people are in the car, and the bus tickets cost $3 to $7 per person. For a family of four, that adds up fast. Also, these independent shuttles generally stop at several hotels, making your commute time much longer than if you stayed at a hotel offering a direct shuttle or drove your own car. Don't pay for this abuse.

Money-Saving Tip

If you're touring during the winter when the water parks are often either closed or running abbrevi-ated hours, you may be better off purchasing a Park Hopper Pass. A Park Hopper Plus makes eco-nomic sense only if you're visiting a water park.

Ticket Purchases and Advance Reservations

Tickets

Purchase tickets to the theme parks by calling 407-W-DISNEY. MasterCard, Visa, and American Express are all accepted, and the tickets will be mailed to you. If you'd prefer to pay by check, call first to confirm prices, then mail your payment to

WDW Tickets
P.O. Box 10030
Lake Buena Vista, FL 32830

You can also buy your tickets online at www.Disney World.com.

Money-Saving Tip

If you buy your tickets online you'll receive a discount of about 5 percent on multiday passes. Log on to www.DisneyWorld.com.

Money-Saving Tip

Theme park ticket prices change about every six months. Always call to confirm prices. Once you purchase tickets, however, the price is fixed, so buy in advance when you can.

Many area hotels, including all Disney hotels, allow guests to purchase theme park tickets at check-in. Inquire when you make reservations. Buying tickets at your hotel is generally faster than waiting in line once you get to the theme parks.

Helpful Hint

One of your best sources for information is the Web site at www.DisneyWorld.com. If you'd like to book your room or create a custom package on-line, log on to the "Book Your Trip" section and begin making choices. The system normally works well, but a few families have reported snafus, so it never hurts to confirm room reservations with a follow-up call. You can also use the Web page to purchase advance tickets.

Rooms

Try to make room reservations for on-site hotels at least six months in advance, especially if you're staying at one of the budget hotels or traveling during a busy season. Call 407-W-DISNEY for information on all Disney-owned hotels. Room reservations for off-site hotels can usually be made later, perhaps a month before you plan to arrive in the off-season or three to four months in advance for the on-season.

Money-Saving Tip

If you want to stay off site, a great way to get discounts is to call the Orlando Visitor's Bureau at 800-255-5786 and request its Vacation Planner and Magicard. It takes three to four weeks to get the package, but the card qualifies you for discounts on off-site hotels, off-site dinner shows, and non–Disney area attractions.

Food

You should also make Disney dinner show reservations from home. The shows accept reservations up to two years in advance.

Money-Saving Tip

Members of the Entertainment Club may be surprised to learn that some spiffy off-site hotels offer 50 percent discounts to cardholders, making an upscale resort as inexpensive as an interstate cheapie. But because hotels set aside only a certain number of rooms for club members, you must make reservations well in advance to get the discounts. Becoming a member of the Entertainment Club is as simple as buying one of the discount coupon books in your hometown. The books are best known for their restaurant coupons. Few people seem to realize that a nationwide directory of hotels offering 50 percent discounts can be found in the back.

Disney restaurants do not accept reservations, but you can arrange for priority seating 60 to 120 days in advance. See chapter 11 for details. Priority seating means that if you show up at the specified time, you'll be given the next available table; it's not as good as a reservation but does guarantee you'll be seated before the walk-ins. Wait times average 10 to 30 minutes under this system.

To arrange priority seating from home, call 407-WDW-DINE. Disney changes dining policy frequently, and the representative on the line will be able to explain your options.

If you would like to wait until you've checked in to your on-site hotel so you can see which restaurant looks the coolest, arrange priority seating through Guest Services or press the "dining" key on your hotel room phone.

You can also arrange priority seating in person on the day you visit, by dropping by the actual restaurant in the Magic Kingdom, at the reservations booth at MGM, or at the World-Key Information System beside Spaceship Earth at Epcot. If

Insider's Secret

Priority seating is a must for character breakfasts (these are meals either in the resorts or theme parks during which the Disney characters circulate among diners, pausing for pictures, autographs, and hugs) or if you're traveling in the busy season and would specifically like to try some of Disney World's more popular restaurants.

Helpful Hint

Consider scheduling a character breakfast on the morning you're set to depart. There are two reasons this is a good idea. First of all, mornings are the best time to tour the parks so you don't want to spend all your best touring hours at a long breakfast. Second, and even more important, young kids are often afraid of the characters at first. Plunking a toddler in the arms of a six-foot dog, even Goofy, can terrify him so badly that he'll avoid the characters for the whole trip. But if he's had several days to see the characters in the parks and get used to how big they are, that same toddler may happily run to Goofy for a hug by the end of the trip.

you wait until the last minute in the on-season, you'll likely be closed out of the most popular eateries at peak dining times. But if you're traveling off-season or don't have a strong preference about when or where you eat, waiting until the last minute is okay.

Tours

Likewise, you can arrange tours 60 days in advance. Tours for adults can be arranged through 407-WDW-TOUR. Several of the kid-oriented tours are booked through 407-WDW-DINE. See Chapter 10 for details.

Transportation: With a Rental Car

Decide in advance if you need a rental car. If you're staying off site or if you plan to visit non-Disney attractions, the answer is probably yes.

Some rental car companies—Avis, Dollar, and National—have desks at the Orlando airport, with the cars in an adjacent lot. Others, including Hertz and the huge and popular Alamo, are located away from the airport and require a separate shuttle ride. Waiting for the shuttle adds 20 minutes to your commute, both coming and going from the airport, but Alamo offers slightly lower rental fees to compensate. To reserve a car, call

Alamo	800-462-5226
Avis	800-331-1212
Dollar	800-800-4000
Hertz	800-654-3131
National	800-227-7368

An average weekly rental fee for a compact is around $300. Don't be fooled by the quoted rate of $30 a day; by the time you add taxes and insurance, it's closer to $50. Quite a few families have reported they used their rental car less than they anticipated—"We paid $320 for the privilege of driving from the airport to our hotel and back," wrote one father—so rent a car only if you're staying off site or visiting several non-Disney attractions. Cars can also be helpful if you plan to eat at or visit a variety of on-site hotels.

Don't worry if you've never driven in Orlando; the town is built for tourists, and roads are well marked. It's approximately a 15- to 25-minute drive from the airport to the Disney gates and the roads on Disney property are often circular; if you miss an exit, keep driving, and you'll soon get another chance.

Insider's Secret

At times it may make more sense to use a taxicab than a rental car or Disney's own transportation. Consider taking a cab if:

- You'd like quick, direct transportation from the airport to your hotel. (The rate should be between $30 and $40.)

- You'd like quick, direct transportation from one Disney resort to another. (The rate should be around $10 to $15.)

- You're staying off site and going to one of the minor parks, such as Downtown Disney or a water park. (Rates vary depending on the location of your hotel.)

- You're staying at a Disney hotel but heading for a day at Universal Orlando or Sea World.

- The kids are absolutely exhausted. If you've pushed too far and everyone is too tired to wait for a bus, cabs are a faster way back to your room. They're waiting near the theme park exits. At times, this is $10 worth spending.

Transportation: Without a Rental Car

If you're flying to Orlando, staying on site, and visiting only WDW, you might not need a rental car. Your first problem is how to get from the airport to your hotel. You can always take an independent shuttle such as Mears (407-423-5566). The shuttle cost is around $14 a person or $25 round-trip. If you have more than two people in your party, you'll come out ahead by taking a cab. They're always available outside the airport, and the fare to Disney-area hotels is between $30 and $40. (If you need to pay by credit card, inform the attendant at the airport cab line in advance.)

Once you're at your hotel you can use Disney transportation to get to the major parks. If you're in a hurry or heading for an out-of-the-way destination such as one of the water parks, you can always have the resort bellman call you a cab. Cabs are also waiting near the bus parking areas at the theme parks.

Things to Discuss with Your Kids Before You Leave Home

It's important to include the kids when planning the vacation. Discuss the following topics before you leave home.

The Trip Itself

There are two schools of thought on just how far in advance of the trip you should tell the kids about the plan. Because many families make reservations six months in advance or more, it's easy to fall into a "waiting for Christmas" syndrome, with the kids nearly in a lather of anticipation weeks before you leave. To avoid the agony of a long countdown, one couple packed in secret and then woke the children up at 5 A.M. one morning and announced, "Get in the car, we're going to Disney World." The best method is probably somewhere in between the two extremes. Tell the kids at the time you make your reservations, but don't begin poring over the brochures in earnest until about two weeks before the trip.

The Layout of the Parks

Among the more than 400 families surveyed or interviewed for this book, the amount of advance research they had done directly correlated with how much they enjoyed the trip. Visitors who show up at Disney World without any preparation can still have fun, but their comment sheets were sprinkled with "Next time I'll know . . ." and "If only we had . . ."

Kids 7 or older should have some idea of the layout of the parks. If you're letting preteens and teens roam about on their own, you should definitely brief them on the location of major attractions and where and when to meet up with the family again.

The pleasures of being prepared extend to preschoolers. If you purchase a few Disney World coloring books to enjoy on the trip down to Orlando or watch one of the Disney Channel specials featuring the parks, even the youngest child will arrive able to identify the Swiss Family Robinson Treehouse and Living Seas pavilion. A little knowledge before entering the gates helps you decide how best to spend your time and eliminates those "Whadda we do now?" debates.

The Classic Stories of Disney

If your children are under 7, another good pretrip purchase is a set of Disney paperbacks with audiotapes. Even though parental eyes may glaze over when *Dumbo* rewinds for its thirty-fourth straight hearing, these tapes and books help to pass the trip and familiarize kids with the characters and rides they'll be seeing once they arrive. (If you find kiddie tapes too annoying, you can always bring along headphones for the children to use.)

Some families rent Disney movies just before the trip. The videotape *Disneyland Fun* is especially good for getting the whole family revved up and in the mood. The featured park is Disneyland in California and not the Magic Kingdom in Florida, but the attractions are similar enough to make the tape an exciting preview. Renting *Honey, I Shrunk the Kids* before you leave will vastly improve your children's appreciation of Epcot's *Honey, I Shrunk the Audience* as well as the *Honey, I Shrunk the Kids* Adventure Zone at MGM.

Special Academic Projects

See the section "Should We Take the Kids Out of School?" earlier in this chapter for ideas on special projects and seminars.

Souvenirs and Money

Will you save all souvenir purchases for the last day? Buy one small souvenir every day? Are the children expected to spend their own money, or will Mom and Dad spring for the T-shirts? Whatever you decide will depend on your pocketbooks and your particular interpretation of fiscal responsibility, but do set your rules before you're in the park. Otherwise the selection of goodies will lure you into spending far more than you anticipated.

One excellent technique for limiting impulse buys is to request Disney Dollars at the time you order your theme park tickets. Disney Dollars come in denominations of $1 (Mickey), $5 (Goofy), and $10 (Minnie or Simba) and are accepted throughout the theme parks, shops, restaurants, and resorts of Disney World. Some wily parents have managed to convince their tots that these bills are the only currency the parks accept and have given them an age-appropriate number of Disney Dollars before leaving home, explaining that this money and this money alone is for souvenirs. You can purchase Disney Dollars at all Disney stores or by writing to

WDW Tickets
P.O. Box 10030
Lake Buena Vista, FL 32830-0030

If you're willing to wait until you arrive, it's easy to get Disney Dollars in the theme parks or at on-site hotels.

The Scare Factor

Finally, give some thought to the scare factor. A mediocre meal or boring show can be a disappointment, but misjudging the intensity of a ride can leave you with a terrified or nauseated child and the whole day in ruins.

How frightening a ride is can be tough to gauge, because Disney World scariness comes in two forms. First, there are atmospheric rides, ranging from the shadows and cardboard witch of Snow White's Scary Adventures to the full-throttle scream-o-rama Alien Encounter. The other kind of fear is motion related: Although Space Mountain and the other coasters are obviously risky, don't overlook the fact that some people lose their lunch on sweet little charmers like the Mad Hatter's Tea Party. For some people, the motion simulation rides are more disturbing than the coasters. Body Wars in Epcot, for example, scarcely moves, but the visual effects leave some people wrecked for the day.

Age is often not the determining factor, because some 6-year-olds are fearless and some 11-year-olds are easily unnerved. Disney's only guidance comes in the form of height requirements (listed next), but saying that a 41-inch-tall 5-year-old *can* ride Big Thunder Mountain is no indication that he *should* ride Big Thunder Mountain. Read the ride descriptions to find out what kind of scary you're dealing with; children who are terrified of a creepy ride like the Alien Encounter may adore the high-speed Test Track, and some kids who love the Haunted Mansion panic when Dumbo lifts off. I include scare factor ratings after each ride description, based primarily on feedback I've received from the families I've surveyed.

Height Requirements

The Magic Kingdom

Alien Encounter	44 inches (and child must be 7 years old)
Big Thunder Mountain	40 inches
Space Mountain	44 inches
Splash Mountain	40 inches

Epcot

Test Track	40 inches
Body Wars	40 inches
Mission: Space	Height requirement not yet established.

MGM

Star Tours	40 inches
Tower of Terror	40 inches
Rock 'n' Roller Coaster	48 inches

The Animal Kingdom

Dinosaur	40 inches (and child must be 7 years old)
Kali River Rapids	42 inches
Primeval Whirl	48 inches

If you're still unsure, employ these strategies:

@ *Do a baby swap.*

No, this does not mean you can trade your shrieking 1-year-old for that angelically napping infant behind you!

If you have doubts whether a ride is appropriate for your child, inform the attendant that you may need to do a baby swap. As you approach the attraction, one parent rides and returns with the verdict. If the first parent thinks the child will do okay, the second parent immediately boards and rides with the child.

If the first parent thinks the ride is too wild, the second parent passes the child through to the first and then rides himself. Granted, it's not as much fun as riding together, but it beats starting the day with a terrified child.

Insider's Secret

You can also use the "baby swap" method if you're traveling with a child who is definitely too young to ride major attractions. One parent rides, and then the other hands the baby through and immediately boards the ride.

@ *Build up ride intensity throughout the day.*

Not sure if your 7-year-old is up to a roller coaster? Start her off with something relatively mild like Goofy's Barnstormer or Pirates of the Caribbean. If she handles these okay, proceed on to Splash Mountain or Big Thunder Mountain Railroad. Who knows, you may close out the day on Space Mountain.

This advice runs counter to the touring tips you'll find later in the book that recommend you ride the big-deal attractions first thing in the morning. But it's better to ease a nervous kid in slowly, even if you risk long lines at the end of the day. You can reduce the wait somewhat if you ride major attractions during the evening parade, which draws most of the crowd back to Main Street.

@ *Avoid motion sickness.*

Obviously, avoid riding a bumpy attraction just after eating. If you begin to feel sick on a ride like Star Tours, where the visual effects are so convincing that many people become queasy, stare at something inside the cabin instead of the screen. If you focus on the back of the seat in front of you, your nausea will likely subside. Some families routinely take motion sickness pills in the morning before heading to the parks.

Don't Leave Home Without ...

✔ *Comfortable shoes.* This is no time to be breaking in new Nikes.

✔ *Minimal clothing.* Many hotels have laundry facilities, and you can always wash out underwear in the sink. Most families make the mistake of overpacking, not figuring on all the souvenirs they'll be bringing back. (Guest Services reports that many families buy so much stuff that they end up shipping their dirty clothes home via UPS.) Disney T-shirts are not only great for touring but can serve as swimsuit cover-ups and pajamas as well. And unless you're planning a special evening out at Victoria and Albert's, casual clothing is acceptable everywhere.

✔ *Lightweight jackets.* It rains in Orlando off and on year-round, so jackets should be water-resistant.

✔ *Basic necessities.* These include disposable diapers, baby formula, film, and blank camcorder tapes. All these are available within Disney World, but at premium prices.

✔ *Sunscreen.* Keep a tube with you, and reapply it often. Sunburn is the number-one complaint at the first-aid clinic in the Magic Kingdom. You need sunburn protection all through the year in Orlando, not just during the summer.

✔ *A waist pouch or fanny pack.* This is a good alternative to dragging along a purse while touring, and it frees up your hands for boarding rides, pushing strollers, and holding on to your kids.

✔ *Ziploc bags.* These are ever so handy for leftover food. Disney serves such large portions, even on kiddie meals, that some parents report they save some of the fruit or chips for a later snack.

✔ *Sunglasses.* The Florida sun is so blindingly bright that more than once I've reached into my purse for my sunglasses only to realize I already had them on. Kids too young for sunglasses need wide-billed caps to cut down the glare.

✔ *Strollers.* Most Orlando hotels are huge so if you have an infant or toddler you'll need your own stroller just to get around your hotel. But if your children are preschoolers and will need a stroller only one or two days of the trip (most likely at Epcot), rental is not a bad option.

Helpful Hint

Planning to take your pet along? The Walt Disney World Kennel Club is located near the Magic Kingdom. Call 407-824-6563 for reservations; the cost is $9 a night for those staying on site and $11 a night for off-site visitors' pets. Never, repeat, never, leave an animal locked in a car in the Florida heat and humidity, no matter what time of the year you're visiting.

How to Get Up-to-Date Information Before You Leave

If you need further information before you leave home, write to

Walt Disney World Guest Information
P.O. Box 10040
Lake Buena Vista, FL 32830-0040

or subscribe to Disney Magazine. To order, write to

Disney Magazine
P.O. Box 37263
Boone, IA 50037-2263

If you want to get information online, try www.Disney
World.com or www.Disney.com. If you still have questions, call
407-824-4321. You'll go through minutes of button-pushing
torment, but eventually a real live person will come on the line
to tell you what time Epcot closes on May 7, the price of the
Polynesian Revue for a 10-year-old, and how tall you have to be
to ride Splash Mountain.

Get maps of the theme parks and general touring information by calling 407-W-DISNEY. If you're traveling with
someone who is elderly or in a wheelchair, request the *Guidebook for Disabled Visitors.*

Getting Info at the Hotel

If you need information once you check into your hotel, both
on-site and off-site hotels provide material at check-in. Study
the maps and brochures on your first evening. Guest Services in
both on-site and off-site hotels are equipped to answer most
questions. The on-site hotels offer nonstop Disney program-
ming about the parks—including laughably obvious "tips" like
"You'll need a ticket to enter the theme parks."

Some of the large off-site hotels have their own entertainment information channels, which keep you up-to-date not
only on Disney but also all other Orlando-area attractions.
Magic Kingdom radio is 1030 AM. Epcot is 810 AM. Tune in
as you drive into the parks.

Getting Info in the Parks

If you need information once you're in the parks, check with Guest Services, located near the main gates of all four major theme parks.

Pal Mickey

You can actually turn your kids into theme park experts by renting a Pal Mickey. Pal Mickey may look like a cuddly friend, but he's also a smart toy whose purpose is to serve as your theme park tour guide. Mickey giggles and vibrates when he has something to say, and you hold him to your ear and squeeze his hand to get the message. But this isn't just random chatter—oh no, Mickey is one savvy mouse. As you walk through the parks, Mickey knows where he is, and different messages are triggered by location. He might remind you about show times and parade routes or tell you where the characters are by saying, "Hey, Goofy's on Main Street, let's drop by and say hi."

Pal Mickey is available to rent for $8 a day and you can find him at 34 locations throughout Walt Disney World, including all four parks and each resort. For a $50 deposit you can keep him for your length of stay, turning him in at any location you choose. Can't bear to say goodbye? If you want to keep Mickey, the deposit becomes your purchase price.

Mickey knows about the attractions you're approaching and can make recommendations, such as telling you about height restrictions, warning you about the witch in Snow White's Adventures or that he might get wet on Splash Mountain. Mickey prompts you when it's time to find a seat for the parade or an upcoming show, and gives tips like "Italy is a great place to watch Illuminations." Since he knows what's going on in "real time" he can update you on what's going on in the park, such as when lines are short for certain attractions.

Most of Mickey's messages are about the parks, but he also spontaneously tells jokes and fun facts. And when a child is waiting in line for a ride or restaurant service is slow, he steps in to entertain. Squeeze both hands and he plays three child-oriented games.

With messages coming about every two minutes, parents may fear Pal Mickey overload, but if you don't want to hear the message you can ignore the giggle. If Mickey is in a backpack (and thus can't "see") he won't send messages at all. Also, if you walk past a location twice, he remembers that he's been there before, so he doesn't tell you the same thing over and over.

I must confess that when I first heard about Pal Mickey I was a little skeptical. It just seemed like one more thing to pay for. But once I tried the toy out I was hooked and your kids probably will be too. The only drawback is that each kid may want his own Pal Mickey, so it's best to set up some sharing ground rules before you rent him.

The Frantic Factor

Although I'll rate rides throughout this book according to their "scare factor," I've often thought that I should include ratings on the "frantic factor" as well, measuring how hysterical the average parent is apt to become in any given situation.

I'm often asked to speak to parent groups on the topic of family travel. Almost inevitably, someone asks me how to make a Disney vacation relaxing. These people are very earnest, but they might as well be asking me to recommend a nice ski lodge for their upcoming trip to Hawaii. The only honest response is, "If you want to relax, you're going to the wrong place." Disney World is a high-stimulation environment, a total assault on all five senses mixed in with a constant and mind-boggling array of choices. This is not the week to take your kids off Ritalin. This is not the week to try to come off cigarettes or discuss marital issues with your spouse. This is not the week to relax.

Actually, high stimulation and a lively pace can be fun and may even be the reason most people go to Disney World in the first place. Families who slip over the line from stimulated to frantic often do so because (1) they forget to build in adequate rest breaks, (2) they've planned their trip for the busiest times, (3) they're confused about the logistics of touring, or (4) they are hell-bent on taking it all in because "We're paying through the nose for this" and "Who knows when we'll get back?" This book is full of tips to help you avoid the first three mistakes, but your attitude is pretty much up to you. Just remember that doing it all is not synonymous with having the most fun, and if time is tight, limit your touring to those attractions that have the most appeal to your particular group. As for when you'll get back, who knows? But using this as a rationale for pushing anyone in the family past their personal exhaustion limit only guarantees that you'll never want to come back.

And if you're fried at the end of the day, don't fret. Nearly every hotel in the Orlando area has a hot tub, and impromptu emotional support groups for parents tend to gather there from 5 to 7 P.M. every day.

CHAPTER

2

Choosing a Hotel

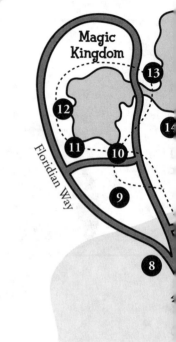

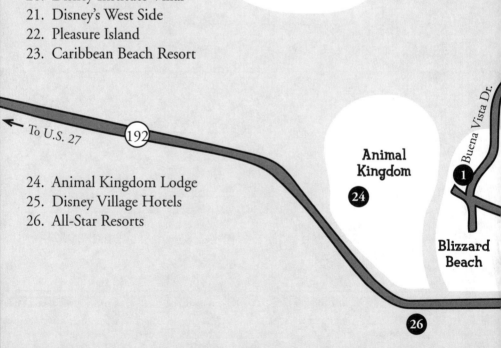

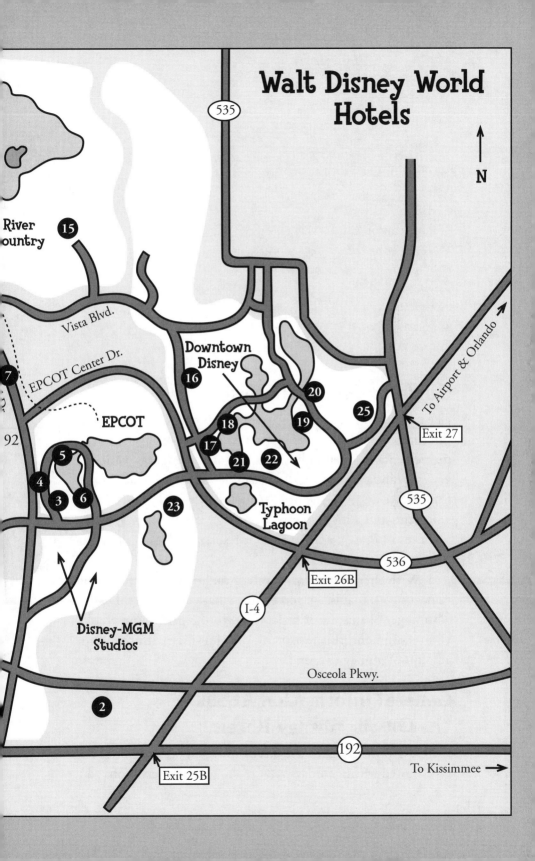

Walt Disney World Hotels

N

River Country **15**

Vista Blvd.

EPCOT Center Dr.

7

92

EPCOT

Downtown Disney **16**

20

18

17

19

25

21 **22**

Exit 27

To Airport & Orlando

5

4

3 **6**

23

Typhoon Lagoon

535

536

Exit 26B

Disney-MGM Studios

I-4

2

Osceola Pkwy.

Exit 25B

192

To Kissimmee

535

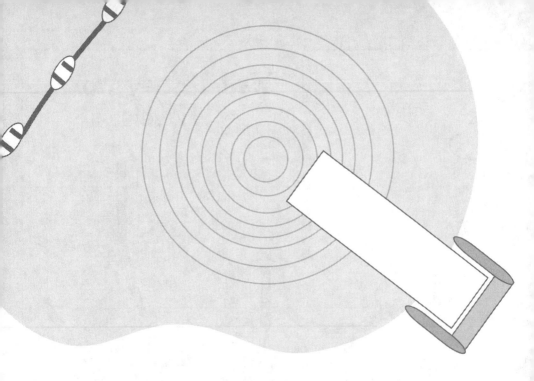

Guide to On-Site Hotels

The ratings for the hotels discussed in this chapter are based on three factors: the responses of families I've personally surveyed; the percentage of repeat business a resort experiences, which is a reliable indicator of guest satisfaction; and the quality of the resort in relation to the price. Obviously, you'd expect more amenities and a higher employee-to-guest ratio at a $250-a-night resort than at a $100-a-night resort, so it's unfair to hold them to the same standard.

With that in mind, I've rated the hotels on the basis of value for cost; that is, are you getting what you paid for? Do the advantages of this resort make it worth the price? And would you recommend this resort to other families with the same amount of money to spend?

General Information About the On-Site Disney Hotels

@ A deposit equal to the price of one night's lodging is required within 14 days after making your reservation. You may pay by check or credit card. If you cancel at least 5 days in advance, your deposit will be fully refunded.

@ All Disney hotels operate under the family plan, meaning that kids 18 and under stay free with parents. The rooms at the budget and midpriced hotels, as well as the Swan, Dolphin, and Wilderness Lodge, are designed for four people; the other on-site hotels can easily fit five in a room. If your family is larger, consider either a villa or a trailer home.

@ Check-in time is 3 P.M. at most Disney resorts but 4 P.M. at the villas and All-Stars. You can drop off your bags and pick up your tickets and resort IDs in the morning, tour

Time-Saving Tip

Checkout time is 11 A.M., but once again, you need not let this interfere with your touring. Check out early in the morning, and store your bags with the concierge or valet parking. Then enjoy your last day in the parks. If you pay with a credit card, you can arrange for automatic checkout; an itemized charge statement is slipped under your door early on the morning you'll be leaving—a definite timesaver.

Helpful Hint

Booking mistakes are rare—in fact, I've never heard from anyone having a problem if they use Disney's own phone service to reserve an on-site room. But several families have reported problems with online booking. The Internet is a good way to comparison-shop for rates, but if you use it to book your room, be sure to make a follow-up call to confirm your reservation before you leave home.

Quick Guide to

Hotel	Description
All-Star Resorts	Very popular, great price
Animal Kingdom Lodge	New and exotic
Beach Club Resort	Homey, lovely, and not one bit fancy
Beach Club Villas	Great location, and brand new
BoardWalk Inn	Rooms are spacious, modern, and attractive
BoardWalk Villas	Great location for both Epcot and MGM
Caribbean Beach Resort	The price is right
The Contemporary Resort	Convenient and lively
Coronado Springs Resort	Great pool area
Dolphin Resort	Geared toward convention trade
Fort Wilderness Campground	Great for families who like to camp
The Grand Floridian	Expensive, but luxurious
Old Key West Resort	Lots of room, quiet
The Polynesian Resort	Relaxed and casual with a loyal, repeat clientele
Pop Century Resort	5,760 more budget rooms
Port Orleans Resort	Transports guests to the heart of the French Quarter or Riverside
Swan Resort	Adult-oriented and expensive
Wilderness Lodge	Rustic looking, with an intimate feel
Wilderness Lodge Villas	Great setting, a bit more space
Yacht Club Resort	On the door of the Epcot World Showcase

NOTE: *The central reservations number for on-site hotels is 407-W-DISNEY.*

On-Site Hotels

Location	Rating	Price Range	Details on
Animal Kingdom	★★	$77–$124	Page 73
Animal Kingdom	★★★	$194–$815	Page 78
Epcot	★★★	$194–$815	Page 64
Epcot	★★★	$224–$990	Page 64
Epcot	★★★	$194–$815	Page 65
Epcot	★★★	$224–$990	Page 66
Epcot	★	$133–$219	Page 67
Magic Kingdom	★★	$194–$815	Page 61
Animal Kingdom	★★	$133–$219	Page 77
Epcot	★	$194–$815	Page 68
Magic Kingdom	★★	$36–$229	Page 62
Magic Kingdom	★★	$194–$815	Page 60
Downtown Disney	★★	$224–$990	Page 72
Magic Kingdom	★★★	$194–$815	Page 57
Animal Kingdom	★★	$77–$124	Page 76
Downtown Disney	★★★	$133–$219	Page 70
Epcot	★	$194–$815	Page 68
Magic Kingdom	★★★	$194–$815	Page 58
Magic Kingdom	★★★	$224–$990	Page 58
Epcot	★★★	$194–$815	Page 64

until midafternoon, and then return to your hotel to check in.

@ When you check in, you'll be issued a resort ID that allows you to charge meals, drinks, tickets, and souvenirs to your room and also gives you access to all Disney World transportation.

Is It Worth the Expense to Stay On Site?

Staying at one of the Disney-owned hotels is very convenient—and with rates as low as $77 a night at the All-Star Resorts, it's becoming more affordable each year.

Off-site hotels are fighting back with special price promotions and perks of their own, arguing that the Disney hotels still cost more and bring you only slightly closer to the action. On site or off site? Ask yourself the following questions; your answers will help you decide.

@ *What time of year are you going, and how long are you staying?*
If you're going in summer or during a major holiday, you'll need every extra minute, so it's worth the cost to stay on site. (Another reason to book on site in summer: In the Florida heat, it's nearly a medical necessity to keep young kids out of the sun in midafternoon, and a nearby hotel room makes that easier.) Likewise, if your visit will be for fewer than four days, you can't afford to waste time commuting, so staying on site is worth considering.

@ *Are you flying or driving?*
If you're flying and doing only Disney World, it may make more economic sense to stay on site and use Disney World's transportation system in lieu of a rental car. But if you're driving to Orlando, consider an off-site location.

You'll be able to drive into the parks at the hours that suit you without being dependent on those sometimes less-than-prompt off-site buses.

Insider's Secret

If your kids are still young enough to take naps, staying on site makes it much easier to return to your room after lunch for a snooze. If they're pre-teens who are up to a full day in the parks, commute time is less of a factor.

@ *How strapped are you for cash?*

If money isn't a major issue, stay on site. If money is a primary consideration, you'll find your best deals at the budget hotels along Interstate 4. The exits that flank the Disney exit are chock-full of chain hotels and restaurants. Exit 68 alone has three Days Inns within two blocks of one another.

Money-Saving Tip

Disney isn't exactly known for deep discounts, but when times are slow they're as eager to fill their rooms as any other hotelier. The trouble is, they don't always announce these discounts to people who seem ready and willing to pay the full price. When you call in to make your resort reservations, always be sure to ask, "Are there any special offers available during the time I'll be visiting?"

@ *How much do your kids eat?*

Food is expensive at Disney World, both in the parks and at the on-site hotels. If you're staying off site, you can always eat at the numerous fast-food and family-style restaurants along Interstate 4, Route 192, and International Drive. If you book a suite, fixing simple meals in your room is even cheaper, and kids can really load up at those complimentary buffet breakfasts so frequently offered at the off-site hotels.

@ *Do you plan to visit other attractions?*

If you'll be spending half your time at Sea World, Universal Orlando, or the other non–Disney World attractions, stay off site, at least during those days. There's no need to pay top dollar for proximity to Disney if you're headed for Islands of Adventure.

@ *Will your party be splitting up at times?*

Does Dad want to play golf in the afternoon? Do you have teenagers who can spend a day at Blizzard Beach on their own? Will there be times when it would make sense for Dad to take the younger kids back to the hotel while Mom stays in the park with the older ones? Is your 5-year-old raring to go at dawn, whereas your 15-year-old sleeps until noon? If so, stay on site, where the use of the Disney World transportation system makes it easy for all of you to go your own way.

@ *What's your tolerance level for hassles?*

If you simply don't want to be bothered with interstate traffic, parking lots, carrying cash, and maps, stay on site.

The Advantages of Staying On Site

Extra Magic Hour

Extra Magic Hour is the current manifestation of Disney's Early Entry program that was dropped for several months during the economic slowdown of 2002. But Early Entry was so popular and such a huge part of why families opted to stay in Disney hotels in the first place that there was a great protest from resort guests. The program was reinstated, albeit under a different name.

It works like this: Each day, one of the four major theme parks opens for Disney resort guests an hour early, providing them the chance to ride some featured attractions and greet the characters in a relatively uncrowded park. (Note the word "relatively." There are so many Disney resort guests that there are still plenty of people around, just not as many as you find when the parks reach peak capacity later in the day.) You get information on which park is featured which day when you check into your hotel. If you need this information in advance to help you create your touring plan, you can call Guest Services at the resort where you'll be staying and ask them.

Generally, only a few attractions per park are open for the Extra Magic Hour, but at least one major ride is always operative, so this can be your chance to get the jump on the crowd for a big-deal ride like Space Mountain or Kilimanjaro Safaris. Just as important, when the ropes drop to the general public, you're already deep inside the theme park, not lined up outside the main entrance, so you can dash to other big-deal attractions before the rest of the crowd get there.

At present, the following schedule applies, but you should always confirm which park opens early on which day when you make your resort reservations.

Magic Kingdom	Sundays and Thursdays
Animal Kingdom	Mondays and Fridays
Disney–MGM Studios	Tuesdays and Saturdays
Epcot	Wednesdays

Priority Seating

On-site guests can arrange for priority restaurant seating both within the theme parks and at on-site hotels up to 60 days in advance. (Some restaurants allow for 120 days in advance, so ask when making arrangements.) Because there are so many on-site guests, this perk has the effect of freezing off-site visitors out of the most popular restaurants at the most popular times.

Length-of-Stay Passes

These tickets, which can be tailored to fit the length of your stay, offer you unlimited access to the major and minor parks and are slightly cheaper than comparable multiday passes.

Transportation

On-site guests have unlimited use of the monorails, buses, and boats of the Disney World transportation system, which is your best bet for getting to the major parks. The buses for the on-site hotels, for example, can deliver riders right to the Magic Kingdom gates, eliminating the need to take a ferryboat or monorail from the Ticket and Transportation Center (TTC)—and cutting at least 15 minutes off the commute.

Using Disney transportation can save you money, because many families staying on site don't rent a car.

Use of Other On-Site Hotel Facilities

If you want to use the child care or sports facilities of other Disney hotels or dine at their restaurants, you'll receive preferential treatment over off-site visitors. (Of course, each hotel, reasonably enough, allows its own guests first shot at its services.) This means that even if you're staying at the midpriced Port Orleans, you can use the kids' club at the Polynesian or take a tennis lesson at the Grand Floridian.

Free Parking at the Theme Parks

If you opt to drive your car to the theme parks, you don't have to pay to park. Just show the attendant your resort ID. Hey, every buck counts.

Package Delivery

If you're buying lots of souvenirs in the parks, you don't have to lug them around while you're touring. Disney will deliver your purchases directly to your hotel. (The packages were once delivered directly to your hotel room, but as part of Disney's cost-cutting measures, they are now delivered to your hotel gift shop. It still beats trying to hang on to a bunch of souvenirs.) It's often the next day before the stuff is delivered, so don't use the package delivery service on the last day of your visit.

Charging Privileges

If you're staying on site, everyone in your party will be issued a resort ID the day you arrive. The ID allows you to charge tickets, souvenirs, and food at sit-down restaurants—either at the hotels or within the parks—to your hotel room. (The vendors selling small things like ice cream or bottled water still require cash.) It's certainly better not to have to carry huge amounts of cash all the time, especially at the pools, water parks, and marinas.

Helpful Hint
If an ID with charging privileges is lost, it should be reported to the front desk immediately to avoid unauthorized charges.

It's up to you whether or not your older kids have charging privileges. Giving them this privilege makes it easier to send Johnny to the snack bar for a round of Cokes. If you do opt to give the minors charging privileges, be sure to impress on them that these IDs work like credit cards; they are not an open invitation for the kids to ingratiate themselves with the gang in the arcade by ordering pizza for everyone, purchasing all seven dwarfs from the hotel gift shop, or heaven forbid, obtaining cash advances.

Insider's Secret

When you get to your hotel, ask if it's possible to get a room upgrade. If the property isn't full, they'll often upgrade you to a better room at no additional cost.

Family Atmosphere

All the on-site hotels are designed with families in mind—the ambience is casual, security is tight, and there are always other kids around to play with. The on-site hotels have laundry facilities, generally located near the pools and arcades so that you can run a load while the youngsters play; there is late-night pizza delivery to your room, or you can visit fast-food courts; and if there is not a child care facility at your particular hotel, Guest Services can help you arrange for an in-room sitter. The emphasis at the Disney hotels is on making life more convenient for parents.

Insider's Secret

The on-site resorts, especially the luxury ones, often have special activities for kids such as scavenger hunts, unbirthday parties, and contests for prizes. These activities are usually posted around the pool areas or child care centers.

Cool Themes

All the on-site hotels have themes that are carried out in mega-detail. At the Polynesian, staff always greet you with "Aloha," jazz music plays all day at Port Orleans, and the dressers in rooms at All-Star Sports look like gym lockers. This makes staying at an on-site hotel almost as exciting for kids as being inside the parks.

In fact, because the on-site hotels are so unspeakably cool, it can be fun to just visit other hotels when you need an afternoon break from touring. Many families told us that they ate meals at several different on-site hotels during their visit; the restaurants carry out the themes too, so if three days at the Polynesian have left you burned out on pineapple juice, go Mexican at Coronado Springs.

Insider's Secret

The Disney resorts tend to be huge and sprawling—especially the All-Stars, Caribbean Beach, Port Orleans Riverside, and Coronado Springs. In other words, the less expensive the resort the more spread out it tends to be. (That said, even luxury resorts like the Yacht and Beach Clubs and Animal Kingdom Lodge have unbelievably long hallways.) If you have young kids with limited stamina, consider one of the smaller resorts. For families with older kids who might enjoy renting boats or bikes and exploring a bit, the wide open spaces of the larger resorts might actually be an advantage.

Rating the On-Site Disney Hotels

Not content with merely dominating the entertainment market, the Walt Disney Company has begun turning its attention to lodging the 10 million visitors who stream into Orlando each year. Orlando has more than 100,000 hotel rooms, and an increasing percentage of these rooms are Disney owned—that is, on site.

The majority of these new Disney hotels fall into the budget and midpriced categories. Until now, cost has been the primary reason for visitors to stay off site; with the explosion in on-site budget and midpriced resorts, Disney is working to eliminate even that objection. Each time Disney opens a new resort, your options increase.

And the need to make decisions multiplies as well. All this expansion means that even if a family has decided to stay on site, it still faces a bewildering number of choices. Does the convenience of being on the monorail line justify the increase in price? Do you want to stay amid turn-of-the-century Victorian splendor, or is a fort more your style? Is it important to be near swimming, golf courses, stables, and other sports activities, or do you plan to spend most of your time in the parks? As with all of Disney World, making the best choice hinges on your awareness of what your family really wants.

On-Site Luxury Hotels

Luxury hotels are actually full-scale resorts, with fine dining, amenities such as health clubs and spas, and a variety of sports options. You can have valet parking, bell service, room service, and other perks that make the mechanics of checking in and out much easier. There's a price attached—the Disney luxury hotels cost, on average, twice as much a night as the midpriced hotels. Luxury hotels include the BoardWalk, Yacht and Beach Clubs, Contemporary, Grand Floridian, Polynesian, Swan, Dolphin, Wilderness Lodge, and Animal Kingdom Lodge.

On-Site Midpriced and Budget Hotels

"Midpriced" is something of a misnomer because both the price and the quality are higher than for a typical chain hotel in Orlando. You'll pay about $30 more a night than you would at a comparable off-site hotel, but you get a mood that's pure Disney. As you sip a drink and watch your kids zoom down the tongue of the beloved sea serpent slide at the Port Orleans pool,

Best On-Site Choices at a Glance

BEST MAGIC KINGDOM RESORT: WILDERNESS LODGE

This resort knocked off the longtime champ, the Polynesian. The Wilderness Lodge has a lot of repeat business; once families stay here, they report that they have no interest in going anywhere else.

BEST EPCOT RESORT: THE BEACH CLUB

You like Epcot? It's a stroll away— and the pool is to die for.

BEST MODERATELY PRICED RESORT: PORT ORLEANS

Relaxed and homey, Port Orleans has the charm of a full-priced hotel at a reduced cost. Because it has a full-service restaurant, the Riverside section edges out its sister, the French Quarter.

BEST BUDGET RESORT: ALL-STAR SPORTS, MUSIC, AND MOVIES

The All-Star Sports, Music, and Movies have the distinction of being both the winners and the only entries in this category—but they're still worth mentioning because of strong reader support. The popularity of these resorts is why Disney is opening a new budget complex, Pop Century Resort.

BEST VILLA: VILLAS AT WILDERNESS LODGE

Families stay loyal to the Wilderness Lodge in any form. The BoardWalk Villas also got a lot of votes.

BEST NEWCOMER: ANIMAL KINGDOM LODGE

Families love this exotic locale, with its unique proximity to the animals and great food choices.

you certainly won't feel like you're slumming. The hotels are well maintained and landscaped, with gobs of atmosphere thrown in that carry their motifs to the nth degree. Resorts that fall into the midpriced description include the Caribbean Beach, Port Orleans, and Coronado Springs Resorts.

The budget hotels are the All-Star Resorts—three mega-hotels, including All-Star Music, All-Star Sports, and All-Star Movies—and, when it opens, the new Pop Century Resort.

It's worth noting that the budget and midpriced hotels don't run with quite the legendary efficiency of the more expensive resorts. I recently endured a 40-minute check-in procedure at All-Star Sports, something that would be unheard of at the Grand Floridian. A woman behind me was grousing that there was no freebie Mickey Mouse lotion in her room like they had at the Yacht Club. But these minor inconveniences pale when you consider that most of the on-site benefits—easy transportation to the parks, help with tickets and reservations, early admission to the theme parks—are just as available to those paying $77 a night at All-Star Sports as to those paying $377 at the BoardWalk. And, hey, the housekeepers still leave your kids' stuffed animals in the window to greet them in the evening, so who can complain?

Villa-Style Accommodations

Larger families or those who like to prepare their own meals may want to rent a villa. Resorts included in this category are the Wilderness Lodge Villas, BoardWalk Villas, and Disney's Old Key West.

On-Site Camping

Want to stay on site but can't afford one of the resorts? Camping at the Fort Wilderness Campground may be your best option.

Definition of Star Ratings for Hotels

★★★ This resort was a favorite among families surveyed and offers solid value for the money.

★★ Surveyed families were satisfied with the service and amenities at this property and felt they got what they paid for.

★ This resort is either more adult oriented, with fewer amenities designed to appeal to families, or is more expensive than you'd expect considering the location or level of service.

Magic Kingdom Hotels

If you'll be spending most of your time at the Magic Kingdom—and you're willing to spend the bucks—consider one of these resorts.

The Polynesian Resort	★★★ 407-824-2000

Designed to emulate an island village, the Polynesian is relaxed and casual. The main desk, as well as most of the restaurants and shops, is in the Great Ceremonial House, along with orchids, parrots, and fountains. Guests stay in one of the 863 rooms in the sprawling "long houses."

Proximity to the Magic Kingdom	Excellent, via direct monorail, launch, or ferryboat
Proximity to Epcot	Good, via monorail with one change at the TTC
Proximity to MGM	Fair, via bus
Proximity to the Animal Kingdom	Fair, via bus

Pluses

+ The Polynesian offers the most options for transport to the Magic Kingdom. You're on the monorail line as well as within walking distance of the ferryboats, and launches leave from the docks regularly. Your best route to the Magic Kingdom depends on the location of your room. Near the lagoon? Take the launch. Near the Great Ceremonial House? The monorail is faster. On the beach? Walk to the ferryboat.

+ A private beach, with an attractive pool and several boating options, is available. Like the beach at the Grand Floridian, the Polynesian beach has canvas shells that provide shade for napping babies and toddlers digging in the sand.

+ The Kona Cafe is one of the best places for breakfast in all of Walt Disney World.

+ The Neverland Club is the best on-site child care in WDW.

Minuses

– Without a discount, expect to pay $194 a night and up.

– Like the Contemporary, it's an older resort. The color scheme screams 1970s.

Overall Grade: ★★★ The Polynesian enjoys a loyal repeat clientele, and that says it all.

The Wilderness Lodge and Villas

★★★
407-824-3200

Starting at $194 a night, the rustic-looking, western-spirited Wilderness Lodge is aimed at filling the gap between the mid-priced and luxury hotels. (The Villas at Wilderness Lodge, part of the Disney Vacation Club time-share program, opened in 2000 and quickly sold out.)

The theme of Wilderness Lodge extends into every aspect of the hotel's design. The pool begins indoors as a hot spring and then flows into a meandering creek, culminating in a waterfall into the rocky caverns of the outdoor pool. The awe-inspiring lobby, which looks like a Lincoln Log project run amok, centers on an 82-foot fireplace that blazes all year round. The Native American–themed wallpaper and quilted bedspreads in the guest rooms, the staff dressed like park rangers, and even the stick ponies children ride to their tables in the Whispering Canyon Café all combine to evoke the feel of a National Park Service lodge built a hundred years ago.

When you check in, you're given a brochure on Wilderness Lodge lore, which will help you find the 100 animals hidden in the lobby, many of them carved in totems or branded in chandeliers. And you'll learn that "it took over two billion years to build the fireplace," because the rock represents strata from all the layers of the Grand Canyon.

Proximity to the Magic Kingdom	Good, via launch
Proximity to Epcot	Fair, via bus
Proximity to MGM	Fair, via bus
Proximity to the Animal Kingdom	Fair, via bus

Pluses

+ The lodge is heavily themed. The pool area is especially dramatic.

+ You are close to River Country and have all the down-home fun of Fort Wilderness without having to camp out.

+ On-site child care.

+ Tons of happy quasi-campers here. The Wilderness Lodge enjoys a loyal repeat business.

Minuses

− At $194 and up a night, it's not cheap.

− This is the only Magic Kingdom resort without monorail access to the Kingdom. The boat takes slightly longer.

– The rooms sleep only four people (the other full-priced resorts sleep five).

Overall Grade: ★★★ A great family-pleasing setting and a favorite with many of our readers.

The Grand Floridian   ★★
                                          407-824-3000

Modeled after the famed Florida beach resorts of the 1800s and possibly the prettiest of all Disney hotels, the Grand Floridian has 900 rooms ensconced among its gabled roofs, soaring ceilings, and broad white verandas.

Proximity to the Magic Kingdom	Excellent, via direct monorail or launch
Proximity to Epcot	Good, via monorail with a change at the TTC
Proximity to MGM	Fair, via bus
Proximity to Animal Kingdom	Fair, via bus

Pluses

+ Convenient location on the monorail line.

+ A private beach on the Seven Seas Lagoon and numerous boating options.

+ On-site child care center.

+ Phenomenal dining. Citricos and Victoria and Albert's are among the finest restaurants in all Disney World. If you have the kids along, check out 1900 Park Fare, which serves a buffet with Disney characters.

+ On-site health club and full-service spa.

+ Exceptionally lovely rooms. The Grand Floridian is a favorite with honeymooners and others seeking a romantic ambience. (It's within sight of Disney's wedding chapel.)

+ The Grand Floridian offers lots of special little touches, such as live music in the lobby at night and tea parties for the kids. Young girls are especially thrilled at the chance to nibble cookies and sip tea with Alice in Wonderland and her friends.

Minuses

– Room prices tend toward the higher end of the deluxe range.

– The elegance puts off some families who feel funny trooping in dripping bathing suits past a grand piano.

Overall Grade: ★★ Expensive but luxurious.

The Contemporary Resort

★★
407-824-1000

You'll either love or hate the Contemporary, which has 1,050 rooms surrounding a mammoth, high-tech lobby full of shops and restaurants. This place is always hopping.

Proximity to the Magic Kingdom	Excellent, via direct monorail
Proximity to Epcot	Good, via monorail with a change at the TTC
Proximity to MGM	Fair, via bus
Proximity to the Animal Kingdom	Fair, via bus

Pluses

+ Located on the monorail line.

+ Fairly easy to book, and discounts are available.

+ The Contemporary is home to the Fiesta Fun Center, a giant arcade.

+ Standard water sports are available, along with tennis and a spa.

+ The California Grille is Walt Disney World's premier restaurant.

Minuses

— It's loud, with a big-city feel that is exactly what many families come to Florida to escape. "Like sleeping in the middle of Space Mountain," wrote one mother. *Note: The Garden Wings are quieter and cheaper than the main building.*

— Like the other hotels on the monorail line, the Contemporary is expensive. Expect to pay $194 and up a night.

Overall Grade: ★★ Convenient and lively. Perhaps a little too lively.

Fort Wilderness Campground   ★★
407-824-2900

A resort unto itself, Fort Wilderness offers campsites for tents and RVs as well as air-conditioned trailers for rent. The wide-open spaces, perfect for volleyball, biking, and hiking, are a relief for families with kids old enough to explore on their own.

Proximity to the Magic Kingdom   Good, via bus or launch

Helpful Hint

Fort Wilderness Campground is so sprawling that many families rent a golf cart to make it easier to get around.

Proximity to Epcot	Fair, directly via bus, or via bus to the TTC, where you can change to the monorail
Proximity to MGM	Fair, via bus
Proximity to the Animal Kingdom	Fair, via bus

Pluses

✦ Fort Wilderness offers a huge variety of activities for kids, such as hayrides, horseback and pony riding, and a petting farm with pigs, goats, and geese.

+ Proximity to River Country and the Hoop-Dee-Doo Musical Revue.

+ Hookups and tent sites are as low as $36 a night. Trailers rent for up to $229 a night but sleep six people and offer full kitchens.

+ Groceries are available at the on-site trading post.

+ Daily housekeeping service is free in the rental trailers.

Minuses

– Camping may not seem like a vacation to you.

– A large number of people are sharing relatively few facilities, and the pools and beach can get very crowded.

– Some families have reported that the rental trailers are shabby and not up to Disney standards. One woman wrote that the first time she entered her rental trailer, the doorknob fell off in her hand!

– The place is so spread out that it requires its own in-resort bus system to get guests from one area to another. You can rent golf carts or bikes, but make no mistake: Fort Wilderness is large and hard to navigate.

Overall Grade: ★★ If you like to camp and are willing to put up with a little inconvenience for great savings, this is a good option.

Epcot Hotels

The Epcot resorts share their own "backdoor" entrance into Epcot's World Showcase. Water taxis and walkways link the resorts to Epcot, where guests can enter the park, buy tickets, get maps, and rent strollers from the World Traveler shop. The World Showcase does not open until 11 A.M., so guests have a bit of a walk to Future World.

The Yacht and Beach Clubs   ★★★
407-934-7000

Designed to resemble a turn-of-the-century Nantucket seaside resort, the Yacht and Beach Clubs are situated on a 25-acre freshwater lake. The Yacht Club, with 635 rooms, is the more elegant of the two, but the sunny gingham-and-wicker-filled Beach Club, with 580 rooms, is equally charming. The Yacht and Beach Clubs hit the perfect balance for families with young kids in tow—homey, lovely, and not one bit fancy.

Proximity to the Magic Kingdom	Fair, via bus
Proximity to Epcot	Excellent, via a short stroll over a bridge
Proximity to MGM	Excellent, via water taxi
Proximity to the Animal Kingdom	Fair, via bus

Pluses

+ Stormalong Bay, the water recreation area that separates the two resorts, is like a private water park. The sand-bottomed "bay" contains pools of varying depths, waterslides, and a wrecked ship for atmosphere. It's especially fun to climb the shipwreck nearly to the top of its rigging and then zoom through a long tube into the middle of the pool. In fact, the water areas at the Yacht and Beach Clubs are so nice you'll have no trouble convincing the kids to return "home" for a dip in lieu of a more time-consuming trek to Typhoon Lagoon or Blizzard Beach.

+ The Yacht and Beach Clubs are literally on the doorstep of the Epcot World Showcase and an easy boat commute to MGM as well.

+ The Sandcastle Club offers on-site child care for children ages 3 to 12.

+ Disney characters are on hand for breakfast at the Cape May Cafe in the Beach Club.

+ The two resorts share an on-site health club.

+ Bayside Marina offers a wide choice of watercraft.

Minuses

– Rates run $194 and up a night, but discounts do apply in the off-season.

Overall Grade: ★★★ These hotels enjoy a large repeat business from satisfied families. If your kids like hanging out at the pool, and you all like Epcot, try the Yacht or Beach Clubs on your next trip down.

The BoardWalk Inn   ★★★
407-939-5100

The BoardWalk Inn and the BoardWalk Villas form the hub of a large complex with convention space, four restaurants, and the ESPN sports club, as well as a dance and comedy club. The mood? Turn-of-the-century Atlantic City. Cheery, attractive rooms are clustered above an old-fashioned boardwalk, and the action on the waterfront goes on until late at night.

In fact, some readers have written that the BoardWalk is a far more affordable version of Pleasure Island. The two night-clubs, Atlantic Dance and Jellyrolls, charge a slight cover during the on-season, but even with this you'll be paying far less than the $21 admission fee to Pleasure Island.

The midway-style games, carnival barkers, and arcades can keep older kids busy. A fun extra is renting a surrey bike ($10.75 for a half-hour) and taking the whole gang for a loop around the lagoon. (You'll be gasping for air by the time you pass the Yacht Club.) The BoardWalk area is stunningly beautiful at night.

Proximity to the Magic Kingdom	Fair, via bus
Proximity to Epcot	Excellent, via a short stroll
Proximity to MGM	Excellent, via water taxi
Proximity to the Animal Kingdom	Fair, via bus

Pluses

+ Great location for both Epcot and MGM.

+ A wider selection of restaurants and entertainment than at the other resorts.

+ On-site health club.

+ You'll have no trouble keeping older kids entertained here—although you may go broke in the process.

+ On-site kids' club.

Minuses

− Expensive, at $194 and up a night.

− May be too lively and hopping for families with very young kids. The rooms facing the boardwalk are loud at night.

Overall Grade: ★★★ You'll feel like you're right in the middle of the action—because you are.

BoardWalk Villas
★★★
407-939-5100

The villa side of the BoardWalk complex offers the same lively activities and great restaurant selection—as well as more rooms upstairs. Many of the suites have whirlpool tubs, and the mini-kitchens are well stocked. Villa units are a bit more expensive than the regular rooms.

Proximity to the Magic Kingdom	Fair, via bus
Proximity to Epcot	Excellent, via a short stroll
Proximity to MGM	Excellent, via water taxi
Proximity to the Animal Kingdom	Fair, via bus

Pluses

+ Lots of space for large families.

+ Food can be prepared in the room—saving you money.

+ Great location for both Epcot and MGM.

+ A wider selection of restaurants and entertainment than at the other resorts.

+ On-site health club.

+ Plenty of activities to keep older kids entertained.

+ On-site kids' club.

Minuses

− Expensive, starting at $224 a night for a suite.

− May be too lively and hopping for families with very young kids.

Overall Grade: ★★★ Fresh and fun—and a great option if you have a large family and need the space of a villa.

Caribbean Beach Resort

★
407-934-3400

This family-priced 2,112-room resort is located on 200 acres with a private lake and white-sand beaches. Each section of this mammoth hotel is painted a different tropical color and named after a different Caribbean island. Each "island" has its own shuttle bus stop, private beach, and pool. The rooms, although small, are attractively decorated.

Proximity to the Magic Kingdom	Fair, via bus
Proximity to Epcot	Fair, via bus
Proximity to MGM	Fair, via bus
Proximity to the Animal Kingdom	Fair, via bus

Pluses

+ The price is right, at $133 to $219 a night.

+ Parrot Cay, an artificial island with a playground, climbing fort, and small aviary, is fun for young kids.

+ The standard selection of watercraft.

+ The new restaurant, Shutters, is a vast improvement over the resort's previous full-service restaurant.

Minuses

− Although the buses are regular, they're not as swift as the water taxis or monorails, and they stop at all the resort "islands." Expect a longer commute time.

− The place is huge. It may be a major hike from your hotel room to the food plaza or marina. If you have young kids, bring your own stroller.

− Caribbean Beach is the oldest of the midpriced hotels, and many of the rooms show it. The resort is in a constant state of refurbishment, with some rooms being recently updated and others looking old and tired. Ask for a recently refurbished room when you book.

− No on-site child care.

Overall Grade: ★ Solid value for the money, but try the newer midpriced resorts first.

Swan and Dolphin   ★
407-934-3000

This convention/resort complex is connected to Epcot and MGM by water taxi and bridges. The Swan and Dolphin are "twin" hotels (like the nearby Yacht and Beach Clubs), which means that although they have separate check-ins (and are in fact owned by separate companies), the resorts are alike in architecture and mood. Despite their emphatically sophisticated feel, both have made great strides to become more family oriented and to offer amenities directed toward the parents of young children.

Proximity to the Magic Kingdom	Fair, via bus
Proximity to Epcot	Excellent, via tram or water taxi
Proximity to MGM	Excellent, via water taxi
Proximity to the Animal Kingdom	Fair, via bus

Pluses

+ Disney is aggressively going after the convention trade with the Swan and Dolphin. If a working parent is lucky, he or she can score a free family vacation here.

+ On-site child care.

+ The expanded beach area offers a playground, kiddie pools, water slides, and a small marina with swan-shaped paddleboats.

+ Bike rentals, tennis courts, and a health club are also available.

Minuses

− Expensive, at $194 and up a night.

− Although considered on site, these hotels are not owned by Disney and have less of a Disney feel. It's an intangible, but you notice the difference immediately.

− Because of the proximity to Epcot and MGM and the fact that they're gunning for the convention trade, these are adult-oriented resorts, with a citified atmosphere.

Overall Grade: ★ A great place to go if the company is picking up the tab. Otherwise, try the Yacht and Beach Clubs first.

Downtown Disney Hotels

Port Orleans
★★★
407-934-5000

The former sister resorts called Port Orleans and Dixie Landings have now been merged into one giant resort called Port Orleans. The New Orleans–themed section (formerly called Port Orleans) is now called the French Quarter; the Old South section (formerly called Dixie Landings) is now known as Riverside. What hasn't changed is that the resort still offers a great deal for the money.

The French Quarter has manicured gardens, wrought-iron railings, and streets with names such as Rue d'Baga. The Mardi Gras mood extends to the pool area, dubbed the "Doubloon Lagoon," where alligators play jazz while King Triton sits atop the water slide, regally surveying his domain.

Riverside is a bit more down-home, with a steamboat-shaped lobby, general stores run by gingham-clad girls in braids, and "Ol' Man Island," a swimming area based on the Disney film *Song of the South*. A bit schizophrenic in architecture, with white-columned buildings encircling fishing holes and cotton mills, Riverside manages to mix in a variety of Southern clichés without losing its ditzy charm. If Huck Finn ever married Scarlett O'Hara, this is where they'd come on their honeymoon.

Comparatively speaking, the French Quarter is only half the size of Riverside, which means the odds are that you'll be close to the pool, lobby, food court, and shuttle bus station; at Riverside, getting around is more of a headache. Both resorts have a fast-food court and a bar that offers live entertainment, but only Riverside has a sit-down restaurant.

Proximity to the Magic Kingdom	Fair, via bus
Proximity to Epcot	Fair, via bus

Proximity to MGM   Fair, via bus
Proximity to the Animal Kingdom   Fair, via bus

Pluses

+ Great pools (especially at the French Quarter), which can easily keep the kids entertained for an afternoon. Riverside also has on-site fishing.

+ So cleverly designed and beautifully maintained that you won't believe you're staying on site for half the price of the other resorts. (Rooms are $133 to $219.)

+ Both hotels have marinas with a selection of watercraft as well as bike rentals.

+ Horse and carriage tours are available around the resort.

+ The Sassagoula Steamboat offers easy water access from both resorts to Downtown Disney and Pleasure Island.

Minuses

– Unless you drive your own car, you are dependent on buses for transport to the major and minor parks, which means a slightly longer commuting time. The fact that the two resorts share buses slows you down a bit.

– No on-site child care.

Overall Grade: ★★★ You get a good deal here in more ways than one.

Insider's Secret

If you can't decide which section of Port Orleans is best for your family, be advised that the French Quarter is much quieter and there's more activity at Riverside.

Disney's Old Key West
★★
407-827-7700

Originally sold as time-shares, the villas of Old Key West are available for nightly rentals. You'll get all the standard amenities of a Disney resort—plus a lot more room. The setting is pleasant and airy, very Floridian in spirit.

Proximity to the Magic Kingdom	Fair, via bus
Proximity to Epcot	Fair, via bus
Proximity to MGM	Fair, via bus
Proximity to the Animal Kingdom	Fair, via bus

Pluses

+ If you have more than two children and need to spread out, or if you'd like a kitchen where you can prepare your own meals, Old Key West is a good on-site option.

+ Tennis, pools, a cute sand play area with a permanent castle, and a marina are on site. There's an arcade, a fitness room, and tandem bikes and movies for rental.

+ Prices run from $224 for a studio with a kitchenette to $990 and up for a three-bedroom Grand Villa, which can easily accommodate 12 people. A roomy two-bedroom villa with full kitchen is about $495, which compares with a room at the Grand Floridian or Yacht Club. If you're willing to swap proximity to the parks for more space and the chance to cook your own meals, Old Key West may be just what you need.

+ The Trumbo Ferry offers swift transit to Downtown Disney.

Minuses

– Still much pricier than such off-site villas as Embassy Suites.

– Quieter, with less going on than at the resorts.

– No child care options.

Overall Grade: ★★ Very homey with nice touches such as tennis courts, shuffleboard courts, and a small basketball court. One of the best options for families seeking peace and quiet at the end of the day.

Disney Institute Villas

The Disney Institute is currently closed and is in the process of becoming Disney's Saratoga Springs and Spa, a Vacation Club time-share and mixed-use facility. About 200 Vacation Club condos will open in 2004 and the rooms of the former Institute will be available for corporate retreats and conventions.

In other words, the property is evolving and thus is no longer available to your average vacationing family. (Unless they're members of the Vacation Club, of course.) Families seeking full suites should consider the villas at the Beach Club, BoardWalk, Wilderness Lodge, or Old Key West.

Animal Kingdom Hotels

All-Star Sports, All-Star Music, and ★★
All-Star Movies Resorts   407-939-5000/939-6000

The All-Star Resorts have rapidly built such a loyal following that despite having nearly 6,000 rooms, they fill up quickly. There are three reasons for the resort's success—price, price, and price. The All-Star Resorts make staying on site possible for families who previously could only dream of such a splurge.

All-Star Sports contains five sections—tennis, football, surfing, basketball, and baseball—with the decor themed appropriately. At the Music Resort, you can choose between jazz, rock 'n' roll, country, calypso, and Broadway tunes. All-Star Movies offers The Love Bug, Toy Story, Fantasia, 101 Dalmatians, and The Mighty Ducks.

Insider's Secret

If your child adores the 101 Dalmatians or is a big football buff, you can indeed request what section of what hotel you'll be lodged in when you make your reservation. Disney won't guarantee you'll get your request, but they'll try.

The in-your-face graphics of the brightly colored buildings and the resort's general zaniness appeal to kids. There are giant tennis ball cans and cowboy boots, a walk-through jukebox, and footballs the size of houses. At the calypso pool in All-Star Music, the buildings are lime green and punctuated with maracas; pitcher Goofy throws water in the diamond-shaped baseball pool at All-Star Sports and stands as goalie at the hockey rink of the Mighty Ducks pool at All-Star Movies. Palm trees are positioned like basketball players set to tip off before a gargantuan backboard in the basketball section of All-Star Sports, Mickey conducts sprays of water in the Fantasia pool of All-Star Movies, and show tunes play all day under the marquee on the streets of the Broadway district at All-Star Music. It's budget, but it ain't boring.

Proximity to the Magic Kingdom	Fair, via bus
Proximity to Epcot	Fair, via bus
Proximity to MGM	Fair, via bus
Proximity to the Animal Kingdom	Good, via a short bus ride

Pluses

+ In a word, cost. Rooms start at $77 during the off-season.

+ All-Star Resorts offers an affordable option for families with a disabled member. For $89 a night, you can have a slightly larger ground-floor suite with roll-in showers.

+ The shuttle buses are a good transportation option, considering the price. When you get into this price range at the off-site hotels, you often have to pay for a shuttle. They run every 15 minutes, and service is prompt.

+ Proximity to Blizzard Beach and the Animal Kingdom.

+ The food court, although crowded, provides a fair selection.

Minuses

— Food options are limited. Fast-food courts only, with no restaurants or indoor bars.

— Sports options are limited; swimming is about it.

— The rooms are very small; they sleep four, but you'll be bunched.

— By breaking each resort into five separate sections, Disney is striving to eliminate that sleeping-in-the-middle-of-Penn-Station feel. But there's no way around the fact that it takes more effort to get around a huge hotel than a small one.

— Longer check-in than is typical for Disney resorts.

Overall Grade: ★★ Lots of bang for the buck here.

Time-Saving Tip

The All-Star Resorts are enormous, and check-in time (3 to 4 P.M.) is a madhouse. If you arrive early, go ahead and try to check in. You may have to return later if your room is not yet available, but at least you'll wait in the shorter, swifter-moving "key pick-up" line.

Helpful Hint

If you don't care what All-Star section you're in, request a room near the lobby when you call to make your reservation. This can save you lots of walking each time you leave your room to catch a bus or eat a meal.

Disney's Newest Resort: ★★
Pop Century Resort

Note: The Pop Century Resort was nearing completion when the September 11, 2001, attacks on the World Trade Center and the Pentagon brought sudden and drastic changes to the travel and tourism industry. Faced with empty rooms at their existing hotels, Disney halted construction on the Pop Century Resort for almost two years, but the resort is scheduled to open by the beginning of 2004. It will be fully reviewed in our next edition.

Because of the incredible popularity of the All-Star Resorts—they are so hot that rooms are sold out months in advance—Disney is adding another mammoth budget hotel. The Pop Century Resort will have 5,760 rooms spread across 20 buildings. Each pair of buildings will be themed to a different decade, from the 1900s to the 1990s. Expect the same larger-than-life icons and bright colors that earmark the All-Stars. Cultural touchstones from each decade—a huge jukebox from the 1950s and an oversized yo-yo from the 1960s, for example—will mark the entrances. The roofs are lined with catchphrases from the era, as well as silhouettes illustrating dances of the time.

At $77 to $124 a night, the Pop Century Resort is in the same price range as the All-Stars. All the budget resorts offer the same basics, that is, swimming pools but not a lot of other sport options, a food court but no sit-down restaurant, and bus service to the parks. Still, despite the lack of frills, the Pop Century Resort will offer all Disney amenities such as free transportation to the theme parks, possible early entry, and so on.

Coronado Springs Resort

★★
407-939-1000

Disney's first moderately priced convention hotel has a Mexican theme, with Spanish tiled roofs, adobe walls, and a pool area that is dominated by an imposing Mayan temple. The rooms are scattered around a 15-acre lake and a series of rocky streams. Most of the action centers on the 95,000-square-foot convention space, but the resort is open to regular vacationers as well.

Proximity to the Magic Kingdom	Fair, via bus
Proximity to Epcot	Fair, via bus
Proximity to MGM	Fair, via bus
Proximity to the Animal Kingdom	Good, via a short bus ride

Pluses

+ Dramatic pool area with water slide, arcade, bar and fast-food stand, and a themed playground. The Dig Site is the heart of all the resort action.

+ Marina with standard boat and bike rentals.

+ On-site health club—a rarity in this price range.

+ Close to the Animal Kingdom and Blizzard Beach.

Minuses

– Coronado Springs is designed as a convention hotel, meaning it has more businesspeople and fewer families than is typical for a Disney resort. You might actually hear cursing by the pool here.

– The food court is far too small to accommodate nearly 2,000 rooms. Some families have reported that they had to leave the resort to get a quick breakfast during peak hours.

– The resort is quite spread out, even by Disney standards. If you're in one of the more far-flung rooms, you may face a 15-minute walk to the pool area and food court. Definitely bring strollers for little ones, and rent bikes for the older kids or have them bring their in-line skates.

Overall Grade: ★★ The price is right, and the resort is gaining in popularity.

Insider's Secret
The good news is that because of the resort's convention trade, Coronado Springs has more amenities than your typical midpriced hotel. The bad news is that because of the convention trade it also has less of a family atmosphere.

Animal Kingdom Lodge
★★★
407-938-4760

Step inside the massive lobby of the new Animal Kingdom Lodge and you'll be transported . . . outdoors. From the thatched roof to the enormous mud fireplace, streams, rope bridges, and lighting created to accentuate sunrises and sunsets, Disney's newest luxury resort, opened in April 2000, creates the feel of a game lodge in the middle of a wildlife preserve.

Designed by Peter Dominick of Wilderness Lodge fame, the architecture is authentically East African, but the real show takes place through the four-story observation windows. The Animal Kingdom Lodge is located in the middle of a 33-acre savanna, where more than 200 animals freely roam. Thirty-six species of mammals, including giraffes, zebra, and gazelles, and 26 species of birds, such as the sacred ibis and African spoonbill, live within the working wildlife preserve. The kopje, a series of rock outcroppings, serves as a natural barrier but is also an elevated walkway, offering panoramic views of the landscape and the chance for guests to come within 15 feet of the animals.

Perhaps you'd rather safari from the comfort of your own room? The six-story lodge is built in the semicircle "kraal" design of an East African village; more than 90 percent of the 1,293 guest rooms have a view of the savanna. Rooms are decorated with hand-carved furnishings, tapestries, and the vibrant jewel tones of East Africa.

Adventure extends to the eating areas. Swahili for "cooling place," Jiko features two wood-burning ovens to simulate the effect of cooking in the open bush. Bona, the family buffet restaurant, showcases an exhibit kitchen and pays tribute to the multicultural influences within Africa, including French, Malaysian, Indian, and English. Named for the river that flows from Kenya to Tanzania and located poolside, Mara is the largest quick-service restaurant at Walt Disney World. Victoria Falls, perched beside a waterfall in the mezzanine lounge, serves a variety of beverages, including gourmet coffees, teas, and, of course, South African wines.

Proximity to the Magic Kingdom	Fair, via bus
Proximity to Epcot	Fair, via bus
Proximity to MGM	Fair, via bus
Proximity to the Animal Kingdom	Excellent, via bus or a short walkway

Pluses

+ This new resort is one of the most dramatic on the property. For sheer romance and ambience, you can't beat the views of the savanna.

+ Lots of extras for the kids, including tours about the animals and games held in the lobby.

+ The lodge includes a child care center, spa, and health club.

+ Close to Animal Kingdom and Blizzard Beach.

+ Jiko is one of the best restaurants on Disney property.

Minuses

- The lodge is pricey, at $194 and up a night. Because the newest resorts are often the most popular, discounts rarely apply.

- The out-of-the-way location means longer-than-average bus rides, especially to the Magic Kingdom, Epcot, and MGM.

Overall Grade: ★★★ The most unique resort on the property.

Helpful Hint

The Florida Department of Transportation renumbered the I-4 exits to Disney World in 2002, causing some confusion for tourists who relied on the old exit numbers. Be sure to confirm directions if you'll be arriving in Orlando by car.

Disney Village Hotel Plaza

The Disney Village Hotel Plaza hotels include the Buena Vista Palace, the Grosvenor, Doubletree Suites, the Hilton, the Hotel Royal Plaza, Courtyard by Marriott, and the Travelodge Hotel.

Because they're neither owned by Disney nor built on Disney property, the Disney Village Hotel Plaza hotels are somewhat of a hybrid between the on-site and off-site lodgings. Located just across the road from the Downtown Disney Marketplace, these hotels are also considered to be "official" Disney World hotels, meaning they run frequent shuttles to all Disney theme parks and offer price breaks on admission tickets. Nonetheless, I have trouble recommending the Disney Village Hotel Plaza hotels with a clear conscience. They're quite expensive for what you get, especially when less pricey accommodations are available just a couple of minutes away at Exit 68.

Proximity to the Magic Kingdom	Fair, via bus
Proximity to Epcot	Fair, via bus

Proximity to MGM	Fair, via bus
Proximity to the Animal Kingdom	Fair, via bus
Proximity to Downtown Disney	Excellent, via a short walk

Off-Site Hotels: Which Location Is Best?

Here's the scoop on three main off-site areas that tourists frequent: Exits 62 and 68 off Interstate 4 and International Drive. Both Exit 62 and Exit 68 are within a 10-minute drive of the theme parks. Exit 68 (US 535) backs up to the hotels of the Disney Village Hotel Plaza, and any number of upscale eateries and hotels are nearby, mixed in with the Days Inns and fast-food places. The Hyatt Regency Grand Cypress, Embassy Suites, Lake Buena Vista, and Holiday Inn Sunspree are all at Exit 68. This area has undergone major expansion in the last few years. On Palm Parkway, just off Exit 68, there are several new suite hotels, including Homewood Suites and Sierra Suites, as well as a recently opened Hampton Inn and Courtyard by Marriott. As chain hotels go, these are all fresh and bright, and Exit 68 is your best bet if you want to be close without paying Disney prices.

Exit 62, which leads to US 192, is a bit less expensive, probably because the hotels are in general older and you don't see the resort area as you're driving down Interstate 4. Hotels there run about $30 a night cheaper than at a comparable hotel at Exit 68.

International Drive is farther out, about 20 minutes from the theme parks, but it is modern and well kept. International Drive boasts every chain restaurant you've ever heard of, as well as ice skating, miniature golf, shopping and entertainment complexes, and a three-story McDonald's. International Drive is the conduit that runs between Sea World, Universal Orlando, and Wet 'n Wild and is your most central location if you'll be spending lots of time at these three parks.

Time-Saving Tip

Many off-site hotels boast that they run shuttles to the theme parks but BEWARE. Relying on off-site transportation can make for a long commute. The worst situations are when two or three hotels share a shuttle—you'll have to make stops at all of them. Even if a resort has its own shuttle, it may make stops at all four of the major parks, meaning commutes of up to an hour just to get from your hotel to the theme park of your choice. A lengthy bus ride is maddening in the morning when the kids are eager to get to the rides and can be disastrous in the evening when you're all tired anyway.

If you're staying off site and planning to use your resort's shuttle, be sure to ask if it is their own private shuttle and if service to the major theme parks is direct. If you don't like what you hear, you may need to get a rental car.

How to Get the Best Deals on Off-Site Hotels

Orlando has more hotel rooms than any other city in the country, so there are plenty of beds out there for the taking. Here are a few tips to make sure you're getting the most bang for your buck.

The Orlando Magicard is free and offers discounts of between 20 and 50 percent on area hotels, as well as restaurants and non-Disney attractions. Delivery takes four weeks, so order in advance by calling 800-255-5786, or visit the Web site at www.go2orlando.com.

The *Entertainment Guide* is another source of major discounts; more than 100 hotels in the greater Orlando area offer price breaks of up to 50 percent to cardholders. You get the card by purchasing one of the Entertainment books (usually around $25), which are available in bookstores and are also a major source of fund-raising for schools and civic groups. Most people buy the books for the restaurant coupons—or because their kid's soccer team is selling them—and don't realize they include a list of hotels all over the nation offering half-price rooms to cardholders. For more information, visit the Web site at www.entertainment.com.

If you especially like a particular hotel chain, you can simply call their 800 number and ask for the hotel nearest Disney World. This can eliminate the element of surprise, because one Hampton Inn looks pretty much like another. Be sure to stress that you want a location near Disney World (preferably located off I-4 near Exit 68 or 62, the two exits that flank Disney property). Proximity to Disney raises the rate about 20 percent, but location is important. A hotel near the airport or downtown can mean a major commute, and Orlando traffic, especially in the morning, is brutal.

Another tip: Try calling both the hotel's 800 number and the direct line to the particular resort. You may be quoted different rates.

Some visitors swear that condos or all-suite hotels are the way to go; the rates tend to be slightly higher than individual rooms, but you can save money by fixing breakfast and keeping drinks and snacks in your room. Condolink (800-733-4445) handles many different properties, and several of our readers have mentioned that they liked the Vistana Resort (800-877-8787), which is managed by Sheraton.

Finally, six magic words can save you major bucks. When talking to a hotel reservation clerk, always ask, "Do you have any discounts available?" Remember that the reservation clerk works for the hotel, and if he (or she) can sell you a room at

$85 a night, there's no incentive for him to tell you how you can drop the rate to $59. But if you specifically inquire about discounts, he has to tell you.

Money-Saving Tip

Always ask for a discount. If none is available, ask for an upgrade on your room.

Things to Ask When Booking an Off-Site Hotel

If you decide to stay off site, you should be aware that there is a wide range of amenities and perks among the hundreds of hotels in the Orlando area. To make sure you're getting top value for your dollar, take nothing for granted. Some $250-a-night hotels charge you for shuttle service to the parks; some $75 ones do not. Some hotels count 11-year-olds as adults, and others consider 19-year-olds to be children. Some relatively inexpensive resorts have full-fledged kids' clubs; some larger and far more costly ones are geared to convention and business travel and don't even have an arcade. The moral is, always ask.

Helpful Hint

One note of caution: An extremely cheap hotel rate, say $45 or less, generally means that the hotel is located in a less desirable part of town than those I've listed—in regard to both theme park proximity and general security. Unless you are personally familiar with the location and quality of the hotel, proceed with caution.

The following questions should help you ferret out the best deal.

@ *Does the hotel provide in-room babysitters? What are their qualifications? What's the cost? How far in advance should I reserve a sitter? Do you have on-site child care?*

Several of the larger hotels have their own version of a kids' club, a drop-off child care center with planned activities for the youngsters.

@ *Does the hotel provide bus service to the Magic Kingdom, Epcot, the Animal Kingdom, and MGM? The minor parks? How often? How early—and how late—do the buses run? Is there any charge? Are the buses express, or do they stop and pick up riders at other hotels?*

Careful here. Small off-site hotels often share shuttles, which means lots of stops and a long commute.

@ *Do kids stay free? Up to what age?*

This can be vitally important. On-site Disney hotels allow kids under 18 to lodge free with parents. The policy at off-site hotels varies.

@ *Does the hotel provide a free buffet breakfast?*

@ *What fast-food or family-style restaurants are nearby?*

@ *Do you have any suites with kitchens?*

No one would suggest you should spend a vacation cooking. But many families report that doing the cereal and juice thing in their rooms saved them plenty of money.

@ *Does the hotel provide airport pickup?*

Most off-site hotels can at least direct you to a shuttle service.

Money-Saving Tip

Some hotels, such as the Holiday Inn Sunspree (407-239-4500), have mini-kitchens with small refrigerators and microwaves—all you need for simple meals. And they don't cost any more than a regular room.

🕑 *Is there a laundry facility on the premises?*

🕑 *Can I buy tickets to area attractions through the hotel's Guest Services desk? Are the tickets discounted?*

Many Orlando hotels offer discounts to Universal Orlando, Sea World, and area dinner shows. Not only do you save money, but you also save the time you'd otherwise spend waiting in line. Use caution, however, if the off-site hotels try to sell you Disney tickets. They're only slightly cheaper than the regular-price passes you'd buy at the theme park gates, and they may limit your access to the minor parks.

CHAPTER

3

Once You Get There

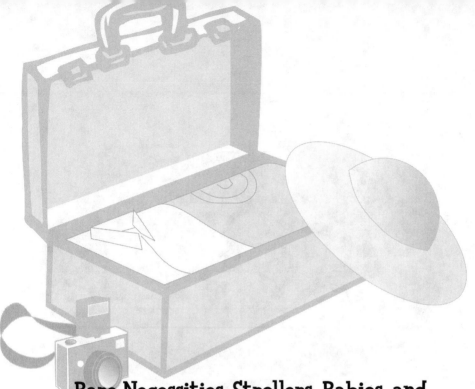

Bare Necessities: Strollers, Babies, and First Aid

Now on to some of the more practical information. Whether you're pregnant, traveling with a baby, or nursing a sore ankle, Disney World is prepared to accommodate your needs.

Strollers

Strollers rent for $8 at all the theme parks, and a double stroller is $15. Wheelchairs rent for $7, and self-powered electric vehicles are available for $30.

@ All kids under age 3 need a stroller, for napping as well as for riding in.

@ For kids ages 3 to 6, the general rule is this: Strollers are a must at Epcot, nice in the Magic Kingdom, and not really needed at the Animal Kingdom or MGM, where the parks are smaller and you'll spend a lot of time in sit-down shows.

@ If you'll need a stroller every day, bring your own from home. But if you have an older child who will need a stroller only at Epcot, rental isn't a bad option.

@ Tie something like a bandanna or a balloon to your stroller to mark it and reduce the chance it'll be swiped while you're inside Peter Pan's Flight. As one mother observed, "Otherwise honest people seem to think nothing about stealing a stroller but stop when they see they might be taking a personal possession as well."

Money-Saving Tip

If you plan to spend time at more than one park, you don't have to pay for a stroller twice: Keep your receipt and show it for a new stroller when you arrive at the next park.

@ Stroller stolen anyway? In the Magic Kingdom, check in at the Trading Post in Frontierland or Tinkerbell's Treasures in Fantasyland. At Epcot, you can get a new stroller at the World Traveler shop located between France and the United Kingdom. Try Oscar's Super Service at MGM and Garden Gate Gifts in the Oasis at the Animal Kingdom. So long as you've kept your receipt, there's no charge for a replacement stroller. Keep in mind that the average number of miles you'll walk in a day of touring is nine, and using a pedometer I've logged as many as 15 miles on a day in the parks. That's a lot.

@ If at 8 A.M. your 5-year-old swears she doesn't need a stroller but at noon she collapses in a heap halfway around Epcot's World Showcase, head for the World Traveler shop between France and the United Kingdom. The World

Traveler is also the place to rent a stroller if you're coming from the Swan, Dolphin, BoardWalk, or Yacht and Beach Clubs and thus using the "backdoor" entrance.

Helpful Hint

Just because your stroller isn't where you left it, don't assume it's been taken. Families often abandon their strollers as they enter an attraction, blocking sidewalks and streets. There are Disney employees whose sole duty it is to rearrange these strollers, lining them up and packing them as tightly together as possible. Keep looking—your stroller may be a few yards away.

@ Likewise, if you're staying at one of the more sprawling resorts, like the Pop Century Resorts, Caribbean Beach, Coronado Springs, Port Orleans, Fort Wilderness Resort, or All-Star Sports, Music, and Movies, bring a stroller from home. It's likely to be quite a trek from your room to the pool or shuttle bus stop.

Baby Services

Rockers, bottle warmers, high chairs, and changing tables are all available at the Baby Services centers; diapers, formula, and jars of baby food are also for sale. The centers are an absolute haven for families traveling with a very young child. (One mother reported that the attendant on duty was even able to diagnose a suspicious-looking rash on her toddler as a reaction to too much citrus juice, evidently a common Florida malady. She later took the child to a doctor and learned the attendant's diagnosis was right on the money.)

In the Magic Kingdom, Baby Services is beside the Crystal Palace at the end of Main Street. It's inside the Guest Services building at MGM, in Safari Village at the Animal Kingdom, and near the Odyssey Restaurant at Epcot.

Diapers are available at the larger shops, but they're behind the counter, so you'll have to ask. Changing tables are available in most women's restrooms and some men's as well. You can always use the Baby Services centers to diaper infants, and there are potty-chairs for toddlers as well.

Nursing Moms

Disney World is so casual and family oriented that you shouldn't feel self-conscious about discreetly nursing in the theaters or restaurants. Some shows, such as the Hall of Presidents in the Magic Kingdom or *Impressions de France* in Epcot, are dark, quiet, and ideal for nursing.

If you're too modest for these methods or if your baby is easily disturbed, try the rockers in the Baby Services centers.

First Aid

Next to the Magic Kingdom's Crystal Palace is the first-aid clinic, staffed by two nurses. Epcot's first-aid clinic is located beside the Odyssey Restaurant, the MGM clinic is in the Guest Services center, and the Animal Kingdom clinic is in Safari Village near the shop called Creature Comforts.

Although the first-aid centers mostly treat patients with minor problems such as sunburn, motion sickness, and booboos, they are also equipped for major emergencies and, when necessary, ambulance service to an area hospital.

If you suffer a medical emergency, take comfort in the fact that the Disney people have received ringing endorsements for their response in times of crisis. One mother who developed an eye infection from a scratched cornea reported that the nurse at the Epcot first-aid clinic, immediately recognizing the severity of the problem, arranged for her transport to Sand Lake Hospital so she could see an ophthalmologist. "We only had a long weekend," she writes, "and I would have felt horrible if the kids spent it in a hospital waiting room. As it was, the nurse handled everything, and my husband and children were able to remain in the park while I was treated. My husband kept phoning in to the nurse for updates, and I met up with them back at Epcot a couple of hours later, looking like Long John Silver."

Helpful Hint
It's worth remembering that any medical problem that can occur at home can also occur in the midst of a vacation. I've received letters from people who have broken bones, fainted from the heat, and come down with chicken pox while in Orlando. Their general advice to others is to seek medical help the minute you suspect there may be a problem. Waiting only makes the solution more painful and more expensive.

Another mother writes, "When our 8-year-old son developed a (repeat) ear infection in the middle of the Magic Kingdom, we went to the first-aid clinic. There, a sweet nurse gently examined him, contacted his doctor back in Ohio to get his regular prescription, and gave him Tylenol for immediate relief. By the time we arrived back at our rooms at Port Orleans, the prescription was there, and by the next morning Nicky was back on his feet and ready to go."

A woman who suffered a miscarriage while staying at an on-site hotel also offered the highest praise to the staff there, both for their swift medical response and for their emotional support.

General First-Aid Tips
    $ If someone begins to feel ill or suffers an injury in the parks, head straight for the first-aid clinic. If the people there can't fix it, they'll find someone who can.

@ Likewise, all on-site hotels and most off-site hotels have physicians on call 24 hours a day. Contact Guest Services or call 407-396-1195 between 8 A.M. and 10 P.M. for in-room health care. Turner Drugs in Orlando (407-828-8125) will deliver to any on-site hotel room (and many off-site ones) 24 hours a day. There's a $5 charge for delivery, with a surcharge between 10 P.M. and 8 A.M.

@ For minor health problems, visit the Medi-Clinic, at the intersection of I-4 and Route 192, or the Lake Buena Vista Clinic, which will pick you up at your hotel room between 8 A.M. and 8 P.M. For more serious illnesses or injuries, head for the emergency room at Sand Lake Hospital.

@ Of course, no matter where you're staying, in a true emergency you should call 911.

Things You Don't Want to Think About

A Rainy Day

Most of the time the parks operate as usual. If there's an electrical storm with thunder and lightning, then outdoor rides and shows are naturally suspended until the weather clears. In the threat of an all-out hurricane, rides totally shut down—but that's really rare.

If it's simply a rainy day or one of those afternoon cloudbursts so common to Florida, then it's business as usual. Just buy one of those $5 rain slickers and go right ahead with your plans. The rain slickers, available throughout the parks and Disney hotels, are much more practical than umbrellas, especially if you're trying to push a stroller or keep your hands free to hang on to young kids. The only problem is that on a rainy day it seems like half the people in the park have them on and thus everyone looks exactly alike. It makes it easier to lose your kids in the crowd, so be especially alert.

Here are some tips to make sure that waking up to a rainy morning doesn't turn the whole day into a washout.

@ MGM is the best park to visit on a rainy day because most of the major attractions are indoors. The big-deal rides—Rock'n'Rollercoaster, Tower of Terror, Star Tours, the Great Movie Ride—are all inside, and MGM also has plenty of indoor shows and tours such as the Animation Tour and Who Wants to Be a Millionaire game.

@ If you don't mind getting wet, the Animal Kingdom is also a good choice when it's a cloudy day. Most of the attractions are outdoors but, assuming there's no thunder and lightning, the animals actually move around more on days when it's cool and overcast. After a rain shower is the best time to ride the Kilimanjaro Safaris, according to the drivers, who claim the animals are far more active when the air is clean and fresh.

@ The Magic Kingdom, which has lots of rides, and Epcot, which requires a lot of walking from one pavilion to the next, are less good choices.

@ There's always plenty to do at Downtown Disney—shopping, movies, DisneyQuest, and the Cirque du Soleil. But be forewarned. These are all popular bad weather activities, and they tend to be very crowded on rainy days. Especially DisneyQuest.

@ Remember, a rainy morning doesn't always mean a rainy day. Weather conditions change quickly in Orlando, and if it clears up later in the day the parks will be less crowded than usual. This is a good time to slip in and ride big-name attractions that draw long lines when the parks are full.

Lost Kids

Obviously, your best bet is not to get separated in the first place. Savvy families will set up prearranged meeting spots.

If you do get separated and your kids are too young to understand the idea of a meeting place, act fast. Lost-kid logs are kept at the Baby Services centers at the major parks. More important, Disney employees are well briefed about what to do if they encounter a lost child, so the odds are good that if your child has been wandering around alone for more than a couple of minutes, he or she has been intercepted by a Disney employee and is on the way to Baby Services.

In real emergencies—if the child is very young or is handicapped or if you're afraid she's been nabbed—all-points bulletins are put out among employees. If you lose a child, don't spend a half-hour wandering around. Contact the nearest Disney employee and let the system take it from there.

Insider's Secret
Everyone designates Cinderella Castle or Spaceship Earth as a meeting place, which is one reason those places are always mobbed. Plan to catch up with your crowd at a more out-of-the-way locale.

Helpful Hint
The one glitch in the system is that lost kids are sometimes so interested in what's going on around them that they don't look lost, and thus no Disney employee intercepts them. It's worth taking a couple of minutes to explain to young children that if they get separated from Mom and Dad, they should tell someone wearing a Disney name tag. The Disney employee can call the child's name in to Baby Services, and, assuming you've contacted Baby Services to report the child as missing, the attendant there can tell you where the child is.

Closed Attractions

Because Disney World is open 365 days a year, there is no downtime for refurbishing and repairing rides. Thus, on any given day, as many as four attractions throughout Disney World may be closed for refurbishment. If an attraction your family eagerly anticipated is closed, it can be heartbreaking. Call 407-824-4321 before you leave home to find out the attractions scheduled for shutdown during the week you're visiting. That way, if Space Mountain or Star Tours is closed, at least you'll know before you get to the gate.

There's still a slight chance that a ride will be malfunctioning and temporarily closed when you visit, but the Disney people are so vigilant about repairs that this happens very, very rarely. (The one exception to this is Test Track at Epcot; it closes for servicing more often than any other Disney attraction.)

Auto Breakdowns

If you return to the parking lot at the end of the day to find your battery dead or your tire flat, walk back to the nearest tram stop. The roads at Disney World are patrolled continuously by security staff who can call for help. Twelve thousand visitors locked their keys in their cars at Disney World last year, so the security people are used to these fun moments.

A full-service gas station and branch of AAA are located near the toll plaza at the Magic Kingdom entrance. Although prices are high, the station does provide towing and minor re-

Insider's Secret

By far the most common problem is forgetting where you parked. Be sure to write down your row number as you leave your car in the morning. Although Pluto 47 seems easy to remember now, you may not be able to retrieve that information 12 brain-numbing hours later.

pairs in an emergency. If the car can't be swiftly repaired, don't despair. The day isn't lost. Disney World personnel will chauffeur you to any of the theme parks or back to your hotel.

Running Out of Money

The Sun Bank, which has branches all around Disney World, gives cash advances on MasterCard and Visa, provides refunds for lost American Express or Bank of America traveler's checks, and exchanges foreign currency for dollars. Guest Services at some hotels will give you cash advances on credit cards as well.

Crime

Use common sense, especially in trying to avoid the most common crime: theft. Make use of the lockers so that you won't have to carry valuables or new purchases around the parks or take cameras and camcorders onto the rides with you, and be extra cautious at the water parks, where you may be tempted to leave your wallet in your lounge chair while riding the waves. It's far better either to wear one of those waterproof waist pouches in the water or rent a locker, returning to it whenever you need money. The locker keys are on elasticized cords that slip around your wrist, so there's no hassle in hanging on to them.

Don't let paranoia ruin your trip—statistically, Orlando is a pretty safe town—but do keep your wits about you, making sure that you bolt the hotel door, lock the rental car, and stick to major roads while exploring.

Saving Time

❧ Prepare as much as you can before you leave home. You should purchase theme park tickets, reserve rental cars, and book shows or special dinners long before you pull out of your own driveway. Every call you make now is a line you won't have to stand in later.

- Visit the most popular attractions before 11 A.M. or after 6 P.M.

- Eat lunch either before noon or after 2 P.M. This system will have you eating while everyone else is in line for the rides and riding while everyone else is eating.

- It also saves time—and money—to make lunch your big meal of the day. Most families opt to eat a large breakfast and large dinner and snack at lunch; go against the crowds by eating your big meal in early afternoon, when the parks are too hot and crowded for effective touring anyway.

- Split up. Mom can make the dinner reservations while Dad rents the strollers. Mom can take the 9-year-old to Space Mountain while Dad and the 4-year-old try out the Tomorrowland Speedway. Security in Disney World is very tight, so preteens and teens can tour on their own, meeting up with the rest of the family periodically.

- Be aware that once you cross the Florida state line, there is an inverse relationship between time and money. You have to be willing to spend one in order to save the other. One family in our survey proudly listed their cost-saving measures, including staying 30 miles outside of Orlando and cooking every meal themselves. They said it took them six days to tour the major parks, something most families can manage comfortably in four days. Considering the high cost of admissions, it's doubtful that they saved very much money at all—and they certainly wasted time.

Time-Saving Tip

If you have three days or fewer to tour, it is imperative that you go during the off-season. You can see in three days in November what takes six days to see in July.

@ Don't feel you have to do it all. If you study this guide and your maps before you go, you'll realize that not every ride or show will be equally attractive to your family. The world won't come to an end if you skip a few pavilions.

@ The full-service restaurants within the theme parks can be slow. If you're on a tight touring schedule, stick to fast food or sidewalk vendors and order a pizza at night when you get back to your hotel room.

Helpful Hint

How should you spend your arrival day at Disney World? It's tempting to rush straight to the parks but that may not be the best use of your money. Since it'll probably be at least midafternoon by the time you arrive and settle in to your hotel, you'll be using a full day of your expensive ticket for only a few hours in the park. It may make more sense to relax around your resort, enjoying the pool and other perks, and spend the evening at Downtown Disney, which doesn't require a ticket. Then you can start the first full day of your vacation relaxed and raring to go.

Saving Money

Saving money at Disney World is somewhat of an oxymoron, but there are ways to minimize the damage.

@ If the cost of flying the whole family down and then renting a car is prohibitive, consider renting a van in your hometown and driving to Orlando.

@ Eat as many meals as possible outside the parks. If you have a suite, fixing simple meals there is clearly your most economical option. Many Orlando hotels offer free breakfasts to guests, and there are numerous fast-food and family chain restaurants along International Drive and the I-4 exits.

@ If you'd like to try some of the nicer Epcot restaurants, book them for lunch, when prices are considerably lower than at dinner. And remember that restaurant portions are huge, even with kiddie meals. Consider letting two family members share an entrée.

@ Children's value meals run about $4 at the fast-food places and $6 at the sit-down restaurants. Kids sometimes eat free at certain establishments; signs are prominently posted announcing the restaurants that offer this deal.

Money-Saving Tip
Except for maybe an autograph book and a T-shirt, hold off on souvenir purchases until the last day. By then the kids will really know what they want and you won't waste money on impulse buys.

@ Buy film, blank videotapes, diapers, and sunscreen at home before you leave. These things are all for sale in the parks, but you'll pay dearly for the convenience.

@ The All-Star Resorts, Caribbean Beach Resort, Port Orleans, Coronado Springs, Pop Century, and Fort Wilderness Campground provide your most economical on-site lodging. Off site, there are several Comfort Inns and Days Inns along I-4 and International Drive.

@ If you're driving to Orlando and not arriving until afternoon or evening, don't reserve your on-site room until the second day of your visit. It's silly to pay for a whole day of Grand Floridian amenities if you'll be checking in at 10 P.M. Instead, stop your first night at a budget hotel, rise early and check out the next morning, and then go straight to your on-site hotel. They'll let you unload your bags, pick up your tickets and resort ID, and go on to the theme parks.

@ If you move from park to park in your car, save your parking receipt so you'll have to pay the $7 fee only once. (There's no parking charge for on-site visitors.) Likewise, be sure to save stroller receipts.

@ If you plan to try any of the minor parks such as Typhoon Lagoon, Blizzard Beach, or Pleasure Island, buy a Park Hopper Plus pass. Without it, you'll pay separately for each minor park, which can add up very fast. Some families reported that they went to one of the water parks several times during their Disney World stay—a treat that is easy with a Park Hopper Plus pass but totally unfeasible otherwise.

@ The dinner shows are expensive, costing a family of four about $130, and even a character breakfast can set you back $50 or more. If the budget is tight, skip these extras and concentrate on ways to meet the characters inside the parks.

@ Employees of many companies with exhibits inside Disney World are entitled to benefits so if your employer sponsors an exhibit inside Disney World, contact your employee benefits office well before you leave home and see if you are eligible for a discount on park admissions or on-site lodging. (Note: Sometimes employees can enter an attraction through the private lounge and ride without having to get into the line at all. This can be a big bonus if you're a GM employee who wants to ride Test Track.)

@ Buy your tickets when you make your hotel reservations, and you'll be protected in case Disney decides it's time for another price increase.

y-Saving Tip

hotels offer a deal where you buy a souvenir beverage mug the first day of your trip and get free refills at the resort for the remainder of your stay. Because drinks at Disney World are very expensive, this little perk can save you at least $20.

Meeting the Disney Characters

Meeting the characters is a major objective for some families and a nice diversion for all. If your children are young, prepare them for the fact that the characters are much, much larger than they appear on TV, and often overwhelming in person. I once visited Disney World with a 20-month-old whose happy babble of "My Mickey, my Mickey" turned into a wary "No Mickey, no Mickey" the minute she entered the Magic Kingdom gate and saw that everyone's favorite mouse was a good 6 feet tall. Kaitlyn's reaction is not unusual; many kids panic when they first see the characters, and pushing them forward only makes matters worse. The characters are trained to be sensitive and sensible (in some cases more so than the parents) and will always wait for the child to approach them. Schedule a character breakfast on the last morning of your visit; by then, cautious youngsters have warmed up.

Many kids enjoy getting character autographs, and an autograph book can become a much-cherished souvenir on your return home. You might also want to prepare the kids for the fact that the characters don't talk. As many as 30 young people in Mickey suits (mostly women, because the suits are pretty small) might be dispersed around Disney World on a busy day, and they can't all be gifted with that familiar squeaky voice. So the characters communicate, pretty effectively, through body language.

Also be aware that because of the construction of their costumes, the characters can't always see what's beneath them too clearly. Donald and Daisy, for example, have a hard time looking over their bills, and small children standing close by may be ignored. If it appears this is happening, lift your child to the character's eye level.

Times and places for meeting the characters are listed on the theme park maps and timetable that you are given as you enter the parks; each park also has a chalkboard indicating when the characters appear.

Insider's Secret

Disney's Character Caravan goes around to the on-site resorts several times a week. It's a great way to visit with the characters in a relaxed atmosphere. The days, times, and locations are given to you as part of your check-in package.

Camcorder Taping Tips

- If you plan to take your camcorder with you frequently, make use of the lockers located near the main gates of all three parks. Lockers can be especially helpful if you'll be riding Space Mountain and Big Thunder Mountain, where you risk jarring the camera, or Splash Mountain, where there's a very good chance it'll get wet. Never take a camcorder on Kali River Rapids in the Animal Kingdom.

- Don't pan and zoom too much, because sudden camera moves disorient the viewer. If you're filming the kids, say, on the teacups, use the wide-angle setting and keep the camera stationary. Attempting to track them in close-ups as they spin past is too tough for anyone but a pro.

...ul Hint

Camcorders can be a hassle to carry on the rides, but it's way too risky to leave them in strollers while you're inside the attractions. Consider taking your camcorder with you on only one day, preferably the last day of your trip, when you're revisiting favorite attractions—that way you'll leave with a "Disney World Greatest Hits" tape.

@ If you're using vocal commentary such as "We're in Frontierland now, looking toward Big Thunder Mountain Railroad," be sure to speak loudly. If you don't, the background noise of the parks may muffle your words.

Insider's Secret

Remember to ask each time you board the monorail if the driver's cab is vacant. Sooner or later you'll get the chance to ride up front, and one bonus is the chance to film panoramic views of the parks as you enter.

Best Souvenirs

For serious shopping, head to World of Disney at the Downtown Disney Marketplace, which has a little bit of everything. But if you're looking for a slightly unusual souvenir, consider the following:

@ Autograph books, which can be purchased nearly anywhere on the first day of your trip. The signatures of the more obscure characters like Hades or the Queen of Hearts are especially prized.

- Passports, purchased from vendors all around Epcot. Collecting a stamp and greeting from every country in the World Showcase is a good way to keep very young kids interested in this admittedly rather adult section of Epcot.

- Disney watches, with an outstanding selection to be found at Uptown Jewelers on Main Street in the Magic Kingdom. Check out the Goofy watch—it runs backward.

- A piñata from the Mexico pavilion at Epcot.

- Character Christmas ornaments, found at It's a Wonderful Shop at MGM, Ye Olde Christmas Shoppe in the Magic Kingdom, and Days of Christmas in the Downtown Disney Marketplace.

- At MGM, you'll find old movie posters and other campy knickknacks from Hollywood's golden era at Sid Cahuenga's One-of-a-Kind.

- Character cookie cutters and presses that stamp Mickey's visage onto toast and pancakes are at Yankee Trader in Liberty Square in the Magic Kingdom. A Disney-themed breakfast on your first Saturday home is a nice way to fight those post-trip blues.

- There's a cool Hollywood Tower Hotel gift shop complete with bathrobes, towels, ashtrays, and "I survived" T-shirts as you exit the Twilight Zone Tower of Terror.

- Get character-themed athletic gear at Team Mickey in the Downtown Disney Marketplace. You'll find some items here that you won't see anywhere else—such as Mickey golf balls, softballs, and basketballs.

- All the on-site hotels have their own T-shirts, a nice variation from the shirts you see in the parks.

- There are great Disney-themed board games at the new Once Upon a Toy in Downtown Disney Marketplace.

- Animal Kingdom T-shirts are also unique. Try the Outpost near the entrance or the larger Island Mercantile in Safari Village. Stuffed versions of the characters in safari gear are especially adorable. Eeyore's carrying the tent on his back!

- And, of course, mouse ears are sort of retro-chic. Get your name stitched on at the Chapeau in the Magic Kingdom.

Special Tips for Extra-Crowded Times

If your schedule is such that you simply have to go during Easter week or in the dead of summer, the following tips will make the trip more manageable.

- If at all possible, stay at a hotel on Disney property. There are three reasons for this. First of all, it's better to use Disney transportation between your resort and the theme parks than to fight the traffic on the roads and in the parking lots. Secondly, on extremely crowded days the theme parks might actually close their gates to arriving visitors, but guests at Disney resorts who have multiday tickets are always allowed in. Finally, if you're visiting at a crowded time, everything takes longer. You'll exhaust yourself faster, which means it's a good idea to return to your hotel for a midafternoon rest. Breaking up the day is much easier if you're staying on site and can commute back to your hotel room via monorail, boat, or bus.

- Allow an extra day—or two. First of all, you won't be able to see as much in a single day as you would if you were going at a less crowded time. Second, you'll tire more easily when the crowds are thick, and you'll need longer rest periods to recuperate. Many families schedule an entire day off from touring in the middle of their week, which is really helpful when you're going in the busy season.

@ Use FASTPASS whenever possible. This system, which Disney debuted two years ago to cut down on the time guests spend in line for major attractions, is a godsend. Let's say you want to ride Test Track, but by the time you get there at 10 A.M. the line is already 90 minutes long. If you run your theme park tickets through the machines at the FASTPASS kiosk you'll get your ticket back, along with a second ticket, the FASTPASS, that tells you the time when you should return (let's say between 1 and 2 P.M.). When you come back, your FASTPASS allows you to enter a separate, much shorter line. Just be sure to visit the FASTPASS kiosks in the mornings—on really crowded days, the allotted number of FASTPASSes might all be distributed by noon and then you're back in the regular line with the rest of the crowd.

@ Read this book in advance and decide on four or five "must-see" attractions for each park. As I said earlier, visitors at busy times won't see it all, so you want to make sure that you see the things that matter the most to your particular family. Guests who don't list their priorities often arrive at the parks, find them swamped, and then just wander around looking for any attraction with a short line. The result is that they spend all their time in minor attractions. While these can be fun, it doesn't make sense to travel so far and spend so much money and not see any of the big-deal stuff. So make sure you see your top priorities for each park first so that anything else you manage to do after that is a little bonus.

@ If you're traveling at a busy time, you must be at the parks when they open. By 10 A.M. you'll face hour-long waits at many rides, and the parks may even close to arriving guests.

Special Tips for Big Families

If you're down at Disney World with a really big brood, the following tips—all offered by family reunion veterans—might make things a little less hectic.

- Staying on site makes splitting up much easier because you can rely on the Disney World transportation system instead of the family car. This is especially vital if there is wide variation in the age, stamina, or risk tolerance of the family members.

- Best on-site options for large families who want to room together include the trailers at Fort Wilderness Campground and the Old Key West, Beach Club Villas, Villas at Wilderness Lodge, and BoardWalk Villas. If you'd like a little less togetherness, book as many rooms as you need at the resort of your choice, but ask for adjoining rooms. It's easier to get them if you book early.

- Rent a pager at Guest Services in the major theme parks or through Guest Services at your hotel. Because big groups tend to scatter, a pager can be invaluable for getting everyone reassembled when it's time to eat or head for home. Lacking this, you can also leave messages for each other at Guest Services.

Money-Saving Tip

If the adults plan to head out for a night, an in-room sitter is generally less expensive than drop-off child care when more than three kids are involved.

◉ Have everyone wear the same color T-shirt or hat each day. A tour guide operator passed along this tip, which makes it much easier to spot "your people" in a sea of faces.

Special Tips for Grandparents

Many grandparents travel to Disney World with their grand-kids, and although Orlando truly can be the ultimate multi-generational destination, a few pointers may make the trip go more smoothly.

◉ If at all possible, stay on site. It's easier to return to your hotel for rests, and you skip the hassles of commuting.

◉ Be sure to alternate shows and other restful attractions with more active touring.

◉ If you have back or joint problems or are easily tired, rent a wheelchair. All the theme parks offer wheelchair rental from the same spot that rents strollers, located near the main entrance. If your grandchildren are old enough to enjoy pushing you, go the conventional wheelchair route; if not, arrive early enough to guarantee the availability of an electric cart. One huge boon of wheelchair rental is that you and your entire party board rides at a completely different entrance from the ordinary queue, and this line is invariably shorter. For this reason, many young and able-bodied people rent a wheelchair and take advantage of the wheelchair-boarding zones to cut down on their time waiting in line. This obviously unethical little scam is most often played by teenagers, but there is no reason for an older person not to take advantage of the rental wheelchairs, especially at Epcot. Just be sure to get a copy of the *Guidebook for Disabled Visitors,* which is generally available at the place where you rent your wheelchair. Or you can order one by calling 407-824-4321 at least three weeks before your trip to Disney World. The guidebook gives information on how to board each ride.

- Avoid the summer at all costs. Not only are the crowds worse, but Florida heat and humidity can also be hard on senior citizens.

Special Tips for Pregnant Guests

I've personally toured Disney World twice while pregnant and not only lived to tell the tale but honestly enjoyed both trips. However, a few precautions are in order.

- Make regular meal stops. Instead of buying a sandwich from a vendor, get out of the sun and off your feet at a sit-down restaurant.

- If you aren't accustomed to walking nine miles a day—an average Disney World trek—begin getting in shape at home. By taking 30- to 40-minute walks, beginning a couple of months before your trip, you'll be less likely to get sore or poop out early once you're at Disney World.

- Dehydration is a real danger. Drink lots of fluids and keep a juicebox in your tote bag for emergencies.

- This is definitely an occasion when it's worth the money to stay on site. Return to your room in midafternoon to put up your feet.

- If staying on site isn't feasible, the Baby Services centers have rockers and are a good place for mothers-to-be to

Helpful Hint

Standing stock-still can be much more tiring than walking when you're pregnant, so let your husband stand in line for rides. You and the kids can join him just as he's about to enter the final turn of the line.

take a break. And the parks are full of benches—sit when you can.

◉ Once you're inside the holding area for theater-style attractions, such as the *Country Bear Jamboree* or Universe of Energy, find a bench and sit down. If the benches are taken, sit on the floor near the wall and don't stand up when the Disney attendant gets on the loudspeaker and asks everyone to move into the theater; all the people in the holding area will be admitted into the theater, so it's pointless to get up and join the mob at the turnstiles. Let everyone else go ahead and then amble through. (This is a good strategy for anyone who is utterly exhausted, pregnant or not.)

> **Helpful Hint**
> Most important of all, check out restroom locations in advance.

Special Tips for Disabled Guests

◉ Wheelchairs can be rented at any stroller rental booth, and most attractions are accessible by wheelchair. Attendants will be happy to help guests with special needs board and disembark from rides; guests in wheelchairs board through their own gates and can often avoid waiting in line altogether. If someone in your party is in a wheelchair, be sure to request a copy of the *Guidebook for Disabled Visitors*, a specific guide on how to board each ride, either when you order your tickets in advance or at the wheelchair rental booth.

◉ A tip from frequent visitors: If you're traveling with someone in a wheelchair, it's emphatically worth the money to stay on site. Disney does an excellent job of offering disabled guests a number of transportation options. The ferry and monorail are wheelchair accessible, but if needed, you can request a van with a motorized platform. The resorts offer rooms with specially equipped bathrooms and extra-large doors; life jackets for the handicapped are available at resort pools and water parks. The Polynesian gets high marks from readers with special needs, while for those seeking a less expensive option, the All-Star Resorts have several rooms especially designed to meet the needs of the disabled for $84 a night.

@ Portable tape players and cassettes for sight-impaired guests are available, as are TDDs for the hearing impaired. Check with Guest Services in the theme parks. Deaf guests can call Florida Relay Services at 800-955-8771 for information.

@ All on-site hotels are equipped to refrigerate insulin.

Finally, not a tip but a word of reassurance: If you're traveling with someone who has a chronic health problem or disability, rest assured that Disney World cast members will help you in any way they can. Because Disney World is frequently visited by children sponsored by the Make-a-Wish Foundation and other programs like it, the personnel are accustomed to dealing with a wide variety of challenges and have proven themselves able to accommodate visitors who are quite seriously ill. The key is to make everyone at both your hotel and in the theme parks aware of your presence and the possibility that you'll need special assistance.

Birthdays and Special Occasions

While Disney has no set protocol on birthdays, anniversaries, and other special occasions, the general rule is, "Ask and you shall (probably) receive." If you're staying at a Disney resort, inform Guest Relations or the concierge in advance if you'd like flowers, balloons, or a gift delivered on the special day. It's also a good idea to arrange priority seating at your restaurant of choice weeks before the big day and let the manager know if you have any preferences. Most are more than happy to oblige.

For example, one mother wrote to me that her son celebrated his birthday at the character breakfast in Wilderness Lodge. Because Tigger is his favorite character, a Pooh-themed cake was carried to the table by the main tiger himself. Or consider the young man who proposed to his girlfriend at the Coral Reef in the Living Seas pavilion at Epcot. The couple were having dinner next to the mammoth glass aquarium when, at the key moment, one of the divers swam by their table carrying a sign that read, "Will you marry me?" When the girl turned to look at her boyfriend, he was on one knee with the ring. The servers had told all the other diners what was brewing, so the whole restaurant stood up and cheered when she said yes.

What do these stories have in common? The treats and surprises were arranged well in advance. So decide where you'll be staying and eating on your special day and then contact management directly. With their help, you should have no trouble finding a way to make the day memorable.

CHAPTER

4

Touring
Tips and
Plans

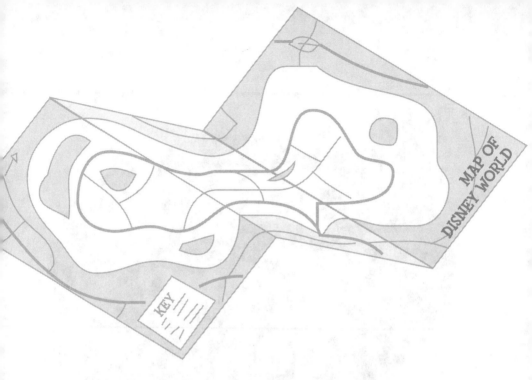

General Disney World Touring Tips

The size of Disney World is often a shock to first-time visitors, many of whom arrive with vague notions that they can walk from Epcot to the Magic Kingdom or even that they are in separate sections of the same theme park. There is also some confusion over the names: Some people use "Walt Disney World" and "Magic Kingdom" synonymously, whereas in reality the Magic Kingdom is a relatively small part of the much larger Disney World complex. There's more to this place than Cinderella Castle and Space Mountain.

Thus an understanding of the Disney World layout and transportation system is vital, because you'll be covering many miles in the course of your touring. Despite the distances involved, the tips in this chapter encourage you to visit more than one park a day, allowing you to follow a morning of bodysurfing at Typhoon Lagoon with an afternoon show at MGM. The best way to avoid overstimulation and burnout is to work a variety of experiences—some active, some passive, some educational, some silly—into each day.

When it comes to touring, families tend to fall into three groups. The first group sleeps in, has a full-service meal at their hotel, and lollygags over to the parks around 11 A.M. They wander around aimlessly, finding the lines for major rides to be so long that their only choices are either to wait 90 minutes for Splash Mountain or spend the whole afternoon riding minor attractions. By the time they get the hang of the system (i.e., they catch on to things like FASTPASS), it's 5 P.M. and they're exhausted. They retreat back to their hotel room—frustrated at how little they've seen, irritated by how much they've spent, and limp from the heat. This is a vacation?

The second group is what I call Disney World Commandos. These hyperorganized types have elaborate tour plans and march determinedly from ride to ride, checking off their "to do" list as they go. Amanda wants to ride Dumbo twice in a row? No way! It'll throw them off schedule. Jeffrey wants to duck into Innoventions? Sorry—it's not on the list. If anything unforeseen happens—Space Mountain opens late or there's a glitch in the bus system—the whole group goes into a major psychological meltdown. This is a vacation?

The most Disney-savvy families find a sweet spot between the two extremes. They have an overall plan but make sure to leave empty spaces in the day to allow for spontaneity. They get an early start each day, and factor in plenty of downtime to rest. Most important, they're familiar enough with each park and its attractions that they arrive with a clear idea of what they want to see, but they don't feel compelled to do it all.

The following tips should help you make the most of your time without pushing anyone, parents or kids, past their endurance level.

- For families with kids, it is especially important to avoid the exhaustion that comes with just trying to get there. If you're staying off site, it can take a full two hours from the moment you leave your hotel to the moment you board your first ride, which is enough to shatter the equanimity of even the most well-behaved kid. Your kids have been waiting for this vacation a long time, and now they've been flying and riding a long time: You owe it to them to get into the parks quickly.

Insider's Secret

Come early! If you follow only one tip from this whole book, make this the one. By beating the crowds, not only can you visit attractions in quick succession but you also avoid the parking and transportation nightmares that occur when the parks fill to peak capacity around 11 A.M.

@ Every touring guide to Disney World tells people to come early, and in the 10 years since I've written my first edition, I've noticed that the mornings have become a bit more crowded. But the majority of the people touring Disney World on any given day still arrive between 10 and 11 A.M., proudly announcing that this is their vacation, and they'll sleep in if they want. (These same people seem to take a strange inverse pride in bragging about how long they stood in line and how little they saw.) Arriving early is like exercising regularly; everyone knows you should do it, but most people don't. So if your 4-year-old wants to take three Dumbo flights back-to-back or your 10-year-old is determined to tackle every coaster in the Magic Kingdom, your best plan is still to get there early.

@ On the evening you arrive, call 407-824-4321 or check with your hotel to confirm the opening time of the theme park you plan to visit the next day. If you learn, for example, that the Magic Kingdom is scheduled to open at 9 A.M., be at the gate by 8:30. Frequently the gates open a half-hour early, and you can head toward the most popular attractions while the other 50,000 saps are still crawling along I-4.

Insider's Secret
What if everyone comes early? They won't.

On most days, guests can enter the first section of the theme park in question before it actually opens. In the Magic Kingdom, you can travel the length of Main Street until you reach the ropes. In Epcot, the central plaza between the two sides of Innoventions is open. At MGM, you can walk down Hollywood Boulevard, and in the Animal Kingdom, you are allowed into the Oasis.

This means that you can transact business—renting a stroller, getting maps, visiting Guest Relations, and so on—before the main park is open. If you haven't had breakfast, grab a quick muffin and juice from a vendor. Make a bathroom stop. The characters are often on hand so kids can visit and get autographs, and at Epcot you can make your dining reservations at the WorldKey Information System beside Spaceship Earth. Most important, however, be at the ropes 15 minutes before the main body of the park is scheduled to open.

Because people were practically stampeding each other after the rope drop, Disney is now controlling how fast

Time-Saving Tip
To maximize your time in the parks, eat breakfast at your hotel. There are plenty of places to get breakfast in the parks, but you don't want to waste the relatively uncrowded morning hours in a restaurant.

you can enter the main body of the park. Even so, once the whole park opens, proceed as quickly as you can to an attraction that is likely to have long lines later in the day.

Helpful Hint

Plan to see the most popular attractions either early in the day, late at night, or during a time when a big event siphons off other potential riders (such as the 3 P.M. parade in the Magic Kingdom).

- Eat at "off" times. Some families eat lightly at breakfast, have an early lunch around 11 A.M., and supper at 5 P.M. Others eat a huge breakfast and a late lunch around 3 P.M., then a final meal after the parks close. If you tour late and you're really bushed, all on-site hotels and many off-site hotels have in-room pizza delivery service.

- Be aware that kids usually want to revisit their favorite attractions. Parents who overschedule to the point where there is no time to revisit favorites risk a mutiny.

  One way to handle revisits is to leave the entire last day of your trip free as a "greatest hits" day, so that you can go back to all your favorites one more time. If you feel like lugging the camcorder around only once, make this the day.

- Use the touring plan to cut down on arguments and debates. It's a hapless parent indeed who sits down at breakfast and asks, "What do you want to do today?" Three kids will have three different answers.

- When making plans, keep the size of the parks in mind. MGM is small and can be crisscrossed to take in various shows. Likewise, the Animal Kingdom can be easily toured in four to five hours. The Magic Kingdom has more attractions and more crowd density, slowing you down; although some cutting back and forth is possible, you'll probably want to tour one "land" fairly thoroughly before heading to another. Epcot is so enormous, you're almost forced to visit attractions in geographic sequence or you will spend all your time and energy in transit.

℮ If you're going to be at the Magic Kingdom for two days or longer, plan to visit the most popular attractions on different days. Many families arrive at the Magic Kingdom determined to take in Space Mountain, Splash Mountain, Big Thunder Mountain, Alien Encounter, and Pirates of the Caribbean their first day—and wind up spending hours in line. Better to try to see a couple of the biggies during the first hour after the park opens. After that, move on to less popular attractions, saving the other biggies for subsequent mornings.

℮ Try park-hopping. Many families with a multiday pass figure: We'll spend Monday at the Magic Kingdom, Tuesday at MGM, Wednesday at Blizzard Beach, Thursday at Epcot, and Friday in the Animal Kingdom. Sounds logical, but a day at the Magic Kingdom is too much riding, 12 hours at Epcot is too much walking, the Animal Kingdom simply doesn't require that much time, a whole day at MGM is too much sitting, and anyone who stays at Blizzard Beach from dusk to dawn will wind up waterlogged. It's especially essential to take Epcot in small doses; if you do all the Future World attractions at once, the Audio-Animatronics will run together in the kids' heads, they'll likely get antsy, and any educational potential will be lost.

℮ If you're trying to predict how crowded a ride or show will be, four factors come into effect:

The newness of the attraction. In general, the newer it is, the hotter it is, particularly if it's a thrill ride like Mission: Space or Rock 'n' Roller Coaster.

The quality of the attraction. Space Mountain, *Voyage of the Little Mermaid, Fantasmic!,* and other Disney "classics" will be mobbed five years from now.

Speed of loading. Continuous-loading attractions, such as Pirates of the Caribbean, It's a Small World, Spaceship Earth, and the Great Movie Ride, can move thousands of riders through in an hour. The lines at the start-and-stop rides such as Dumbo, Triceratops Spin, and the Mad Hatter's Tea Party move much more slowly.

Capacity. Movies like *O Canada!* at Epcot and *MuppetVision 3-D* in MGM, and shows like the *Country Bear Jamboree* in the Magic Kingdom can seat large crowds at once. Lines form and then disappear rapidly as hundreds of people enter the theater. For this reason, theater-style attractions are good choices in the afternoon, when the park is crowded.

@ Take some time to familiarize yourself with the sprawling WDW transportation system.

If you're staying on site, you'll be able to take a direct bus, boat, or monorail to any of the four major theme parks; there is bus service to the minor parks, but it isn't always direct. If you're going to Typhoon Lagoon, for example, you may have to make a stop at Downtown Disney as well.

Trying to get from one on-site hotel to another? Use the nearest theme park as your transfer station. If you're staying at Caribbean Beach and trying to get to your dinner reservations at the Grand Floridian, for example, take the bus to MGM and then get on a Grand Floridian bus.

Off-site visitors can drive directly to Epcot, MGM, the Animal Kingdom, or any of the minor parks, all of which have their own parking lots and shuttle trams. But the parking lot for the Magic Kingdom is so far from the actual park that off-site visitors will have to park, catch the tram, and then go through the TTC in order to catch a monorail or ferryboat to get to the Magic Kingdom. (This is why we recommend that off-site visitors allow 45 minutes to get to the Magic Kingdom, even if their hotel is close to the park.)

It may sound overwhelming, but everything is very well marked, you're given a transportation guide when you check into your hotel, and there are always plenty of Disney employees on hand to answer your questions.

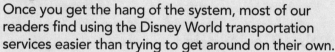

Helpful Hint

Once you get the hang of the system, most of our readers find using the Disney World transportation services easier than trying to get around on their own.

@ If you'll be at Disney World for more than four days, consider planning a "day off" in the middle of your vacation. Families sometimes feel so compelled to do it all that they come back from their trip exhausted and irritable. A day in the middle of the trip devoted to sleeping in, hanging around the hotel pool, taking in a character breakfast, visiting the other hotels, or shopping can make all the difference. You'll start the next day refreshed and energized.

@ You need a strategy for closing time. Except for the Animal Kingdom, the major parks all have nighttime extravaganzas that result in huge logjams as nearly every guest in the park assembles for the show and then mobs the exits en masse when it's over. Your best bet is to be either in the front of the crowd or at the back. If you'd like to clear out fast at the Magic Kingdom, ask an attendant which direction the parade will be coming from and aim to be at the beginning of the route. Once the parade is over, push your stroller out of the way (trying to get back your $1 deposit will just trap you in a line) and head for the exits. At Epcot? Watch IllumiNations from the Mexico or Canada Pavilion if you're leaving by the main gate or by the bridge between France and the United Kingdom if you're leaving by the backdoor. If you're watching *Fantasmic!* at MGM, arrive early enough to be in the top row of the Mickey section, which is nearest the main exit.

If you can't be among the first people to leave the park, be among the last. Shop or snack, and let the bulk of the crowd pass you. Only when the streets have cleared should you head for the exits.

Use Your Time Wisely

This boils down to one thing: Avoid the lines. Biggie attractions draw long lines early, and they stay crowded all day.

Head for the most crowded attractions first. In the Magic Kingdom, this means you should head straight for Space Mountain. The lines will still be half as long as they will be later in the day. At MGM, you can ride the Rock 'n' Roller Coaster and the Tower of Terror with minimal waits in the morning; some thrill junkies ride these two over and over, knowing how hard it can be to get back on later in the day.

If your kids are too young to be drawn to the coasters and other biggie rides, you should still try to see certain attractions

Insider's Secret

Obviously, you won't be able to see all the biggies in the first hour the park is open. If you encounter a wait longer than 30 minutes, move on. The Magic Kingdom and MGM parades draw big crowds, making it easier to sneak on to rides then, and many attractions empty out just before the park's closing time. Or you can try the ride again on a subsequent morning.

first. In the Magic Kingdom, Dumbo, the Many Adventures of Winnie the Pooh, the Mad Hatter's Tea Party, and Goofy's Barnstormer are slow-loading, low-capacity rides capable of producing hour-long lines by midafternoon. These attractions take about 15 to 30 riders at a time, in contrast to a theater-style attraction such as the *Country Bear Jamboree*, which lets in several hundred people at a clip. Ride the rides first; save the shows for later.

Be Willing to Split Up

By this point in the planning process, it is probably beginning to dawn on you that every single member of the family expects something slightly different from this vacation.

Discuss which attractions you'll enjoy as a family; some rides, shows, and parades will be a blast for everyone. The underlying rule is that you respect each other's priority choices, participating cheerfully even if the event might not be your personal first choice.

If you want to maximize your use of an Extra Magic Hour morning, one parent can take the kid who likes scary rides to Space Mountain and Alien Encounter while the other parent takes the less bold child to Fantasyland. When the rest of the park opens, link up and head together to the Haunted Mansion or Splash Mountain.

Especially if an attraction holds appeal for only one or two family members, there's no need to drag the whole crew along. A 13-year-old boy on It's a Small World is not a pretty sight. Teenagers, in fact, often like to split off from the family for an hour or two and hang out in Innoventions or the arcades or simply ride a favorite over and over. Security in the Disney parks is so tight that this is an option worth considering. Just make sure to have a clearly designated meeting time and place.

Must-See List for WDW

AT THE MAGIC KINGDOM

Big Thunder Mountain

Dumbo

Space Mountain

Splash Mountain

AT EPCOT

Honey, I Shrunk the Audience

Test Track

Mission: Space

AT ANIMAL KINGDOM

It's Tough to Be a Bug

Kilimanjaro Safaris

Festival of the Lion King

AT MGM

Star Tours

Twilight Zone Tower of Terror

Rock 'n' Roller Coaster

Voyage of the Little Mermaid

Fantasmic!

The FASTPASS System

Four years ago, Walt Disney World introduced the FASTPASS system, which is designed to reduce the time theme park guests spend waiting in line during peak seasons. Attractions offering FASTPASSes are listed in each theme park chapter.

Here's how it works: You enter the gate and head toward a popular attraction. There, digital clocks show the estimated wait time and the return time for your FASTPASS, usually a one-hour time slot. Let's say you enter the Animal Kingdom gates at 10 A.M. and find that a long line has already formed for Kilimanjaro Safaris, and the return time is 12:30 to 1:30 P.M. If you opt to get a FASTPASS, insert your theme park ticket into the designated turnstile. You'll get the original ticket back, together with the FASTPASS. (Be sure to hang on to that FASTPASS—you'll need to show it to the attendant when you return.) Then go on to tour the rest of the Animal Kingdom. When you return to Kilimanjaro Safaris at 12:30, you'll be allowed to enter through the FASTPASS turnstile and proceed directly to the attraction boarding area. The waits with FASTPASSes average 10 to 15 minutes, a vast improvement over the 90-minute waits that big attractions often post during peak times.

To let as many guests as possible take advantage of the system, you must either use your FASTPASS at the designated time or wait two hours until you can get another one. As we go to press, the rumor is that guests will soon be allowed to hold more than one FASTPASS at a time. If so, this will enable you to cut down vastly on your time in line for popular attractions.

Helpful Hint

Only a limited number of FASTPASSes are available. At the most popular rides on crowded days, FASTPASSes can run out by midafternoon. So if you want to guarantee you'll get a FASTPASS for Test Track or Splash Mountain, visit the kiosk before noon.

Insider's Secret

A finite number of FASTPASSes are issued for each five-minute interval. If a lot of park guests use the FASTPASS system for a popular ride, the time frame between when the FASTPASS is issued and when you can return keeps getting longer. For example, if you get a FASTPASS for Tower of Terror on a relatively uncrowded day, you'll be able to return in about an hour. On a more crowded day, when many people have gotten FASTPASSes before you, your visit to the FAST-PASS kiosk at noon may result in a FASTPASS ticket for 3 P.M. And if you wait until afternoon, you may not get a FASTPASS at all.

Helpful Hint

Four family members will need four FASTPASSes, but that doesn't mean you all have to line up to get the FASTPASS tickets. Let one family member be in charge of holding on to both the theme park tickets and the FASTPASSes. That way you won't find that Tyler has somehow managed to lose his FASTPASS just as you're set to board Test Track.

Touring Tips for Visitors Staying On Site

🅔 By far the greatest advantage to staying at one of the hotels found within Disney World is the easy commute to the theme parks. Visitors with small kids can return to their hotels in midafternoon and then reenter the parks about 5 or 6 P.M. Remember the mantra: Come early, stay late, and take a break in the middle of the day.

If you arrive early, by 1 P.M. you'll have been touring for five or six hours and will be more than ready for a rest. Once "home," nap or take a dip in the pool.

Insider's Secret

In the off-season, the Magic Kingdom, MGM, and the Animal Kingdom sometimes close at 6 P.M., but Epcot stays open later, even during the least crowded weeks of the year. The solution? Spend mornings at one of the parks that close early, return to your hotel for a break, and then spend late afternoons and evenings at Epcot. Not only does this buy you more hours per day in the theme parks, but also many of the best places for dinner are at Epcot anyway.

@ Take advantage of the Extra Magic Hour program. You will be given a brochure upon check-in telling you which park is featured on each day of your visit.

Touring Tips for Visitors Staying Off Site

@ Time your commute. If you can make it from your hotel to the theme park gates within 30 minutes, it may still be worth your while to return to your hotel for a midday break. This is a distinct possibility for guests of the hotels at the Disney Village Hotel Plaza and some I-4 establishments. If your hotel is farther out, it's doubtful you'll want to make the drive four times a day.

@ If it isn't feasible to return to your hotel, find afternoon resting places within the parks. (See the sections headed "Afternoon Resting Places" in each theme park chapter.)

Sometimes kids aren't so much tired as full of pent-up energy. If you suspect that's the case, take preschoolers to the Toontown playground in the Magic Kingdom or let older kids run free among the forts and backwoods paths of Tom Sawyer Island. The *Honey, I Shrunk the Kids* Adventure Zone at MGM and the Boneyard at the Animal Kingdom are also perfect for burning off excess energy.

@ If you're willing to leave the parks in the middle of the afternoon, you have even more options. Cool off in the 24-screen movie theater in Downtown Disney or at a water park. River Country is an easy commute from the Magic Kingdom, because it runs its own launch. If you stash your bathing suits in one of the lockers under the railroad station in the Magic Kingdom, you can retrieve them around lunchtime and go straight to River Country without having to return to your car. *Note:* River Country is closed for refurbishment until spring of 2004.

Helpful Hint

If you take the monorail to a Magic Kingdom hotel for lunch, be sure to line up for the train marked "Monorail to the MK Resorts." Most of the monorails are expresses back to the TTC.

The hotel restaurants in the Magic Kingdom resorts are rarely crowded at lunch, and the dining is much more leisurely than in the parks. An early dinner (around 5 P.M.) can also effectively break up a summer day, when you may be staying at the park until midnight.

@ If you'll be touring all day, get strollers for all preschool-age kids. Few 5-year-olds can walk through a 14-hour day.

@ Spend the morning in the park where you'll be most active (e.g., The Magic Kingdom). In the afternoon, go to a park such as MGM, which has more shows and, thus, more places to sit and rest.

🌀 If you have any kind of multiday ticket, you can use Disney World transportation to move from park to park or to a Disney resort.

How to Customize a Touring Plan

Get Some General Information

In creating a personalized touring plan, your first step is to request maps and transportation information at the time you make your hotel reservations. Familiarize yourself with the overall map of Disney World and the maps of the major theme parks so you can arrive in Orlando with some sense of the proximity and location of major attractions. Getting to Big Thunder Mountain Railroad early is considerably easier if you know where Big Thunder Mountain Railroad is.

Also, request the projected park hours for the week you'll be visiting. There's no point in planning a fun-filled night at the Magic Kingdom if you're going on a day when it closes at 6 P.M.

Ask Yourself Some Basic Questions

Consider how long you'll want to stay at each park. If your kids are under 10, you'll probably want to spend more time in the Magic Kingdom and MGM than at Epcot. Older kids? Plan to divide your time fairly equally among the major parks, but save more time for the water parks and Downtown Disney.

The time of year you're visiting is a factor too; while you may be able to tour MGM thoroughly on a single day in October, it will take you twice as long to see the same number of attractions in July. Likewise, in the summer, the combination of the crowds, the heat, and extended park hours means you'll need to build in more downtime, such as afternoons by the resort pool.

Helpful Hint

If you're traveling in the off-season, when the Magic Kingdom, MGM, and the Animal Kingdom all close early, Epcot becomes almost by default "the evening park."

If you're traveling in the on-season, when all the major parks run extended hours, spend at least one evening in each major park so you can enjoy the closing shows and parades.

Set Your Priorities

Next, poll your family on which attractions they most want to see and then build these priorities into the plan. I'd let each family member choose three "must-sees" per park. For example, at MGM, 10-year-old Jeremy wants to ride the Twilight Zone Tower of Terror and Star Tours and see the *Indiana Jones Epic Stunt Spectacular*. His 6-year-old sister, Elyce, chooses *MuppetVision 3-D* and the *Beauty and the Beast* show and wants to meet the characters at one of the greeting times. Mom thinks the Prime Time Café sounds like a hoot, wants to ride the Great Movie Ride, and agrees that the *Indiana Jones* show sounds great. Dad is all over the Tower of Terror thing, wants to play the Millionaire game, and thinks the Animation Tour sounds interesting.

Helpful Hint

Want to see the characters? Your theme park map indicates when and where they'll appear—where you probably won't see them is just walking down the street. Remember, at Disney the characters are the equivalent of rock stars and security around them is tight. If you want that photo, autograph, or hug, you'll have to line up.

The key is to build all these top priorities into the touring plan first; make sure you do them even if you do nothing else.

With any luck, you'll have a bit of overlap on the must-sees and thus time to do other things. So go on and create a "would be nice" list, too—shows and attractions that you'll enjoy even if they aren't top priorities. If you manage to work in a few of these, so much the better.

Cut Some Deals

Building each family member's must-sees into the touring plan has many advantages: You're seeing the best of the best, you've broken out of that "gotta do it all" compulsion, and the kids feel that they are giving input and are full partners in the vacation planning.

There's another huge advantage: A customized touring plan minimizes whining and fights. Your 12-year-old is more apt to bear a character breakfast with good grace if she knows that you'll be spending the afternoon at Blizzard Beach, one of her top choices. Kids understand fair. They might fidget a bit in Chefs de France, but if you've already covered Test Track, Innoventions, and *Honey, I Shrunk the Audience*, you're perfectly justified in saying, "This is Mom's first choice at Epcot, so be quiet and eat your croquette de boeuf."

Break Up the Days

Next, divide each day of your visit into three components: morning, afternoon, and evening. It isn't necessary that you specify where you'll be every hour—that's too confining—but you need some sense of how you'll break up the day.

Pencil in things that have to be done at a certain time: You have a character breakfast scheduled for Tuesday morning, for example, or you must be in the Magic Kingdom on Friday night because that's the only time the evening parade will be running during your visit, or you've arranged priority seating at the Hollywood Brown Derby for noon on Thursday.

If you're traveling during the on-season, the final product will look something like this:

Monday
Morning: Magic Kingdom
Afternoon: Rest by hotel pool
Evening: Epcot

Tuesday
Morning and afternoon:
   Animal Kingdom
Night: Downtown Disney

Wednesday
Morning: MGM
Afternoon: Blizzard Beach
Evening: Magic Kingdom

Thursday
Morning: Epcot
Afternoon: Rest by pool
Night: MGM

If you're traveling during the off-season, it may look more like this:

Monday
Morning and afternoon:
   Magic Kingdom
Evening: Epcot

Tuesday
Morning and afternoon:
   Animal Kingdom
Evening: Dinner show

Wednesday
Morning and afternoon: MGM
Evening: Epcot

Thursday
Morning: Typhoon Lagoon
Afternoon: Rest at hotel
Night: Downtown Disney

Friday
Morning: MGM
Afternoon and evening:
   Magic Kingdom

Favorite Preschool Attractions

IN THE MAGIC KINGDOM

It's a Small World
Peter Pan's Flight
The Many Adventures of Winnie the Pooh
Cinderella's Golden Carrousel
Dumbo
Mad Hatter's Tea Party
Goofy's Barnstormer
Donald's boat; Minnie and Mickey's houses in Toontown
Tomorrowland Speedway
Buzz Lightyear's Space Ranger Spin
Jungle Cruise
Country Bear Jamboree
The parades
Aladdin's Magic Carpet
Mickey's PhilharMagic

IN THE ANIMAL KINGDOM

Kali River Rapids
Festival of the Lion King
It's Tough to Be a Bug
The Boneyard
Chester & Hester

AT EPCOT

Kiddie games at Innoventions
Family Fun Kidcot Stops
Journey Into Your Imagination
The Living Seas

AT MGM

MuppetVision 3-D
Honey, I Shrunk the Kids play area
Voyage of the Little Mermaid
Bear in the Big Blue House

Whatever you do, save time to meet the characters.
It's a major thrill for kids this age.

Favorite Preteen and Teen Attractions

The following attractions received the highest approval rating from the Disney World visitors we surveyed, ages 11 to 16.

IN THE MAGIC KINGDOM

Space Mountain

Splash Mountain

Alien Encounter

Big Thunder Mountain Railroad

Mad Hatter's Tea Party

Haunted Mansion

AT EPCOT

Test Track

Honey, I Shrunk the Audience

Body Wars

IllumiNations

Mission: Space

Innoventions

AT MGM

The Twilight Zone Tower of Terror

Star Tours

Indiana Jones Epic Stunt Spectacular

Rock 'n' Roller Coaster

Favorite Preteen and Teen Attractions (continued)

IN THE ANIMAL KINGDOM

Kilimanjaro Safaris

DINOSAUR

It's Tough to Be a Bug

IN THE REST OF DISNEY WORLD

Blizzard Beach

Typhoon Lagoon

Water Sprites (the rental speedboats at Downtown Disney and on-site hotels)

Planet Hollywood

DisneyQuest (the arcade at West Side in Downtown Disney)

Cirque du Soleil

CHAPTER

5

The Magic Kingdom®

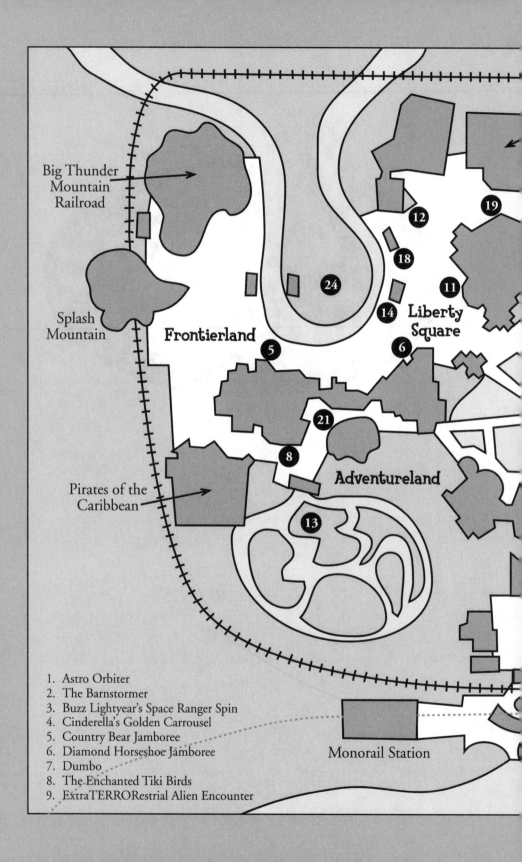

Big Thunder
Mountain
Railroad

Splash
Mountain

Frontierland

Pirates of the
Caribbean

Adventureland

**Liberty
Square**

12

19

18

11

24

14

5

6

21

8

13

Monorail Station

1. Astro Orbiter
2. The Barnstormer
3. Buzz Lightyear's Space Ranger Spin
4. Cinderella's Golden Carrousel
5. Country Bear Jamboree
6. Diamond Horseshoe Jamboree
7. Dumbo
8. The Enchanted Tiki Birds
9. ExtraTERRORestrial Alien Encounter

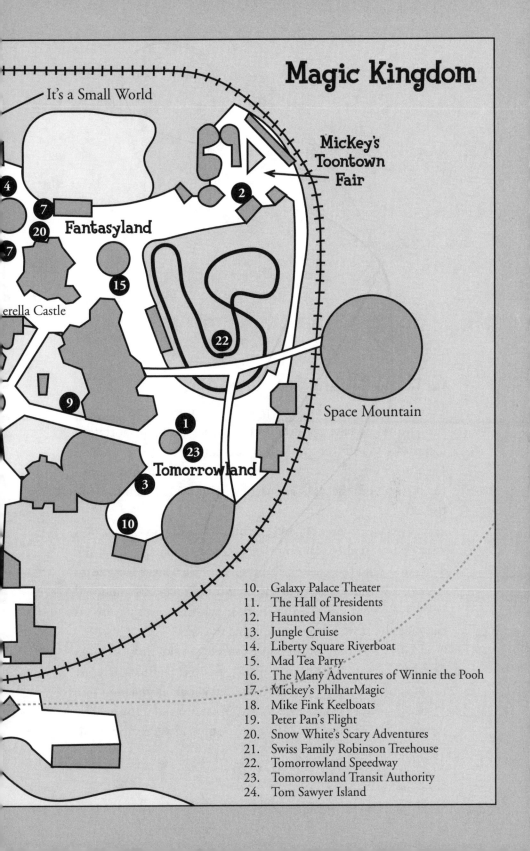

Magic Kingdom

It's a Small World

Mickey's
Toontown
Fair

Fantasyland

erella Castle

Space Mountain

Tomorrowland

Getting to the Magic Kingdom

If you're staying off site, prepare for a complicated journey. Either drive or take a shuttle to the Ticket and Transportation Center (TTC). From the TTC, you can cross the Seven Seas Lagoon by ferryboat or monorail. As you enter the front gates, the turnstiles to the right are usually less crowded than those to the left.

If you're staying on site, getting to the Magic Kingdom is a lot easier. At the Contemporary Resort, you can bypass the TTC and take the monorail directly to the Magic Kingdom. Likewise, if you're staying at the Grand Floridian, the monorail will have you at the Magic Kingdom within minutes. Or you can take the launch from the marina dock.

Guests at the Polynesian Resort have the most choices of all: the launch, the monorail, or the ferryboat. If your room is on the lagoon, walk to the ferryboat. If you're in one of the buildings near the Great Ceremonial House, the monorail is a better bet. If your room is close to the pool, take the launch.

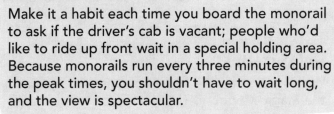

Insider's Secret

Make it a habit each time you board the monorail to ask if the driver's cab is vacant; people who'd like to ride up front wait in a special holding area. Because monorails run every three minutes during the peak times, you shouldn't have to wait long, and the view is spectacular.

Guests at Disney hotels that are not on the monorail line can take shuttle buses that deliver them directly to the Magic Kingdom, bypassing the TTC. This saves you at least 10 minutes of commuting, more during the morning rush hour.

From Fort Wilderness Campground or Wilderness Lodge, take the launch.

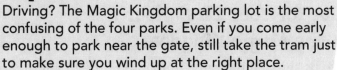

Helpful Hint

Driving? The Magic Kingdom parking lot is the most confusing of the four parks. Even if you come early enough to park near the gate, still take the tram just to make sure you wind up at the right place.

Getting Around the Magic Kingdom

The Disney World Railroad leaves from the main gate with stops near Splash Mountain in Frontierland and Toontown and can save you a bit of time and effort if you happen to hit it right. Don't think, however, that catching the train to Splash Mountain is your fastest way there. The Railroad Station is busy in the morning, and you may have to wait for a second or third train; by that time, you could have walked. If you're arriving in the afternoon or some other time when the station is less crowded, the odds are you can get on the next train. This may save you a few steps, especially if you're headed toward Toontown.

Helpful Hint

Walking is by far the fastest means of transport in the Magic Kingdom. The vintage cars and horse-drawn carriages are fun, but think of them as pleasant rides, not as a serious means of getting around the park.

Be prepared to make frequent rest stops while touring the Magic Kingdom. You won't walk as much as you do in Epcot, but you're likely to spend more time waiting in lines. Standing still is ultimately harder on the feet—and the nerves—than walking.

Tips for Your First Hour in the Magic Kingdom

- Be through the gates 30 minutes earlier than the stated opening time. Get strollers and pick up a map and entertainment schedule as you enter.

Helpful Hint

On crowded days guests are allowed to travel the length of Main Street before the park officially opens. On less crowded days, people may be held in the area in front of the railroad. Either way, a few characters will be on hand to give the kids something to do while you wait for the ropes to drop.

- On Extra Magic Hour mornings, Fantasyland and Tomorrowland open first. Older kids should head straight for Space Mountain, while younger kids should start with Dumbo, Peter Pan's Flight, and The Many Adventures of Winnie the Pooh.

- On regular mornings, all sections of the park open at once. If your kids are up for it, head for Splash Mountain when the ropes drop, then to Big Thunder Mountain Railroad, then across to Space Mountain.

- If there's a gap in the ages of your children and the 9-year-old is ready for the coasters but the 4-year-old isn't, split up. Mom can take one child, Dad the other, and you can meet up again in an hour.

Attractions in the Magic Kingdom that Offer FASTPASSes

Space Mountain

Splash Mountain

Jungle Cruise

Buzz Lightyear's Space Ranger Spin

The Haunted Mansion

Mickey's PhilharMagic

Peter Pan's Flight

The Many Adventures of Winnie the Pooh

Main Street Touring Tips

- Although you might want to spend a few minutes mingling with the characters who greet you as you enter, don't stop to check out the shops or minor attractions of Main Street in the morning; you need to hurry on to the big rides.

@ Return to Main Street to shop in midafternoon. Especially worthwhile are Disney Clothiers, Uptown Jewelers, and the Emporium. Main Street is also a good place for lunch.

Insider's Secret

After shopping, either stow your purchases in the lockers beneath the Railroad Station or, if you're a guest at a Disney resort, have them sent directly to your hotel room. If you're not planning to see the parade, be sure to be off Main Street by 2:30 P.M. After that, it's a mob scene.

@ If you're touring the Magic Kingdom late and your party splits up, make sure you choose a spot on Main Street as your meeting place. Disney employees clear people out of the other sections of the park promptly at closing time, but Main Street stays open up to an hour after the rides shut down. It is the best place to reassemble the family before heading for the parking lot.

@ A blackboard posted at the end of Main Street provides up-to-date information about the approximate waiting times at Magic Kingdom rides, as well as all show times and where to meet the characters. Consult it whenever you're unsure about what to do next.

Fantasyland

Fantasyland, located directly behind Cinderella Castle, is full of kiddie rides. It's the most congested section of the Magic Kingdom.

The Magic Kingdom Don't-Miss List

IF YOUR KIDS ARE 7 OR OLDER

Space Mountain

Splash Mountain

Pirates of the Caribbean

Big Thunder Mountain Railroad

Haunted Mansion

Mickey's PhilharMagic

The parades

Buzz Lightyear's Space Ranger Spin

Any Fantasyland rides that catch their fancy

IF YOUR KIDS ARE UNDER 7

Dumbo

Mad Hatter's Tea Party

It's a Small World

Peter Pan's Flight

The Many Adventures of Winnie the Pooh

Toontown, especially Goofy's Barnstormer

Pirates of the Caribbean

Country Bear Jamboree

Mickey's PhilharMagic

The parades

Splash Mountain, if they pass the height requirement

Big Thunder Mountain Railroad,
if they pass the height requirement

Buzz Lightyear's Space Ranger Spin

Aladdin's Magic Carpet

Quick Guide to Magic

Attraction	Location	Height Requirement
Aladdin's Magic Carpet	Adventureland	None
Astro Orbiter	Tomorrowland	None
Big Thunder Mountain Railroad	Frontierland	40 inches
Buzz Lightyear's Space Ranger Spin	Tomorrowland	None
Carousel of Progress	Tomorrowland	None
Cinderella's Golden Carrousel	Fantasyland	None
Country Bear Jamboree	Frontierland	None
Diamond Horseshoe Jamboree	Frontierland	None
Dumbo	Fantasyland	None
The Enchanted Tiki Birds	Adventureland	None
ExtraTERRORestrial Alien Encounter	Tomorrowland	44 inches
Frontierland Shootin' Arcade	Frontierland	None
Goofy's Barnstormer	Toontown	None
The Hall of Presidents	Liberty Square	None
The Haunted Mansion	Liberty Square	None
It's a Small World	Fantasyland	None
Jungle Cruise	Adventureland	None
Liberty Square Riverboat	Liberty Square	None

Scare Factor

0 = Unlikely to scare any child of any age.
! = Has dark or loud elements; might rattle some toddlers.
!! = A couple of gotcha! moments; should be fine for school-age kids.
!!! = You need to be pretty big and pretty brave to handle this ride.

Kingdom Attractions

Speed of Line	Duration of Ride/Show	Scare Factor	Age Range
Slow	1 min.	0	All
Slow	2 min.	!	7 and up
Moderate	3 min.	!!	5 and up
Fast	6 min.	0	3 and up
Fast	22 min.	0	10 and up
Slow	2 min.	0	2 and up
Moderate	15 min.	0	All
Fast	30 min.	0	All
Slow	1 min.	0	All
Fast	20 min.	0	All
Fast	20 min.	!!!	10 and up
Slow	n/a	0	7 and up
Moderate	1 min.	!	5 and up
Fast	20 min.	0	10 and up
Slow	9 min.	!!	7 and up
Fast	11 min.	0	All
Slow	10 min.	0	All
Fast	15 min.	0	All

(continued)

Quick Guide to Magic

Attraction	Location	Height Requirement
Mad Hatter's Tea Party	Fantasyland	None
The Many Adventures of Winnie the Pooh	Fantasyland	None
Mickey's PhilharMagic	Fantasyland	None
Peter Pan's Flight	Fantasyland	None
Pirates of the Caribbean	Adventureland	None
Snow White's Scary Adventures	Fantasyland	None
Space Mountain	Tomorrowland	44 inches
Splash Mountain	Frontierland	40 inches
Swiss Family Robinson Treehouse	Adventureland	None
Timekeeper	Tomorrowland	None
Tomorrowland Indy Speedway	Tomorrowland	None
Tomorrowland Transit Authority	Tomorrowland	None
Tom Sawyer Island	Frontierland	None

Scare Factor

0 = Unlikely to scare any child of any age.
! = Has dark or loud elements; might rattle some toddlers.
!! = A couple of gotcha! moments; should be fine for school-age kids.
!!! = You need to be pretty big and pretty brave to handle this ride.

Kingdom Attractions

Speed of Line	Duration of Ride/Show	Scare Factor	Age Range
Slow	2 min.	0	4 and up
Moderate	5 min.	0	All
Moderate	20 min.	0	All
Moderate	3 min.	0	All
Fast	8 min.	!!	6 and up
Slow	3 min.	!!	5 and up
Moderate	3 min.	!!!	7 and up
Moderate	10 min.	!!	5 and up
Slow	n/a	0	4 and up
Fast	20 min.	0	3 and up
Slow	5 min.	0	2 and up
Fast	10 min.	0	All
Slow	n/a	0	4 and up

Fantasyland Touring Tips

- ℮ Wait times for Dumbo, Peter Pan's Flight, and The Many Adventures of Winnie the Pooh are always longer than for other Fantasyland rides. Visit these first.

- ℮ Visit Fantasyland either before 11 A.M., after 7 P.M., or during the 3 P.M. parade.

- ℮ Don't eat or shop in Fantasyland. Similar food and toys are available elsewhere in far less crowded areas of the Magic Kingdom.

- ℮ When it opens, *Mickey's PhilharMagic* will undoubtedly be a big hit with all age groups. Go to one of the first shows of the day if possible. If not, lines will probably be somewhat shorter during the afternoon parade and in the evening, when Fantasyland is slightly less crowded.

- ℮ Park your strollers in one spot, and walk from ride to ride. Fantasyland is geographically small, so this is easier than constantly loading and reloading the kids, only to push them a few steps.

Helpful Hint

Stay alert. Because the kiddie rides tempt them to wander off, this is the most likely spot in all of Disney World to lose your child.

Fantasyland Attractions

It's a Small World

During this 11-minute boat ride, dolls representing children of all nations greet you with a song so infectious you'll be humming it at bedtime. The ride loads steadily, so the lines move fast, making this a good choice for afternoon. And it's one of the best attractions to film with a camcorder.

Helpful Hint
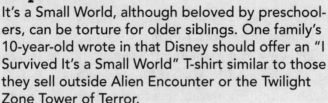
It's a Small World, although beloved by preschoolers, can be torture for older siblings. One family's 10-year-old wrote in that Disney should offer an "I Survived It's a Small World" T-shirt similar to those they sell outside Alien Encounter or the Twilight Zone Tower of Terror.

Peter Pan's Flight
Tinkerbell flutters overhead as you board miniature pirate ships and sail above Nana's doghouse, the sparkling night streets of London, the Indian camp, and Captain Hook's cove. Of all the Magic Kingdom attractions, this one is most true to the movie that inspired it.

Time-Saving Tip

Even if you have younger kids who will be spending most of their time in Fantasyland, you can still use FASTPASSes to help you handle long lines. Peter Pan's Flight and The Many Adventures of Winnie the Pooh both offer FASTPASSes; don't hesitate to get them, because lines at both these attractions often get long by midafternoon.

Mickey's PhilharMagic
A 3-D show projected onto a mammoth screen, *Mickey's PhilharMagic* is Fantasyland's newest attraction and designed to appeal to all age groups. The story line is that maestro Donald Duck loses control of his orchestra and a wide variety of Disney characters spanning the entire age of animation, get into the musical act. You can see Donald falling in love with Ariel or sailing through the skies with Aladdin. The show is funny, the

music is stirring, and the presence of the beloved characters make this a great introduction to 3-D for kids too young to appreciate *Honey, I Shrunk the Audience* at Epcot or even *It's Tough to Be a Bug* at the Animal Kingdom.

The show is not open to the general public as we go to press, so it is too early to see if Disney will make FASTPASS available, although presumably they will if the lines become prohibitive.

Time-Saving Tip

Usually FASTPASS is best reserved for rides, not shows, but *Mickey's PhilharMagic* may be an exception. New attractions are always more crowded than the old standbys, so if FASTPASS is offered for *Mickey's PhilharMagic*, take advantage of it.

The Scare Factor

Although *Mickey's PhilharMagic* is not open to the public as we go to press and we were thus unable to gauge the reactions of children, this show is less frightening than other Disney 3-D movies. That said, there are a couple of startling special effects and, like so many of the shows, it's very loud. Unless your child is afraid of darkness or very sensitive to loud noises, she'll probably love the show. After all, with Donald in charge, what can go wrong?

The Many Adventures of Winnie the Pooh

This upbeat ride follows Pooh and friends through a "blustery" day, meaning your honey-pot-shaped car will swirl and jostle a bit. Designed specially for younger kids, the ride is gentle and fine for any age. Pooh's Thoughtful Shop, located at the exit, has great souvenirs for Pooh fans.

Cinderella's Golden Carrousel

Seventy-two white horses prance while a pipe organ toots out "Chim-Chim-Cheree" and other classic Disney songs. The carousel is gorgeous at night, and benches nearby let Mom and Dad take a breather.

Snow White's Scary Adventures

Don't expect to see much of the dwarfs. This ride focuses on the part of the movie where Snow White is fleeing the witch. You ride mining cars through the dark, and the Wicked Witch appears several times quite suddenly.

The Scare Factor

It's hard to know exactly whom this ride was designed for—it's boring for kids over 6 and unnerving for preschoolers. If you look at the sign, you'll see where the staff slipped the word "Scary" between "Snow White" and "Adventures." Another sign warns you that the witch is inside. In short, although the special effects are very simple, the mood of the ride is foreboding enough to give toddlers the willies.

Dumbo

This happy little elephant has become the center of some controversy: Is he worth the wait or not? Although the lines do indeed move slowly, making a one-hour wait possible for a 90-second ride, there's something special about this attraction. It's frequently featured in the ads, so it has become an integral part of our collective Disney consciousness.

If you visit this ride first thing in the morning, you can cut the wait down, perhaps to only a few minutes. The height of your Dumbo flight can be controlled by a joystick, making the ride appropriate for any age.

Mad Hatter's Tea Party

Spinning pastel cups, propelled by their riders, swirl around the Soused Mouse, who periodically pops out of the teapot. Because you largely control how fast your teacup spins, this ride can be enjoyed by people of all ages.

Time-Saving Tip

Rider volume ebbs and flows at Mad Hatter's Tea Party. If the line looks too daunting, grab a drink or make a bathroom stop. By the time you emerge, the crowd may have dispersed.

Ariel's Grotto Playground

A small play area with squirting fountains, the grotto is a good place for toddlers and preschoolers to cool off on a hot afternoon. Go inside the cave to meet Ariel and get her autograph only if the line is short; some parents report waiting up to 30 minutes for an autograph, far too long for a single character.

Insider's Secret

Visit Storytime with Belle at Fairytale Garden near the Mad Hatter's Tea Party in Fantasyland. This sweet little show, in which Belle herself helps young members of the audience act out the much-loved story of *Beauty and the Beast*, is great fun for younger kids. (Especially if they're tapped to play Mrs. Potts, Lumiere, or another member of the gang.) Check your map for show times.

Mickey's Toontown Fair

Mickey's Toontown Fair (most often referred to as just "Toontown") makes you feel as if you were immersed in a giant cartoon. Attractions are designed to appeal primarily to the 2- to 8-year-old set.

Toontown is full of great photo ops, such as the bright blue car outside Pete's Garage or Minnie's House, where the oven bakes a cake before your eyes and kids can make popcorn pop by pushing a microwave button. Donald's boat, the *Miss Daisy*, is a great play area with squirting fountains, making Toontown a good choice after you've finished Fantasyland and the kids just want to run and play for a while.

Toontown is also the best place in the park to meet the characters: After you tour Mickey's House and meet him in the tent behind it, enter the main tent called Toontown Hall of Fame. You'll see three separate lines marked something like "Mickey's Pals," "The Hundred Acre Wood," "Forest Friends," "Villains," or "Princesses." At least four characters will be waiting in each room. There is plenty of time for photos and autographs, and because guests are admitted 15 at a time, young children can visit the characters without being trampled or mobbed. After you've visited one group, you can always rejoin the line and visit another.

The centerpiece of Toontown is a zippy little roller coaster called Goofy's Barnstormer, which takes you on a wild trip through Wise Acre Farm with you-know-who as the pilot. The ride lasts only 50 seconds and is the sort of ride many kids insist on doing again and again.

Toontown Touring Tips

@ Like Fantasyland, Toontown can become unbearably crowded in midafternoon. By early evening, however, the crowds thin. If you've missed Goofy's Barnstormer in

The Scare Factor

Goofy's Barnstormer is a good choice for kids not quite up to Splash Mountain or Space Mountain; the drops are steep and the thrills are definitely there, but the ride is so short you barely get out one good scream before it's over. You can see the whole path of the ride from the ground, so if you have any doubts, watch the Barnstormer make a couple of trips and then decide.

the morning, check back in the evening, when waits are minimal.

- Donald's boat is a great place to cool off—and get soaked—on a summer afternoon.

- The very best time to visit Mickey and the other Toontown characters is Sunday morning, when your kids are apt to be well rested and the crowds are light.

Tomorrowland

Tomorrowland has a 1950s' sci-fi look that reflects "the future that never was." In this Tomorrowland, the mood is decidedly campy—as evidenced by the robot paperboy hawking tomorrow's news and the street sweepers on rollerblades.

Tomorrowland Touring Tips

- If you don't plan to ride Space Mountain or see Alien Encounter, save Tomorrowland for afternoons, when the park is at its most crowded. Several Tomorrowland attractions, such as *Timekeeper*, are high capacity and relatively easy to get into even in the most packed part of the day.

- On crowded days Tomorrowland has its own tip board across from Alien Encounter, and it lists approximate wait

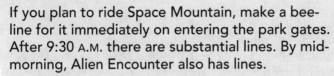

Insider's Secret

If you plan to ride Space Mountain, make a bee-line for it immediately on entering the park gates. After 9:30 A.M. there are substantial lines. By mid-morning, Alien Encounter also has lines.

times for rides. Check the tip board if you're headed for Space Mountain; if the wait is longer than 40 minutes, come back another time.

@ There's an arcade across from Space Mountain that is a good place for the less adventurous members of your party to wait while the coaster warriors tackle Space Mountain.

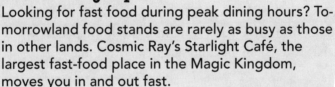

Time-Saving Tip

Looking for fast food during peak dining hours? Tomorrowland food stands are rarely as busy as those in other lands. Cosmic Ray's Starlight Café, the largest fast-food place in the Magic Kingdom, moves you in and out fast.

Tomorrowland Attractions

Space Mountain

This three-minute roller coaster ride through inky darkness is one of the few scream-rippers in the Magic Kingdom. The cars move at 28 miles per hour, a fairly tame pace compared to that of the monster coasters at some theme parks, but the entire ride

Insider's Secret

Ride Space Mountain in the morning and then get a FASTPASS so you can return later and ride again with a minimal wait.

takes place inside, and it's impossible to anticipate the turns and dips in the blackness, which adds considerably to the thrill.

The Scare Factor

Children under 7 must be 44 inches tall and be with an adult to ride. Children under 3 and pregnant women are prohibited. Some kids 3 to 7 like the ride, but most find it far too scary. Kids in the 7-to-11 age group in general give a thumbs-up, and teens adore Space Mountain.

Tomorrowland Speedway

These tiny sports cars circle a nifty-looking racetrack, and although the ride isn't anything unusual, kids under 11 rate it highly, perhaps because even young drivers can steer the cars themselves. (If Jennifer's legs are too short to reach the gas pedal, Mom or Dad can handle the floor pedals while she steers.) Kids 52 inches and taller can drive solo.

Helpful Hint

Try to persuade your child not to rush through Tomorrowland Speedway; loading and unloading the race cars takes time, and you may as well drive slowly rather than sit for five minutes in the pit waiting to be unloaded.

Galaxy Palace Theater

This large outdoor theater hosts shows during the on-season. Check your entertainment schedule or the blackboard at the end of Main Street for details. Because the theater is so huge, you can almost always be seated if you arrive 10 to 15 minutes before show time.

Buzz Lightyear's Space Ranger Spin
This ride is an "interactive fantasy in which riders help Buzz save the world's supply of batteries." More specifically, the ride transports guests into the heart of a video game where they pass through various scenes, shooting at targets. (Hint: You get more points for hitting distant or moving targets, so don't spend all your time taking cheap shots.) Your car keeps your score, and at the end you learn whether you're a Space Ace or a lowly trainee. Buzz is addictive, but the line moves fast. Hardly any kid will let you do it just once.

Astro Orbiter
A circular thrill ride—sort of a Dumbo on steroids—Astro Orbiter is a bit too much for preschoolers and a bit too little for teens. Like Dumbo, it loads slowly; if you wait to ride at night the astro-ambience is even more convincing.

The Scare Factor
Astro Orbiter is a good choice for those ages 5 to 10 who are not quite up to Space Mountain. But this is not, repeat not, a good choice for anyone prone to vertigo or motion sickness.

Tomorrowland Transit Authority
This little tram circles Tomorrowland and provides fun views, including a glimpse inside Space Mountain. The ride is never crowded, and often the attendant will let you stay on for another go-round. The rocking of the train has lulled more than one cranky toddler into a nap.

Timekeeper
In this CircleVision 360 film, Jules Verne and H. G. Wells take the audience from nineteenth-century Paris into the future. The voices of Robin Williams and Rhea Perlman, your time travel pilot and navigator, add to the fun.

While the show is well done, guests stand throughout the presentation. Strollers are not allowed inside the theater, which means babies and toddlers have to be held during the show, and preschoolers often need to be lifted up to have a prayer of seeing the film—a drawback that eliminates it for many families.

Lines disappear every 20 minutes, allowing 1,000 people at a time to enter, making *Timekeeper* a good choice for the most crowded times of the afternoon.

Carousel of Progress

This is another fairly long show (22 minutes), another high-capacity attraction, and thus another good choice for the crowded times of the afternoon. Kids under 10, however, may be bored by this salute to the uses of electricity, especially once they've seen the more high-tech presentations of Epcot.

Helpful Hint

Carousel of Progress, along with *Timekeeper*, is often closed seasonally. In other words, if you're traveling in the off-season, don't expect to see these attractions.

ExtraTERRORestrial Alien Encounter

Alien Encounter is about a time travel experiment that runs amok, "releasing" an alien into your theater. Although you never totally see the beast, you see flashes of parts of his body and hear him rattling around above your head and behind you. Like Epcot's *Honey, I Shrunk the Audience*, some of the special effects are tactile; the shoulder harness gives the sensation that the monster is just behind you, slipping around your shoulders and breathing down your back.

The danger is mostly implied, because the imagineers working on the attraction theorized that the mind can conjure up far worse things than Disney technicians could ever create. At one point in the presentation, when the tactile and aural effects are at their peak, you sit in total darkness for more than a minute.

Kids must be 44 inches to enter. The preshow is misleading; the main show is far scarier. I'd send a parent through first to preview the experience before going in with kids under 10.

Helpful Hint

Alien Encounter has a surprisingly small sign and is not that easy to find. It's directly across from *Timekeeper* as you enter Tomorrowland via the Main Street Bridge.

The Scare Factor

I've received more negative mail on Alien Encounter than on any other attraction at Disney World, most of it indicating that the show is far, far too intense for children under 10. One mother pointed out that the shoulder harness not only gave her 8-year-old the sense he was strapped down but also prevented her from putting her arm around him or comforting him when he panicked. "There is fun scary and scary scary," one 7-year-old wrote. "Alien Encounter is scary scary."

Adventureland, Frontierland, and Liberty Square Touring Tips

@ If you have two days to spend touring the Magic Kingdom, begin your second day in Frontierland, at Splash

Mountain. Move on to Big Thunder Mountain Railroad, then the Haunted Mansion in Liberty Square. All three attractions are relatively easy to board before 10 A.M., and you can return to ride less crowded Liberty Square and Frontierland attractions later in the day.

@ Because most visitors tour the lands in a clockwise or counterclockwise fashion, these three lands reach peak capacity around noon and stay crowded until around 4:30 P.M., when the people lined up to watch the 3 P.M. parade finally disperse. So if you miss Splash Mountain, the Haunted Mansion, or Big Thunder Mountain Railroad in the morning, wait until evening to revisit them.

@ Should you, despite your best intentions, wind up in one of these three sections in midafternoon, you'll find a bit of breathing space on Tom Sawyer Island, with the Enchanted Tiki Birds, in the Hall of Presidents, or among the shops in the shady Adventureland Pavilion. Surprisingly, Pirates of the Caribbean isn't that difficult to board in midafternoon. The lines look terrible, but at least you wait inside, and this is one of the fastest-loading attractions in Disney World.

Time-Saving Tip

Everyone dashes to Splash Mountain the minute the ropes drop in the morning, and on very busy days this means the line may be massive within minutes after the park opens. If you hustle straight to Frontierland and arrive only to find yourself facing a wait longer than 30 minutes, move on to Big Thunder Mountain Railroad; check Splash Mountain again immediately afterward, and you may find that the initial surge of people has moved through and the line is a bit shorter.

Adventureland

Thematically the most bizarre of all the lands—sort of a Bourbon Street meets Trinidad by way of the Congo—Adventureland definitely conveys an exotic mood.

Adventureland Attractions

Jungle Cruise

You'll meet up with headhunters, hyenas, water-spewing elephants, and other varieties of frankly fake wildlife on this 10-minute boat ride. It's very dated looking in comparison to the real-life adventures of the Animal Kingdom. What distinguishes this attraction is the amusing patter of the tour guides—these young adventurers in pith helmets are unsung heroes of Disney casting genius.

The cruise is not at all scary and is fine for any age, but the lines move with agonizing slowness. If you decide to take the cruise, go in the morning—or during the 3 P.M. parade.

Aladdin's Magic Carpet

This new kiddie attraction in Adventureland is a circular aerial ride with the added twist that riders control their carpets, making them tilt, rise, or drop on command. The ride, which is colorful and visually appealing, is a big hit with the preschool and school-age set, but, like Dumbo, it boards slowly. Go in the morning or during the afternoon parade.

The Scare Factor

Aladdin's Magic Carpet should be fine for any age. Because the carpets pitch and tilt a bit, the ride is slightly more intense than Dumbo, but most preschoolers love it.

The Enchanted Tiki Birds

These singing/talking birds, and the singing/talking flowers and statues around them, represent Disney's first attempt at the Audio-Animatronics that are now such an integral part of Epcot magic. The addition of Iago from *Aladdin* and Zazu from *The Lion King* as the new co-owners adds a much-needed shot in the arm to this rather tired old attraction. The music is livelier, and kids enjoy seeing their favorite birds. (*Note:* Stick around for Iago's stream of insults as you exit the theater. It's the funniest part of the show.)

The Scare Factor

A Scare Factor rating for the good old Tiki birds? It's sad but true. An unfortunate side effect of the revamped show is that it is much louder and more intense than the previous version. When the Tiki gods are angered, the theater darkens and a thunder and lightening storm begins. While the show is certainly not as scary as Alien Encounter, the noise and rattling are enough to scare toddlers.

Swiss Family Robinson Treehouse

There's a real split of opinion here—some visitors love this replica of the ultimate treehouse, whereas others rate it as dull. Kids who have seen the movie tend to like it a lot more.

Helpful Hint

One word of warning: The Swiss Family Robinson Treehouse is a tough attraction to tour with toddlers. Lugging a 2-year-old through the exhibit is tiring, but the real problem is that the bamboo and rigging look so enticing the kids want to climb on their own and at their own pace. This may not sit well with the 800 people in line behind you.

Pirates of the Caribbean

This ride inspires great loyalty, and a significant number of guests of all ages name it as their favorite in all the Magic Kingdom. Your boat goes over a small waterfall, and the pirates are remarkably lifelike, right down to the hair on their legs. The theme song is positively infectious, and young buccaneers can stop off at the Pieces O' Eight gift shop on the way out for plastic weaponry.

The Scare Factor

The queue winds through a dark, drafty dungeon and scares more kids than the ride does. Unfortunately, the scariest elements of the ride occur in the first three minutes; there are gunshots, skeletons, cannons, and one segment where you go through about a minute of shadowy darkness; by the time you get to the mangy-looking and politically incorrect buccaneers, the mood is up-tempo, as evidenced by the cheerful theme song. Fine for most kids over 6, unless they're afraid of the dark.

Frontierland

Kids love the rough-and-tumble, Wild West feel of Frontierland, which is home to several of the Magic Kingdom's most popular attractions.

Frontierland Attractions

Big Thunder Mountain Railroad

A roller coaster disguised as a runaway mine train, Big Thunder Mountain is considerably less scary than Space Mountain, but almost as popular. The glory of the ride is in the setting. You zoom through a deserted mining town. If you're wondering if the coaster may be too much for your kids, be advised that Big Thunder Mountain is more in the rattle-back-and-forth than in the lose-your-stomach-as-you-plunge genre.

The Scare Factor

Most children over 7 should be able to handle the dips and twists, and many preschoolers adore the ride as well. Children under 7 must ride with an adult, and no one under 40 inches tall is allowed to board. If you're debating which of the three mountains—Space, Splash, or Big Thunder—is most suitable for a kid who has never ridden a coaster, Big Thunder is your best bet.

Splash Mountain

Based on *Song of the South* and inhabited by Brer Rabbit, Brer Bear, Brer Fox, and the other characters from that film, Splash Mountain takes riders on a watery, winding journey through swamps and bayous, culminating in a 40-mile-an-hour drop over a five-story waterfall. "Zip-a-Dee-Doo-Dah," perhaps the most hummable of all Disney theme songs, fills the air, making the ride both charming and exhilarating—truly the best of both worlds.

Splash Mountain can get very crowded; ride early in the morning or in the last hour before closing. Also, you can get

The Scare Factor

The intensity of that last drop, which momentarily gives you the feeling that you're coming out of your seat, along with the 40-inch height requirement, eliminates some preschoolers. If your kids are unsure about Splash Mountain, watch a few cars make the final drop before you decide. Our mail indicates that most kids over 5 love the ride.

really soaked, which is great fun at noon in June, less of a thrill at 9 A.M. in January. Some people bring big black plastic garbage bags to use as ponchos and then discard them after the ride.

Hidden Mickey

While you and the kids are keeping an eye out for Mickey Mouse, you may not realize that you're walking right past him. No, we're not talking about the life-sized Mickeys, we're talking about silhouettes and abstract images of the main mouse, that are cleverly hidden throughout Walt Disney World.

These "Hidden Mickeys" began as an inside joke among the imagineers, the artists and engineers who design the theme park attractions. But as guests learned that Hidden Mickeys were scattered throughout the parks, they went on a quest to find them, and spotting Mickey can be an added treat.

For example, in the final scene of Splash Mountain, as you pass the "Zip-A-Dee-Lady" paddleboat, look for a pink cloud floating high in the sky. You'll find a silhouette of Mickey lying on his back.

Diamond Horseshoe *Jamboree*

The *Jamboree,* formerly a tame Wild West saloon revue, is being revised to make it more appealing to families. Although the show isn't complete for review as we go to press, the good news is that Woody from the *Toy Story* movies will be headlining, which is bound to thrill his young fans. Since you can buy drinks and munchies while you watch the show, the *Jamboree* is a good place for a light lunch when you're on a tight touring schedule.

In the past you could get into the *Jamboree* simply by lining up 20 minutes before show time, but since the new show is likely to be more popular, Disney will undoubtedly institute a new system to handle the crowd flow. Check with Guest Services as you enter the Magic Kingdom to see if you need tickets or reservations.

Frontierland Shootin' Arcade

Bring your quarters. This is a pretty standard shooting gallery and a good place for the kids to kill a few minutes while adults wait in line for the *Country Bear Jamboree*.

Country Bear Jamboree

Younger kids fall for the funny, furry Audio-Animatronic critters featured in this 15-minute show. From the coy Teddi Barra to the incomparable Big Al, from Bubbles, Bunny, and Beulah (a sort of combination of the Andrews Sisters and the Beach Boys) to Melvin the Moosehead, each face is distinctive and lovable.

The *Jamboree* seats large numbers of guests per show, so you can slip in easily in the evening or during the 3 P.M. parade. (But don't, for heaven's sake, try to get in just after the parade when thousands of tourists suddenly find themselves on the streets of Frontierland with nothing to do.) Kids 9 and up rate the bears as hokey; if there's a split in your children's ages, one parent can take little kids to the *Jamboree* while the other rides nearby Splash Mountain with the older ones.

A different but equally charming show runs at Christmas.

Tom Sawyer Island

A getaway playground full of caves, bridges, forts, and windmills, Tom Sawyer Island is a good destination when the kids become too rambunctious to handle. Adults can sip a lemonade at Aunt Polly's Dockside Inn, the island's fast-food restaurant, while the kids run free.

The big drawback is that the island is accessible only by raft, which means you often have to wait to get there and wait to get back. If your kids are under 5, don't bother making the trip. The terrain is too widespread for preschoolers to play without supervision, and young kids can better blow off steam in Toontown. Likewise, there is little on the island for adults and teenagers to do. But if your kids are 5 to 9 and beginning to get a little squirrelly, stop off at Tom Sawyer's Island, where such behavior is not only acceptable, it's de rigueur.

Liberty Square

Walk on a few feet from Frontierland, and you'll find yourself transported back a hundred years to colonial America, strolling the cobblestone streets of Liberty Square.

Liberty Square Attractions

Liberty Square Riverboat
The second tier of this paddlewheel riverboat offers outstanding views of Liberty Square and Frontierland, but, as with the other Rivers of America crafts, board only if you have time to kill and the boat is at the dock.

The Hall of Presidents
This attraction may remind you that one of the villains in the movie *The Stepford Wives* was a Disney imagineer. The Hall of Presidents is indeed a Stepford version of the presidency, with eerily lifelike and quietly dignified chief executives, each responding to his name in the roll call with a nod or tilting of the head. In the background, other presidents fidget and whisper.

The presidential roll call and the film that precedes it will probably bore most kids under 10. Older children will find the 20-minute presentation educational. Babies and toddlers consider the hall a fine place to nap. A good choice for the afternoon.

Time-Saving Tip
The Hall of Presidents theater holds up to 700 people, and lines disappear every 25 minutes. Ask one of the attendants at the lobby doors how long it is before the next show and amble in about 10 minutes before show time.

The Haunted Mansion

More apt to elicit a giggle than a scream, the mansion is full of clever special effects—at one point a ghost "hitchhikes" a ride in your own "doom buggy." The cast members, who dress as morticians and never smile, add to the fun with such instructions as "Drag your wretched bodies to the dead center of the room." The mansion is full of insider jokes. For example, the tombstones outside name the imagineers who designed the ride. And take a glance at the pet cemetery as you leave.

The Scare Factor
A significant number of kids 7 to 11 list the Haunted Mansion as one of their three favorite attractions, but a few mothers of children under 7 report that their kids were frightened by the darkness. Fine for most kids over 7; the ride is richly atmospheric, but the spooks are played for laughs.

The mansion draws long lines in the afternoons; try to see it midmorning, or—if you have the courage—it's fun to tour at night.

Hidden Mickey
Hidden Mickey alert! Look at the arrangement of dishes on the table in the Haunted Mansion banquet scene.

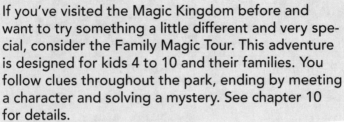

Insider's Secret

If you've visited the Magic Kingdom before and want to try something a little different and very special, consider the Family Magic Tour. This adventure is designed for kids 4 to 10 and their families. You follow clues throughout the park, ending by meeting a character and solving a mystery. See chapter 10 for details.

Food Choices in the Magic Kingdom

Let's face it, the Magic Kingdom is NOT the fine-dining park of Walt Disney World. Even so, some options are far better than others.

If you want to have a sit-down meal and see the characters, try the Crystal Palace and Cinderella's Royal Table, which is actually located in the castle. You can't beat the castle for a great setting, and Cinderella is on hand to greet you. The Crystal Palace has its fans too, both because you can visit Pooh and the gang and because the buffet means you can get your food quickly. The buffet offers good variety, so there's always something for picky eaters.

The only problem with these locales is that 10,000 other people have the same great idea. Cinderella's Royal Table and the Crystal Palace are always so busy that it's necessary to arrange priority seating in advance. If that sounds like too much trouble but you still want a sit-down meal, consider Tony's Town Square Café. This Italian restaurant, based on the romantic spot where Tramp wooed Lady, has good food and a lively, cute atmosphere. Because it's located on Main Street near the park entrance, people often forget about it when they're deep in the park at lunchtime. Ergo, it's usually a bit less crowded than the other sit-down restaurants.

Quick Guide to Full-in the Magic

Restaurant	Description
Cinderella's Royal Table	She'll greet you at the door
The Crystal Palace	Winnie the Pooh characters visit
Liberty Tree Tavern	All-American cuisine, character dining
The Plaza Restaurant	Great ice cream desserts
Tony's Town Square Restaurant	Massive portions of Italian cuisine

For descriptions of ratings, prices, priority seating, and suitability for kids, see chapter 11.

In terms of fast food, Cosmic Ray's Starlight Café in To-morrowland is the largest fast-food spot in the park and the lines move fast. You can get soups and salads as well as the typical fast-food chow. Pecos Bill Café in Frontierland specializes in burgers with a fresh toppings bar that allows you to dress up your burger pretty nicely. For snacks, try the fruit cobblers at Sleepy Hollow in Liberty Square or the Dole pineapple whips at Aloha Isle in Adventureland.

One final thought. The Magic Kingdom is always crowded and can be a bit exhausting. For a true

Insider's Secret

Closed out of priority seating at Cinderella's Castle? Try the lesser-known Princess Breakfast in the Norway Pavilion of Epcot.

Service Restaurants Kingdom

Rating	Price	Priority Seating	Suitability	Details on
★★	$$$	Necessary	High	Page 341
★★	$$	Recommended	High	Page 342
★★	$$	Recommended	High	Page 347
★★	$$	Recommended	High	Page 350
★★	$$	Recommended	High	Page 353

break from all the hubbub—and better food than you'll find in the park—you should visit one of the Magic Kingdom resorts. You don't have to be staying at the resort in question to dine there and, in truth, it doesn't take much longer to hop the monorail to a resort than it does to stay in the Magic Kingdom and deal with the long lines.

It's easy: Exit the park, have your hand stamped for re-entry, and get on the monorail marked "Resorts." Your first stop is the Contemporary, where the Concourse Steak House is, which has pasta, salads, burgers, and great smoothies. The next stop is the Ticket and Transportation Center. Sit tight. Nowhere to eat there. Stop number three is the Polynesian and the tropical-inspired Kona Café—stir-fries, salads, and seriously good desserts. The final option is the Grand Floridian Café in the Grand Floridian Resort, which offers seafood, chicken salads, and yummy Key lime pie. After you eat, reboard the monorail, and you'll be back at the Magic Kingdom within minutes.

Afternoon Resting Places

- The Disney World Railroad (you can rest while you ride)
- The small park across from Sleepy Hollow in Liberty Square
- *Diamond Horseshoe Revue*
- Hall of Presidents
- *Mickey's PhilharMagic*
- Galaxy Palace
- *Country Bear Jamboree*
- The Enchanted Tiki Birds
- Tom Sawyer Island
- Guests with a Park Hopper Plus pass can take the launch marked "Campground and Discovery Island" to either River Country or Discovery Island. If it's hot, bring your bathing suits along or wear them under your clothes. An hour or two in River Country can cool you off and revive your spirits.

Best Vantage Points for Watching the Parades

The Magic Kingdom has two basic parades: the 3 P.M. parade that runs daily and the nighttime parade that runs nightly in the on-season and periodically during the off-season. On crowded days the evening parade often runs twice, once from Main Street to Frontierland and then from Frontierland back to Main Street. If you're visiting during the on-season, ask an attendant what direction the parade will be coming from and try to be near the beginning of the route; those near the end of the route will have to wait an additional 20 minutes before they see their first float.

One good location is at the very beginning of Main Street, along the hub in front of the Railroad Station. (The parade usually begins here, emerging from behind City Hall.) You do lose the vantage point of the floats coming down Main Street, but it's worth it not to have to fight the crowds.

The crowds grow less manageable as you proceed down Main Street and are at their worst in front of Cinderella Castle. In fact, if you find yourself behind four layers of people on Main Street, send one of your party toward the entrance gate to check out the situation at the hub; you may find there's still curb space there even when the rest of the route is mobbed.

If you find yourself deep in the bowels of the theme park at parade time, don't try to fight your way up Main Street to the hub—you'll never make it. Instead, go to the end of the route in Frontierland. The crowds here are thinner than in front of Cinderella Castle or in Liberty Square.

The parade (or the first parade of the evening if two are scheduled) is immediately followed by fireworks.

Insider's Secret

If you're stuck in Frontierland during the parade, be aware that there is a second pathway that runs right along the riverbank. It's still crowded but preferable to trying to pick your way along the parade route.

Best Restroom Locations in the Magic Kingdom

By "best" I mean least crowded. You can get in and out of these rather quickly.

@ Behind the Enchanted Grove snack bar near the Mad Hatter's Tea Party.

@ In the passageway between Adventureland and Frontierland. This one draws traffic but is so huge that you never have to wait long.

@ Near Space Mountain in Tomorrowland.

Insider's Secret

As you leave Pirates of the Caribbean, make a stop at the restroom located at the back of the market stalls. This one is so secluded that I didn't find it until my seventeenth fact-finding trip to Disney World.

@ If you're in the Baby Services center for other reasons, make a pit stop.

@ The sit-down restaurants have their own restrooms, which are rarely crowded.

Tips for Your Last Hour in the Magic Kingdom

@ Some rides—most notably Big Thunder Mountain Railroad, Cinderella's Carrousel, Astro Orbiter, Dumbo, and Splash Mountain—are particularly beautiful at night.

@ If you're visiting on an evening when a parade is scheduled, ask an attendant which direction it will be coming from. If it begins on Main Street, move as far as possible up Main Street and stake your curb space near the hub. Make a final potty run before the parade starts so you'll be ready to make a fast exit once the final float rolls by. If you're on Main Street near the hub, you may want to go ahead and turn in your rental stroller. If you're farther back, just park the stroller out of the way, pick up the babies, and hoof it. Pushing a stroller down Main Street in the crush of departing people is at best difficult and sometimes impossible.

- If the parade is coming from Frontierland, line up in front of the *Country Bear Jamboree*. But don't try to exit the park just behind the parade; people will still be waiting to watch it on Main Street, and the entire park bottlenecks there, causing frightening crowds. Instead, stop for a snack or do a bit of window-shopping and aim to leave after the main surge of people has exited the park. The rides stop running at the official closing time, but Main Street stays open up to an hour longer.

- Just before the parade is scheduled to start, look toward the castle to see a magical little extra called Tinkerbell's

Helpful Hint

Planning to skip the parade? Be off Main Street by at least 20 minutes before it is scheduled to begin. If you're deep in the park you can catch the railroad in either Frontierland or Toontown and disembark at Main Street, thus avoiding the waiting Main Street crowd altogether. But the train stops running 10 to 15 minutes before the parade begins, so allow yourself plenty of time. Otherwise you'll have to wait out the parade and be stuck BEHIND the exiting Main Street crowds. Definitely not what you want!

Flight, in which a young woman dressed like Tink descends via wire from the top of the castle. After the parade be sure to stick around for the fireworks, which are a perfect closing to a Disney day.

Insider's Secret

The best place to watch the Magic Kingdom fireworks isn't in the Magic Kingdom at all—it's the California Grill, located high atop the Contemporary Resort. The California Grill is a definite splurge restaurant, with some of the best cuisine in Orlando, if not all of Florida. Despite the restaurant's culinary reputation, however, it isn't formal or stuffy. In other words, kids are welcome.

To see the fireworks, arrange a priority seating time about 30 minutes before the Magic Kingdom parade is due to start. (This needs to be done before you leave home: After you've called 407-824-4321 to determine the evenings and times the parade is scheduled, arrange priority seating at the California Grill by calling 407-WDW-DINE.)

You won't see much of the parade, but once the fireworks begin the restaurant dims its lights, pipes in the theme music, and you have a fabulous and unique vantage point on the pyrotechnic display. There's also an outdoor balcony where you can get a great view.

Tips for Leaving the Magic Kingdom

❧ On leaving at the end of the day, visitors staying off site should pause for a second as they exit the gates. If a ferryboat is at the dock to your far left, that's your fastest route back to the TTC. If there's no boat in sight, queue up for the monorail that runs directly back to the TTC.

- Guests at the Contemporary Resort should take the resort monorail. Guests at Wilderness Lodge or Fort Wilderness should take the hotel launch. Guests staying at the Polynesian Resort or the Grand Floridian should glance down at the launch dock, which is straight ahead as you exit the Magic Kingdom gates. If a launch is in sight, take it back to your hotel; otherwise head for the resort monorail.

- Guests at the other Disney hotels should return to the shuttle bus station.

CHAPTER

6

Epcot®

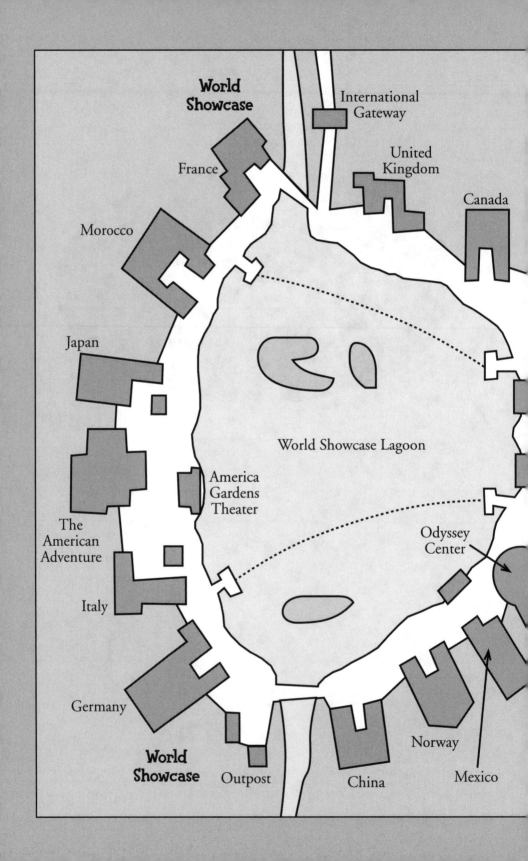

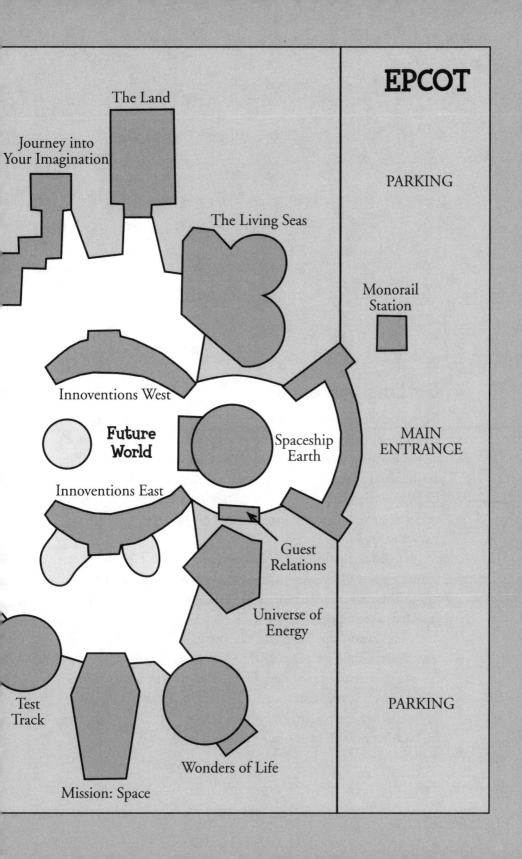

EPCOT

The Land

Journey into
Your Imagination

PARKING

The Living Seas

Monorail
Station

Innoventions West

Future
World

Spaceship
Earth

MAIN
ENTRANCE

Innoventions East

Guest
Relations

Universe of
Energy

Test
Track

PARKING

Wonders of Life

Mission: Space

Getting to Epcot

Many off-site hotels and most on-site hotels offer shuttle buses to Epcot, and Epcot is also easy to reach by car. If you arrive early in the morning, you can park very close to the main entrance gate and forgo the tram ride. If you arrive a bit later, however, the trams do run quickly and efficiently. Just be sure to write down the number of the row where you parked your car.

If you're staying at the Polynesian, Grand Floridian, or Contemporary Resort, your fastest route is to take the monorail to the Ticket and Transportation Center (TTC) and then transfer to the Epcot monorail.

The Swan, the Dolphin, the BoardWalk, and the Yacht and Beach Clubs are connected to a special "backdoor" World Showcase entrance by bridge. Either take the shuttle tram or a water taxi or, if you're staying at the Yacht or Beach Clubs, simply walk over the bridge.

Other on-site hotels run buses to Epcot.

Getting Around Epcot

As any Disneyphile can tell you, Epcot is an acronym for the Experimental Prototype Community of Tomorrow. But as one of the players at the Comedy Warehouse on Pleasure Island suggests, maybe Epcot really stands for "Every Person Comes Out Tired."

Epcot is indeed sprawling—more than twice the size of the Magic Kingdom—but the FriendShips that crisscross the World Showcase Lagoon and the double-decker buses that encircle the lagoon should be viewed as fun rides, not transportation. Your fastest means of getting around is walking.

Tips for Your First Hour at Epcot

- At present, on-site guests can enter Epcot one hour early on Wednesday. Only a few attractions will be open, but you can ride them with virtually no wait. Ride Spaceship Earth first and then go to *Honey, I Shrunk the Audience*. Lines for Mission: Space and Test Track may be forming before the entry ropes are actually dropped. If the posted wait time is less than 40 minutes, line up now. If you're not visiting on an Early Entry morning, the scenario changes a bit.

- As soon as you enter the main gate, veer left to rent a stroller. Pick up a map/entertainment schedule. If you haven't arranged priority seating, enter the WorldKey Information System and do that now.

- If you have time before the rest of the park opens, browse through Innoventions. It's probably a mistake to let the kids at the games—once they start, it will be hard to get them out—but scope out the exhibits you'd like to return to later.

- After the ropes are dropped and you're allowed to enter the body of the park, veer sharply left and ride Mission: Space if it's open, then Test Track.

- Next, head for the first showing of *Honey, I Shrunk the Audience*. If Test Track and Mission: Space are too wild for you, go to *Honey, I Shrunk the Audience* first.

Insider's Secret
The newer the ride, the hotter it is—so ride Mission: Space as early as possible.

Attractions at Epcot that Offer FASTPASSes
Test Track

Honey, I Shrunk the Audience

Mission: Space

Epcot Touring Tips

- Take Epcot in small doses if your kids are young; three to four hours at a time is enough.

- When Test Track opened it was prone to technical problems. Chances are, Mission: Space will also go through a similar "breaking in" period. Check the Epcot tip board between Communicores East and West to make sure Mission: Space is running before you sprint over there.

- In the off-season, Epcot hours are often staggered. Future World is generally open from 9 A.M. to 7 P.M. and the World Showcase from 11 A.M. to 9 P.M.

- You can avoid crowds by touring Future World until midmorning and then drifting toward the World Showcase in the afternoon, where you can escape to the films and indoor exhibits during the hottest and busiest times.

Time-Saving Tip

Avoid the high-capacity shows such as *Universe of Energy* or *O Canada!* in the morning. Your time is better spent moving among the continuous-loading attractions such as Body Wars, Test Track, the Land, the Living Seas, and Journey Into Your Imagination. With the exception of *Honey, I Shrunk the Audience*, save the theater-style attractions until afternoon.

@ After an early dinner, head back into Future World. It's easier to ride anything there, even Mission: Space and Test Track, if you wait until after 8 P.M. when people begin to gather for IllumiNations.

@ If you are touring off-season and plan to spend mornings in the other parks and evenings at Epcot, make your dinner priority seating times as early as possible, leaving yourself several hours to tour after dinner.

@ Another alternative: If your children have had a good afternoon nap and can keep going until 10 P.M., make your dinner reservations for very late. The restaurants accept their final seating just before the park shuts down, and all the transportation stays operative for at least 90 minutes after the official park closing time. Eating late buys you maximum hours in the park, assuming your kids can handle the schedule— and assuming you're seeing IllumiNations on another night.

@ On entering a World Showcase pavilion that has a show or film—France, Canada, America, or China—ask the attendant how long you have until the show begins. If your wait is 10 minutes or less, queue up. If the wait is longer, browse the shops of the pavilion until about 10 minutes before show time. The World Showcase theaters are so large that even people near the back of the line will be seated.

☙ Innoventions and the interactive exhibits in the Wonders of Life, Journey Into Your Imagination, and Spaceship Earth pavilions are very worthwhile—and a nice break from the enforced passivity of all the rides. But ride the rides first and save the interactive games for midafternoon or early evening.

☙ If you're not staying for IllumiNations, begin moving toward the exit gates while the show is in progress.

Insider's Secret
Most people circle the World Showcase Lagoon in a clockwise fashion, beginning with Mexico. You'll make better time if you move counterclockwise, beginning with Canada.

Helpful Hint
If you miss the chance to exit before the IllumiNations crowd or you've opted to stay for the show, don't join in the throngs that mob the exit turnstiles and shuttle buses just after the show ends. Pick up dessert before the show and then, after IllumiNations, find a table, sit down, relax, and let the crowds pass you by. The trams and monorails will still be running long after you finish your snack, and the lines waiting for them will be far shorter.

Future World

Future World comprises nine large pavilions, each containing at least one major attraction, and is very much like a permanent World's Fair, mixing educational opportunities with pure entertainment. Most visitors are drawn first to the rides with their spectacular special effects, but don't miss Innoventions and the chance to play with the smaller, interactive exhibits. Many of these encourage young visitors to learn while doing, and stopping to try them out helps kids avoid what one mother termed "Audio-Animatronics overload."

The Epcot Don't-Miss List

Mission: Space

Spaceship Earth

Cranium Command in the Wonders of Life pavilion

Test Track

Honey, I Shrunk the Audience

The American Adventure in the America pavilion

IllumiNations

Innoventions

The Epcot Worth-Your-While List

Universe of Energy

Body Wars in the Wonders of Life pavilion

The Living Seas

The Making of Me in the Wonders of Life pavilion

Living with the Land and *Food Rocks!*
in the Land pavilion

Journey Into Your Imagination

Wonders of China in the China pavilion

O Canada! in the Canada pavilion

Maelstrom in the Norway pavilion

Impressions de France in the France pavilion

Quick Guide to

Attraction	Location	Height Requirement
The American Adventure	World Showcase	None
Body Wars	Future World	40 inches
Circle of Life	Future World	None
Cranium Command	Future World	None
El Rio del Tiempo	World Showcase	None
Food Rocks!	Future World	None
Honey, I Shrunk the Audience	Future World	None
Impressions de France	World Showcase	None
Innoventions	Future World	None
Journey Into Your Imagination	Future World	None
Kodak's "What If" Lab	Future World	None
The Living Seas	Future World	None
Living with the Land	Future World	None
Maelstrom	World Showcase	None
The Making of Me	Future World	None
Mission: Space	Future World	n/a
O Canada!	World Showcase	None
Spaceship Earth	Future World	None
Test Track	Future World	40 inches
Universe of Energy	Future World	None
Wonders of China	World Showcase	None

Scare Factor
0 = Unlikely to scare any child of any age.
! = Has dark or loud elements; might rattle some toddlers.
!! = A couple of gotcha! moments; should be fine for school-age kids.
!!! = You need to be pretty big and pretty brave to handle this ride.

Epcot Attractions

Speed of Line	Duration of Ride/Show	Scare Factor	Age Range
Fast	30 min.	0	All
Moderate	5 min.	!!	6 and up
Fast	20 min.	0	All
Fast	20 min.	0	6 and up
Fast	9 min.	0	All
Fast	15 min.	0	All
Fast	25 min.	!!	5 and up
Fast	20 min.	0	10 and up
n/a	n/a	0	3 and up
Fast	13 min.	!	3 and up
Fast	n/a	0	All
Moderate	8 min.	0	All
Fast	10 min.	0	All
Moderate	15 min.	!!	4 and up
Slow	15 min.	0	4 and up
Slow	15 min.	0	4 and up
Fast	20 min.	0	10 and up
Moderate	15 min.	0	All
Slow	25 min.	!!!	7 and up
Slow	30 min.	!!	3 and up
Fast	20 min.	0	10 and up

Future World Attractions

Spaceship Earth

Whatever their age, few travelers can remain blasé at the sight of Spaceship Earth, the most photographed and readily recognizable symbol of Epcot.

The ride inside, which coils toward the top of the 17-story geosphere, traces developments in communication from cave drawings to computers. The voice of Jeremy Irons croons in your ear as you climb past scenes of Egyptian temples, the Gutenberg press, and a performance of Oedipus Rex. Even preschoolers rated Spaceship Earth highly, probably because of the excitement of actually entering the "Big Ball" and the impressive finale, which flashes a planetarium sky above you as you swirl backward down through the darkness.

Hidden Mickey

We all know Mickey is a star, and he actually has his own constellation in Spaceship Earth. Look for him in the starry sky at the beginning of the ride, just after you load.

The Living Seas

The Living Seas pavilion features a saltwater aquarium so enormous that Spaceship Earth could float inside it. You board a hydrolator that takes you through an underwater viewing tunnel. More than 200 varieties of marine life, including stingrays, dolphins, barracuda, and sharks, swim above you. Unfortunately, the hydrolator ride is so brief that there's not much time to look.

The most enjoyable part of the attraction comes after you disembark at Seabase Alpha. You can remain here as long as you choose, wandering through two levels of observation

Time-Saving Tip

At the beginning of the Living Seas, you're given a choice between watching a film in the briefing room or heading directly to the hydrolators. The film, *The Sea,* is geared toward adults, so if you have kids along, head directly for the hydrolators.

Time-Saving Tip

If you plan to devote a day to Sea World while in Orlando, you'll find much of the same stuff there, so hold your time at the Living Seas pavilion to a minimum.

tanks that allow you to view the fish and the human divers at close quarters. (A diving program allows visitors ages 10 and up to suit up and enter the tank with a guide for $140. Children ages 10 to 14 must be accompanied by an adult. Call 407-WDW-TOUR for details.)

The Land

This cheerful pavilion, sponsored by Nestlé and devoted to the subject of food production and the environment, is home to three separate attractions as well as a rotating restaurant and fast-food court. Because there are so many places to eat here, the Land is crowded from 11 A.M. to 2 P.M., when everyone heads in for lunch.

@ *Living with the Land.* Visitors travel by boat past scenes of various farming environments, ending with a peek at fish farming, drip irrigation, and other innovative agricultural technologies. Perhaps because there are few special effects, this attraction is less interesting to preschoolers. But, as is the case in all of Future World, the presentation moves swiftly. In short, this won't be your children's favorite attraction, but they won't complain either. (Hour-long guided tours of the greenhouse are also available, at a price of $6 for adults and children over 10, $4 for kids ages 3 to 9. Ask a host for details.)

@ *Circle of Life.* This film, in the Circle of Life Theatre, graphically illustrates how we interact—positively and negatively—with our environment. *Circle of Life* was revamped to make it more appealing to kids, with Pumbaa, Timon, and Simba from *The Lion King* as the new stars; the resulting film is both educational and entertaining.

Helpful Hint

Circle of Life is in a large theater with comfortable seats, making it a good choice for the afternoon.

Insider's Secret

The Garden Grill Restaurant in The Land offers character dining at both lunch and dinner and is a great alternative for families who don't want to spend a morning at a character breakfast but who'd still love to see Mickey and the gang.

Insider's Secret

In The Land pavilion food court look for the Junior Chef booth where kids can bake—and eat—Nestlé Toll House cookies. The adult chefs are there to help the kids bake the cookies several times a day, usually around lunchtime and the afternoon. Exact times are posted on a board in the food court.

@ *Food Rocks!* A funny 15-minute show featuring famous rock 'n' roll stars masquerading as foods, *Food Rocks!* is another good choice for afternoon. The Peach Boys sing about "good nutrition," an eggplant is dubbed "Neil Moussaka," and the Refrigerator Police oversee "every bite you take."

Journey Into Your Imagination

Journey Into Your Imagination debuted a new look in 1999— a look that cut out the popular character Figment and tried to make the attraction more adult-oriented. It didn't work. The Imagineers revamped the ride again and it's much more fun for kids now that Figment is back.

As you exit Journey Into Your Imagination, stop off at Kodak's "What If" lab, where interactive exhibits allow you to distort your facial image, produce sounds by stepping on pictures of lightning and lions, and picture yourself skydiving high above Cinderella Castle. The most popular experiment lets you transfer your own face onto a koala, sunflower, or dozens of other images . . . and then e-mail the results home to yourself and three friends free of charge. It's a fresh new way to say "Wish you were here."

> **Helpful Hint**
>
> As you leave the Journey Into Your Imagination pavilion, take time to check out Splashtacular, a fun fountain show that gives kids the chance to get wet.

Honey, I Shrunk the Audience

Beside Journey Into Your Imagination is Epcot's sleeper hit, the 3-D film *Honey, I Shrunk the Audience.* This show is so much fun that several families reported that their kids insisted on seeing it more than once. Based on the popular movie series, the presentation begins as Dr. Wayne Szalinski is about to pick up the award for Inventor of the Year. The scene quickly dissolves into mayhem as the audience is accidentally "shrunk," one son's pet snake gets loose, and the other's pet mouse is reproduced 999 times. Although the 3-D images are dazzling, the effects go far beyond the visual—you actually feel the "mice" running up your legs, and the kid-pleasing, dog-sneezing finale is not to be missed.

Insider's Secret

Closer is not always better, especially when it comes to a 3-D show like *Honey, I Shrunk the Audience*. For best viewing, sit in the center, about two-thirds of the way back.

The Scare Factor

Honey, I Shrunk the Audience is very, very highly rated by the families we surveyed. If your child does happen to be unnerved by the special effects, have him (or her) take off the 3-D glasses and either pull up his legs into the seat or sit in your lap. That way he won't see the images clearly and won't feel the tactile sensations.

Test Track

Test Track is the longest, fastest ride in all of Disney World.

The idea is that guests are testing automobiles before they leave the factory. You begin the ride inside, checking out how your vehicle responds to conditions of cold, heat, and stress. The stress level of the passengers soars when you move to the speed test, break through a barrier, and burst outside of the building. Once outside, the cars reach speeds of up to 65 miles per hour on hills, curves, and hairpin turns. Twenty-eight cars are on the track at the same time, each with its own on-board computer. In other words, the track isn't pulling the cars, as is the case in most driving rides; the Test Track cars are driving themselves. The track is almost a mile long, adding up to a powerfully exciting ride.

The Scare Factor

Children must be 40 inches tall to ride, and an adult must accompany children under 7. It's all about speed, with no flips or plunges, and kids we surveyed love Test Track.

Insider's Secret

Test Track draws some of the longest lines in Walt Disney World. How do you spell relief? F-A-S-T-P-A-S-S! Just don't wait too long to get your FASTPASS. At Test Track, a whole day's supply of FASTPASSes is often gone by midafternoon.

Insider's Secret

Is the line for Test Track unbearably long? If your kids are older, consider going through the Singles Line. You won't end up riding together, but your wait time will be about one-third as long. It's a great option for a busy day.

Coming in late 2003—Mission: Space

Epcot will be debuting a new thrill ride in the winter of 2003, in the space where Horizons used to be, and the premise is a fascinating one.

Mission: Space will launch guests into a simulated space adventure, from the excitement of lift-off to the wonder of

The Scare Factor

Mission: Space is not open as we go to press, and height requirements have not been established. Therefore, we're basing our scare factor rating solely on the ride description. The lift-off sequence sounds extremely intense, so we're suggesting that if children are 7 or under a parent should ride first to determine if their child should ride. Expect an updated scare factor rating, based on surveys of families, in next year's guide.

weightlessness. Set decades into the future, guests enter the International Space Training Center, where they will encounter the sort of challenges real astronauts face. Presented by the

Insider's Secret

Mission: Space is expected to debut in late fall of 2003. The rule of thumb, however, is that the more complex the ride's technology, the more snafus the imagineers are apt to encounter as it goes into production. This happened with Test Track, which had a very delayed opening and was frequently shut down for repairs during the first six months after it opened.

The moral is, don't promise Mission: Space to your kids during early 2004. If you get there and it's open, or in a ride-testing phase, that's a wonderful bonus—and much better than running to the gates only to find that this highly anticipated ride isn't yet on line.

When the ride does operate, expect enormous crowds and long lines. Use FASTPASS, and make sure you get to the kiosk as soon as possible after you enter.

Compaq Computer Corporation, Mission: Space will be Disney's most technologically complex attraction, overshadowing even Test Track in its sophistication.

Wonders of Life

Devoted to celebrating the human body, the Wonders of Life pavilion resembles a brightly colored street fair full of hands-on exhibits. You can check out your health profile via computer, get advice on your tennis or golf swing, and test your endurance on a motorized bike. Like the Land pavilion, the Wonders pavilion houses three major attractions and is crowded by 11 A.M.

- *Body Wars.* Body Wars uses flight simulation technology to take riders on a turbulent high-speed chase through the human body. After being miniaturized to the size of a pinhead and injected into a patient, the crew is briefed to expect a routine medical mission for the purpose of removing a splinter from the "safe zone just under the skin." But when shapely Dr. Lair is sucked into a capillary, your crew is off on a rescue chase through the heart, lungs, and brain.

- *The Making of Me.* This 15-minute film provides a fetus-eye view of conception, gestation, and birth. Martin Short

The Scare Factor

No expectant mothers or kids under 3 are allowed to board, and Body Wars does indeed have its queasy moments, more because of the accuracy of flight simulation technology than the bouncing of the spaceship. Those prone to motion sickness should skip the trip, as well as anyone put off by the subject matter. More people reported losing their lunch on Body Wars than on Star Tours, the major motion simulation ride at MGM. The height requirement is 40 inches.

travels back in time to show us his own parents as babies and then chronicles how they met and ultimately produced him. (One glaring anachronism: Martin must have been the only kid born in America in the 1950s who was delivered through Lamaze.) Although the film is direct and unflinching, it's appropriate for any age.

☉ *Cranium Command.* One of the funniest presentations in Epcot, Cranium Command mixes Audio-Animatronics with film. The preshow is vital to understanding what's going on: General Knowledge taps an unfortunate recruit, Fuzzy, to pilot "the most unstable craft in the fleet"—the brain of a 12-year-old boy. If he fails in his mission, Fuzzy will be demoted to flying the brain of a chicken or, worse, a talk show host.

Fuzzy tries to guide his boy through a typical day of junior high school without overloading his system— which isn't easy, especially when the body parts are played by this cast: Charles Grodin as the right brain, Jon Lovitz as the left brain, Hans and Franz from *Saturday Night Live* pumping it up in the role of the heart, Norm from *Cheers* as the stomach, and, in a particularly convincing performance, Bobcat Goldthwait as adrenaline.

Time-Saving Tip
The Wonders of Life pavilion is drastically in need of updating and it is rarely crowded—even including Body Wars. Visit in the afternoon when other pavilions are busy.

Universe of Energy
This technologically complex presentation can be enjoyed by any age on any level. Ask the attendant at the door how long

until show time, and don't queue up until the wait is 10 minutes or less; this is an almost-30-minute presentation, and there's no point in wearing out the kids before you begin.

Disney has made the preshow and postshow a lot snappier by bringing in Ellen DeGeneres, Alex Trebek, and Jamie Lee Curtis. The premise is that after Ellen dreams she goes on *Jeopardy!* and is thoroughly skunked in the science category by smarty-pants Jamie Lee, Bill Nye the Science Guy convinces her that we all need to know more about energy.

The Disney twist comes when the 97-seat theater begins to break apart in sections that align themselves in sequence and move toward a curtain. Your theater has become your train, and the curtain slowly lifts to reveal an Audio-Animatronics version of the age when coal deposits first began to form. The air reeks of sulfur as it presumably did during the prehistoric era, the light is eerie blue, and all around you are those darn dinosaurs.

The Scare Factor

Few families report that their kids were afraid of the dinosaurs; in fact, for most kids the dinosaurs are by far their favorite part of the attraction.

After your train has once again metamorphosed into a theater, there's a final film segment in which a newly educated Ellen gets her *Jeopardy!* revenge.

Despite its proximity to the front gate, this is not a good choice for the morning; save it for afternoon or early evening, when you'll welcome the chance to sit for a half-hour. The *Universe of Energy* theater seats a large number of people at a time, meaning that lines form and dissipate quickly. If the line looks prohibitive, check out nearby pavilions and return in 20 minutes. You may be able to walk right in.

Innoventions

Innoventions is the arcade of the future, where you can try out new video games before they hit the market, experience virtual reality, and play with beyond-state-of-the-art technology such as video controller chairs and computers that translate voice dictation directly into the printed word.

Innoventions is a showcase for such corporations as Apple, IBM, Motorola, Sega, and AT&T. The products displayed have either just come on the market or are straight from the inventor and not yet available. There are games and quiz shows to pull guests of all ages into the action.

Insider's Secret

Don't be overwhelmed by Innoventions. Almost all the games and exhibits are interactive, so just wander over to a likely kiosk and start playing.

Well-informed cast members are on hand to answer questions or help you get the hang of the games and experiments. Exhibits change frequently, which keeps things fresh, and lately Epcot has introduced more kid-friendly stations. Now even preschoolers can find plenty of games suited to them.

If the blinking and beeping become too overwhelming, parents can take a break outside at the nearby Expresso and Pastry Café. The Fountain of Nations between Innoventions East and West—so named because it contains water from all the countries of the World Showcase—puts on a lovely show.

Helpful Hint

Innoventions becomes crowded in midmorning, as people enter the gates and make a dash for the first thing they see. Visit in early evening or during IllumiNations.

World Showcase

Pretty by day and gorgeous by night, the World Showcase comprises the pavilions of 11 nations—Mexico, Norway, China, Germany, Italy, America, Japan, Morocco, France, the United Kingdom, and Canada—stretching around a large lagoon. Some of the pavilions have full-scale attractions (listings follow); others have only shops and restaurants. Demonstrations, musical presentations, and shows are scheduled throughout the day.

Most important from an educational and cultural perspective, each pavilion is staffed by citizens of the country it represents. Disney goes to great pains to recruit, relocate, and, if necessary, teach English to the shopkeepers and waiters you see in these pavilions, bringing them to Orlando for a year and housing them with representatives from the other World Showcase nations. It's a cultural exchange program on the highest level. (One Norwegian guide told me that her roommates were from China, Mexico, and Canada.)

These young men and women save the World Showcase from being merely touristy, add an air of authenticity to every aspect of the experience, and provide your kids with the chance to rub elbows, however briefly, with other cultures. So even if pavilions such as Morocco and Japan don't have a ride or film,

Helpful Hint

The World Showcase used to be a big yawn for kids under 8. But if you buy them a World Showcase Passport at Port of Entry, they can collect stamps and a handwritten message from each World Showcase nation they visit. Given kids' passion for collecting, a desire to fill their passport will motivate them to move from country to country. It's the equivalent of collecting character autographs and makes a great souvenir.

don't rush past them: Stop for a pastry and chat with the person behind the counter.

In addition, *Family Fun* magazine sponsors Kids' Zones, where children can learn a craft appropriate to the country they're visiting, such as making a mask or collage. The hands-on interaction with a World Showcase employee is a real kick, and stopping at the Kids' Zones is a great way to break up the afternoon.

World Showcase Attractions

O Canada!

This 20-minute Circle-Vision 360 film is gorgeous, stirring, and difficult to view with kids under 6. In order to enjoy the effect of the circular screen, guests must stand during the presentation, and no strollers are allowed in the theater. This means babies and toddlers must be held, and preschoolers, who can't see anything in a room of standing adults, often clamor to be lifted up as well. So we regretfully suggest that families with young kids pass up this presentation, as well as the equally lovely *Wonders of China.* If you're dining at Epcot during your parents' night out, this would be a good time to take in those World Showcase attractions that just aren't oriented toward kids.

Impressions de France

What a difference a seat makes! Like all the Epcot films, *Impressions de France* is exceedingly well done, with lush music and a 200-degree wide-screen feel. It's fairly easy to get in, even in the afternoon, and no one minds if babies take a little nap.

The American Adventure

This multimedia presentation, combining Audio-Animatronics figures with film, is popular with all age groups. The technological highlight of the show comes when the Ben Franklin robot actually walks up stairs to visit Thomas Jefferson, but the entire 30-minute presentation is packed with elaborate sets that rise from the stage, film montages, and moving music. It's worth noting that some people find the patriotism of *The American Adventure* a little heavy-handed. There seem to be two primary reactions to the show—some people weep through it, and other people sleep through it.

Helpful Hint

The America pavilion becomes quite crowded in the afternoon, but because it's located at the exact midpoint of the World Showcase Lagoon, it's impractical to skip it and work your way back later. If you're faced with a half-hour wait, enjoy the excellent Voices of Liberty preshow or have a snack at the Liberty Inn next door.

Wonders of China

Another lovely 360-degree film—when Disney directors and photographers went to China to shoot it, they were the first Westerners ever allowed to film many of these sites. Once again, the theater for this film was not really designed with families in mind.

Maelstrom

In this Norwegian boat ride, your Viking ship sails through fjords and storms, over waterfalls, and past a threatening three-headed troll—all within four minutes. Riders disembark in a North Sea coastal village, where a short film is presented. A Viking ship–styled play area is located to the left of the Norway pavilion—a welcome addition for kids.

Hidden Mickey

Check out the mural of Vikings in the queue line before you board. Believe it or not, one of them is wearing mouse ears.

The Scare Factor

Maelstrom sounds terrifying, but the reality is far tamer than the description. The much-touted "backward plunge over a waterfall" is so subtle that passengers in the front of the boat are not even aware of the impending doom. Some preschoolers are put off by the darkness, the swirling mists, and the troll, but the ride is generally fine for kids 6 and up.

El Rio del Tiempo: The River of Time

There's rarely a wait at this little boat ride, located inside the romantic Mexico pavilion. Reminiscent of It's a Small World in the Magic Kingdom, El Rio is especially appealing to younger riders.

Insider's Secret

Don't miss the live entertainment around the World Showcase Lagoon. Especially noteworthy are the following: the acrobat show in China; Off Kilter, a high-energy rock band in Canada; the silly skit "King Arthur and the Knights of the Round Table" in the United Kingdom; the Beatles clones known as the British Invasion, also in the UK; and the remarkable human statues called "The Living Statues" in Italy. Bring your cameras for this one!

General Information About Epcot Restaurants

A while back Disney changed the reservation system it had employed for years, replacing it with "priority seating," which basically means that if you show up at a restaurant at the prearranged time, you'll receive the next table available that fits the size of your party. The problems begin when 15 families of four show up all at once with the same priority seating time; our readers report waits of anywhere from 10 minutes to an hour, with about 20 minutes being typical.

Still, it's better than being a walk-in, the lowest life form in the Disney World food chain. So if you'd like to try a certain restaurant, arrange priority seating up to 120 days in advance by calling 407-WDW-DINE, or, if you're staying on site, press the dining button on your hotel room phone.

Here are some general tips for the obligatory Epcot dining experience:

@ If you haven't arranged priority seating before dining, either dial from your on-site hotel room or, if you're staying off site, make your plans first thing in the morning at the WorldKey Information Center to the left of Spaceship Earth. (If the center is closed, go next door to Guest Relations.) Visitors who have no priority seating commitment sometimes get seated by simply showing up at the restaurant door, especially if they try a large restaurant like the Biergarten or eat dinner very early.

@ The Epcot dining experience doesn't come cheap. Dinner for a family of four will run about $60 without alcohol. However, as throughout Disney World, portions are very large, even on items from the kiddie menu. Two children can easily share an entrée; for that matter, so can two adults.

@ Kids are welcome at any Epcot eatery, although some are more entertaining for youngsters than others. (See the following section for details.) High chairs, booster seats, and kiddie menus are universally available.

@ The World Showcase restaurants offer "Mickey's Child Deals" for about $4. The food is a nod to the country whose

Money-Saving Tip

If you're trying to save money, remember that lunchtime selections are just as impressive as dinner, and the fare is much cheaper.

cuisine is being represented—for example, skewered chicken in Morocco and fish and chips in the United Kingdom. But the entrées are smaller, less spicy, and look enough like chicken nuggets and fish sticks that the kids will eat them.

@ Casual attire is acceptable anywhere in the park. It may seem strange to eat oysters with champagne sauce while wearing a Goofy sweatshirt, but you'll get used to it.

@ Be bold. Your hometown probably has good Chinese and Italian restaurants, but how often do you get to sample Norwegian or Moroccan food?

Food Choices at Epcot

Epcot is THE food park. It has an embarrassment of riches—so many wonderful spots to grab a bite that it's hard to choose.

For sit-down dining, two perennial favorites are the San Angel Inn in Mexico and Bistro de Paris in France. The San Angel Inn, located inside the dark, atmospheric Mexico pavilion, is a great escape on a hot sunny day. El Rio del Tiempo gurgles by and the scene is that of an evening marketplace. Bistro de Paris recreates the feel of a Parisian sidewalk café—white tablecloths, bustling waiters, beautifully prepared food. The escargot is so delicious that my kids actually ate every bite. (And didn't ask what it was until later!)

In terms of fast food, you have plenty of possibilities. The Tangierine Café in Morocco serves Mediterranean wraps, hummus salads, and Shawarma, tasty platters of chicken and lamb. The Café has a great patio area with tiled tables, fountains, and the perfect view of the entertainment outside. Don't miss the pastry counter in the back for baklava and other honeyed delights—not to mention Turkish coffee so strong that you'll set a land-speed record on your next lap around the World Showcase Lagoon.

While the Tangierine Café is right in the middle of the action, the Yakitori House is tucked away in the back of the Japan pavilion with a beautiful view of the manicured gardens and koi ponds. Try the Kushi Yaki, broiled skewers of chicken, shrimp, and beef with rice and teriyaki sauce. Another good choice is Kringla Bakeri Og Kafé in Norway, which has wonderful open-faced salmon sandwiches and a Viking ship for the kids to play on while the adults sip their beer.

The Yorkshire County Fish and Chip stand in Great Britain is always popular. No lovely patio here, so carry your food into the back garden and sit on a park bench while you listen to the fun 60s-style group, the British Invasion, sing Beatles classics.

Money-Saving Tip

If you want to save both time and money, stick to the fast-food places for meals—but arrange priority seating at a sit-down restaurant for a truly off time, say 4 or 10 P.M., and just have dessert. You can soak up the ambience for an investment of 30 minutes and 20 bucks.

The Boulangerie Patisserie in France emits such phenomenal smells of coffee and croissants that there's always a line there, even though the shop is located in an out-of-the-way back alley. Queue up for sandwiches, quiche, and a wide selection of decadent pastries, which are so good that they make the Boulangerie a favorite with Disney employees. Bon appétit!

Quick Guide to Full-

Restaurant	Description
Akershus (Norway)	Lots of fish, picky eaters may rebel
Biergarten (Germany)	Rousing, noisy atmosphere
Bistro de Paris (France)	Classic French cuisine, very elegant, very adult
Le Cellier Steakhouse (Canada)	A good spot for beef and salmon— as well as buffalo
Les Chefs de France (France)	The ambience of a Paris sidewalk café
Coral Reef Restaurant	Great view of the Living Seas tank
The Garden Grill Restaurant	American food, restaurant rotates
Marrakesh (Morocco)	Exotic surroundings, belly dancers
Nine Dragons (China)	Cuisine representing every region of China
L'Originale Alfredo di Roma (Italy)	Most popular restaurant in the World Showcase
Rose & Crown Dining Room (United Kingdom)	Pub atmosphere and charming service
San Angel Inn Restaurant (Mexico)	Service is swift and friendly
Teppanyaki Dining Room (Japan)	Chefs slice and dice in the best Benihana tradition

For descriptions of ratings, prices, priority seating, and suitability for kids, see chapter 11.

Service Restaurants at Epcot

Rating	Price	Priority Seating	Suitability	Details on
★★	$$	Recommended	Moderate	Page 329
★	$$	Recommended	High	Page 338
★★★	$$$	Necessary	Low	Page 339
★★	$$	Recommended	Low	Page 340
★★★	$$$	Necessary	Moderate	Page 340
★★	$$$	Necessary	High	Page 342
★★	$$	Recommended	High	Page 344
★★	$$	Suggested	Moderate	Page 348
★★	$$	Suggested	Moderate	Page 348
★★	$$$	Necessary	Moderate	Page 349
★★	$$	Recommended	Moderate	Page 351
★★	$$	Recommended	Moderate	Page 351
★★	$$$	Necessary	High	Page 353

Insider's Secret

Just want a snack? We like the pastries in Kringla Bakeri Og Kafé in Norway, the Boulangerie Patisserie in France, and the Tangierine Café in Morocco. The Tangierine Café has an especially lovely patio area—a great place to relax and people-watch while you eat your baklava and drink your strong Turkish coffee.

Money-Saving Tip

In many of the World Showcase eateries, a child's combination plate is more than adequate for an adult, especially if you'll be snacking in a couple of hours.

Epcot Extras

The Magic Kingdom isn't the only place to see the characters, catch a show, watch fireworks, or buy souvenirs. Epcot provides all that entertainment, but with an international spin.

Characters

The character shows at the World Showcase Lagoon bring as many as 20 characters to a single spot, and the crowds of kids vying for their attention are never as large as those at the Magic Kingdom—especially if you choose the first show of the day. Check the entertainment schedule on your map for times. The characters also sometimes appear in "their" country of the World Showcase—Aladdin in Morocco, Mary Poppins in the United Kingdom, and so on. Again, times are marked on the entertainment schedule.

Insider's Secret

Fueled by the clamor of young girls who want their princesses, and want them now, Disney has added a princess character breakfast to Epcot. While the Restaurant Akershus in the Norway pavilion doesn't quite have the panache of Cinderella Castle—it's a fort, after all—the setting has plenty of stone and steel and once the princess characters show up, the kids are content.

As word gets out about this new princess character breakfast, it will undoubtedly get harder to book. Call (407) WDW-DINE 120 days before your trip to ensure a seat.

World Showcase Performers

Singers, dancers, jugglers, and artisans from around the globe perform throughout the World Showcase daily. Most of these presentations (which are detailed in your daily entertainment guide) are not especially oriented toward children—although kids over 7 will catch the humor of the World Showcase Players in the United Kingdom, who put on wacky farces with lots of audience participation. The extraordinary young Dragon Legend Acrobats in the China pavilion appeal to children of all ages.

Older kids will enjoy the pop group British Invasion, also in the United Kingdom. Or check out Off Kilter, who offer "High Energy Progressive Celtic Music," in Canada. This translates to rock music with bagpipes, and the show is a must-see. Another crowd-pleaser is the Imaginum in Italy, where remarkably unlifelike actors pose as classical statues and interact with guests.

IllumiNations

This display of laser technology, fireworks, syncopated fountains, and classical music is a real-life *Fantasia* and an unqualified Disney World classic. Very popular, very crowded, and a perfect way to end an Epcot day, IllumiNations takes place on the World Showcase Lagoon, and the performance coincides with the park closing time. Try to watch from the Mexico or Canada pavilion so you'll be able to beat most of the crowd to the exits afterward. (If you're staying at the Swan, Dolphin, BoardWalk, or Yacht and Beach Clubs and thus leaving via the "backdoor" exit, try the United Kingdom or France pavilion.)

Shopping

You'll see things in Epcot that aren't available anywhere else in Disney World: German wines, silk Chinese robes, a collection of piñatas that puts any Mexican marketplace to shame, and a shop devoted to English teas are all within strolling distance of each other. However, you don't want to end up carrying those hand-knit Norwegian sweaters and that Venetian crystal around the park with you, so if you make major purchases, either have them sent to Package Pickup near the front gate or, if you're staying on site, have them delivered to your hotel.

Epcot Food and Wine Festival

Dining your way around Epcot's World Showcase is always a treat but it gets even better during the Epcot Food and Wine Festival, which is held for approximately a month each year sometime between mid-October and mid-November. (To verify exact dates for the year you're visiting, call 407-WDW-FEST.) Open-air booths representing the cuisine, wine, and beer of more than 60 nations are set up around the World Showcase, offering everything from New Zealand lamb to Bavarian apple strudel. The sample-size servings range between

$1 and $4 in price so you can happily nosh your way around the World Showcase Lagoon, indulging in what is actually WDW's biggest buffet.

If you want to learn more about what you're eating and drinking, cooking demonstrations and wine tastings are also available daily and are usually free of charge. True foodies and wine enthusiasts should consider one of the special event dinners, which are beautifully done and an absolute bargain considering the quality of the events. To reserve a seat, call 407-WDW-FEST as soon as possible: These events sell out well in advance, especially the ultra-exclusive Reserve Dinners.

Grand Tastings

A variety of food stations and the vintages of 15 wineries are offered at the Grand Tastings, which are a great chance to sample a splash of this and a taste of that. Grand Tastings are held in the Odyssey Restaurant on selected evenings. The cost is $60.

Food and Wine Pairings

Not sure if you should serve a Pouilly-Fuissé or a Pinot Noir with the barbecue? Classes on food and wine pairings are held on selected afternoons throughout the festival in the Coral Reef Restaurant. The cost is $25 per person and includes both food and wine tastings.

Winemaker Dinners

Five courses, each prepared by a different chef with five accompanying wines, are offered at the Winemaker Dinners for $75 a person. The themed dinners are held in the Odyssey Restaurant on selected evenings and are extremely popular.

Reserve Dinners

Ready for an even headier dining experience? The Reserve Dinners are $125 a person and take place in an Epcot VIP lounge. Only 30 guests will enjoy five food courses prepared by different chefs, accompanied by reserve quality wines chosen by celebrated vintners. Themes include Champagne: Les Grande Marques, Truffles and Terroir, and French Cellars and Foie Gras.

Afternoon Resting Places at Epcot

- *Universe of Energy*
- *Circle of Life* or *Food Rocks!* in the Land pavilion
- *Honey, I Shrunk the Audience*
- *The Making of Me* in the Wonders of Life pavilion
- *The American Adventure*
- *Impressions de France*

Best Restroom Locations at Epcot

The restrooms within the Future World pavilions are always crowded, and those around Innoventions aren't much better. But there are places where you can take a relatively quick bathroom break:

- At Baby Services, located on the bridge between Future World and the World Showcase
- Behind Kringla Bakeri Og Kafé in the Norway pavilion
- Between the Morocco and France pavilions
- Near the Group Sales Booth at the Entrance Plaza (a good place to stop as you exit the park)
- In Future World, the restroom near the Garden Grill Room in the Land pavilion

Tips for Your Last Hour at Epcot

@ If you're staying for IllumiNations, you'll need to find a good spot around the World Showcase Lagoon 30 minutes in advance during the off-season, 45 to 60 minutes in advance during the on-season. If the idea of such a long wait dismays you, you can bring desserts and have an evening snack to pass the time. Or one parent can hold the turf while the other takes the kids souvenir shopping.

@ Not staying for IllumiNations? The show pulls a lot of people to the World Showcase Lagoon, so this is an excellent chance to ride any Future World attractions you may have missed earlier, especially Test Track or Mission: Space. Or drop by Innoventions on your way out. Just be sure to be at the exit gate before IllumiNations ends and the onslaught of people begins.

Tips for Leaving Epcot

@ Families staying for IllumiNations should prepare themselves for a crush of people. You may want to abandon rental strollers before the show begins and just carry younger kids to the exits; it can be nearly impossible to maneuver a stroller in the mob. On top of everything else, in order to make the fireworks more effective, the lights are dimmed during and after IllumiNations, so you are exiting in the dark. Whatever their age, hold on to

Time-Saving Tip
If you're not staying for IllumiNations, be out of the park before it ends. Once you see the fireworks begin in earnest, you have about five minutes to get to the exits ahead of the crowds.

your children's hands; this is the time of the day when you're most apt to be separated from your party.

- If you're not in the first wave of people to hit the exits (which is most likely if you're watching from the areas near the Mexico or Canada pavilions), have a snack, browse the stores, and aim to exit about 20 minutes behind the main crowd.

CHAPTER 7
Disney-MGM Studios Theme Park

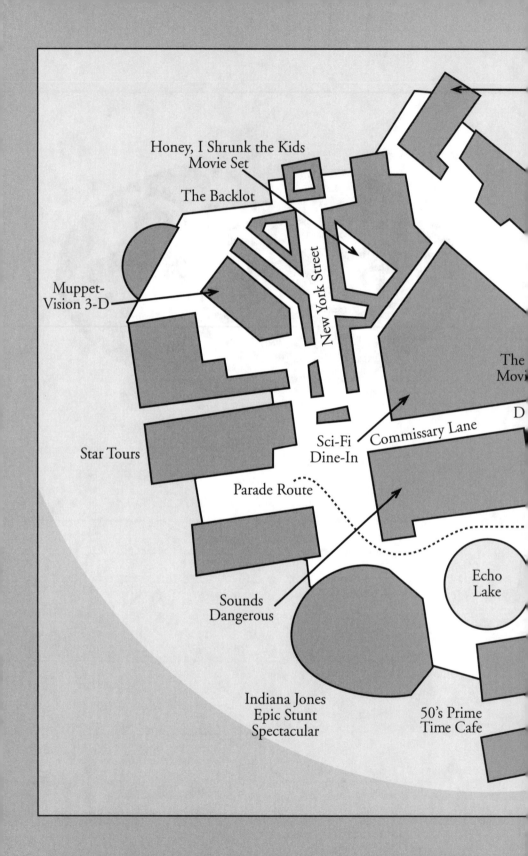

Honey, I Shrunk the Kids
Movie Set

The Backlot

Muppet-
Vision 3-D

New York Street

Star Tours

The
Movi

D

Sci-Fi   Commissary Lane
Dine-In

Parade Route

Echo
Lake

Sounds
Dangerous

Indiana Jones
Epic Stunt
Spectacular

50's Prime
Time Cafe

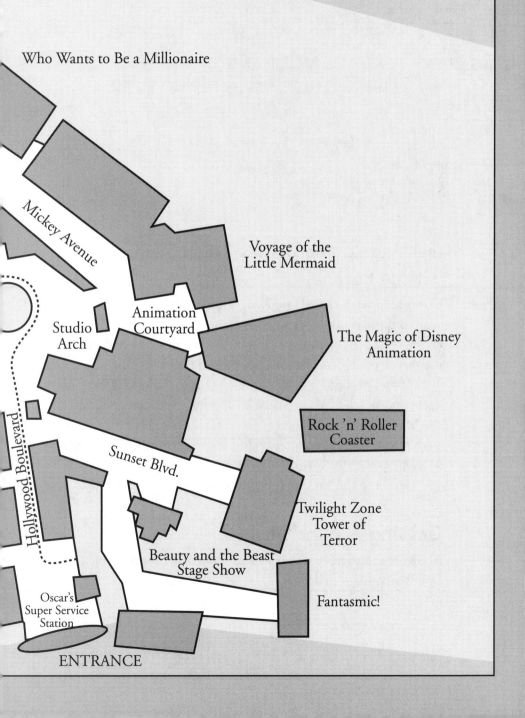

Studios
Backlot Tour

Disney-MGM Studios

Who Wants to Be a Millionaire

Mickey Avenue

Voyage of the
Little Mermaid

Studio
Arch

Animation
Courtyard

The Magic of Disney
Animation

Rock 'n' Roller
Coaster

Hollywood Boulevard

Sunset Blvd.

Twilight Zone
Tower of
Terror

Beauty and the Beast
Stage Show

Oscar's
Super Service
Station

Fantasmic!

ENTRANCE

DISNEY WORLD
SCENE 1
TAKE 17

Getting to the Disney-MGM Studios Theme Park

Compared with the Magic Kingdom, getting to MGM is a snap. Shuttle buses run approximately every 15 minutes from all on-site hotels. (Remember that on-site guests who drive to the theme parks don't have to pay for parking.)

If you're staying at the Swan, Dolphin, BoardWalk, or Yacht and Beach Clubs, you're a 15-minute water taxi ride from the MGM gate.

If you're staying off site and have a car, note that the MGM parking lot is small. If you get there at opening time, you can forgo the parking lot tram and walk to the front gate.

Getting Around MGM

MGM is a relatively small park with no in-park trains or buses. In other words, you'll walk.

Tips for Your First Hour at MGM

- At present, on-site resort guests can enter MGM one hour early on Tuesday and Saturday. The blackboard halfway down Hollywood Boulevard lets you know the attractions that are operative; the whole park doesn't open early, but several major attractions will be ready to ride.

- One parent can handle stroller rental at Oscar's Super Service Station while the other picks up a map and entertainment schedule at Guest Relations or Crossroads of the World.

Helpful Hint

Need a quick MGM breakfast? Stop by Starring Rolls Bakery for a great selection of pastries. If you have more time and would like a full meal, head to the cafeteria called Hollywood & Vine. Hollywood & Vine holds a character breakfast buffet during the on-season.

- If your kids are old enough and bold enough for a big-deal ride, go straight to the Rock 'n' Roller Coaster. Then move on to the Twilight Zone Tower of Terror on Sunset Boulevard.

  Younger kids? If an early show of *Voyage of the Little Mermaid* is scheduled, you should head there the minute you enter the gate. Your entertainment schedule will tell you if an 8:30 or 9 A.M. show is planned.

- If you haven't made dining plans yet, pause at the Hollywood Junction Red Car Station, where Sunset Boulevard meets Hollywood Boulevard, to arrange priority seating for any restaurant you'd like to try. The booth has sample menus.

@ Board the Great Movie Ride.

@ Board Star Tours.

MGM Touring Tips

@ With the exception of *Voyage of the Little Mermaid*, save theater-style presentations such as *Beauty and the Beast*, *Indiana Jones Epic Stunt Spectacular*, Playhouse Disney, and Sounds Dangerous for afternoon. Tour continuous-loading attractions such as the Tower of Terror, the Great Movie Ride, the Rock 'n' Roller Coaster, and Star Tours early in the day.

@ Save the Backlot and Animation tours for after lunch or early evening.

@ MGM is small and easily crisscrossed, so don't feel obligated to tour attractions in any particular geographic sequence. Those 4- and 5-year-olds who need a stroller at the Magic Kingdom or Epcot can do without one here.

Helpful Hint

The Disney people post a gigantic blackboard at the end of Hollywood Boulevard to keep visitors updated on approximate waiting times at various attractions. Consult it whenever you're in doubt about what to do next.

@ Also, after the dinner hour, popular restaurants such as the Sci-Fi Dine-In Theater Restaurant sometimes will accept walk-ins, especially if you're just dropping by for dessert.

As at the other theme parks, the restaurants are still serving food as the park officially closes, so if you didn't make it into one of the big-deal restaurants earlier in the day, now's your chance.

@ *Fantasmic!*, a 25-minute evening spectacular, is an absolute must-see. Performances take place on a lake beside the Tower of Terror. You should be in place 90 minutes before the stated show time to guarantee a good seat in the on-season. Show up an hour early in the off-season.

Attractions at MGM Offering FASTPASSes

Rock 'n' Roller Coaster (starring Aerosmith)

The Twilight Zone Tower of Terror

Star Tours

MuppetVision 3-D

Voyage of the Little Mermaid

Indiana Jones Epic Stunt Spectacular

Who Wants to Be a Millionaire—Play It!

MGM Attractions

Twilight Zone Tower of Terror

The Twilight Zone Tower of Terror combines the spooky ambience of a decaying, cobweb-covered 1930s-style Hollywood hotel with sheer thrills. The clever preshow, for which Disney spliced together clips from the old TV series in order to allow the long-deceased Rod Serling to narrate the story, invites you to enter an episode of *The Twilight Zone*. The story begins on Halloween evening in 1939 when five people board the hotel elevator: a movie star and a starlet, a child actress and her nanny, and the bellboy. The hotel is struck by lightning, the elevator drops, and the five passengers are transported into the Twilight Zone.

After watching the preshow, guests are directed to a cage "freight" elevator that will ascend—you guessed it—13 stories. Your seat has a lap bar, and each elevator holds about 25 people. On the way up, the elevator will stop to reveal a hallway that literally vanishes before your eyes.

It's the second stop that will really get you. The elevator will move forward past a series of holographic images, the doors eventually opening on to a panoramic view of the park from more than 150 feet in the air. Then you free-fall—it's a squealer—and then they haul you up and do it again.

Hidden Mickey

Look fast, and you might notice that the child actress in the preshow is holding a Mickey Mouse doll when she boards the doomed elevator.

Originally, I recommended this ride for ages 7 and up, and many kids in the 7 to 11 age range will still love it (or perhaps even love it more) in its newer, wilder form. But it's no longer true that the scary part of the ride lasts a mere three seconds; now you're in the shaft for long enough to get out a couple of real good screams.

Rock 'n' Roller Coaster

The Rock 'n' Roller Coaster, starring Aerosmith, features a soundtrack perfectly synchronized to reflect the movements of the coaster. The story is that guests are headed for a concert by their favorite band in 24-passenger stretch limos.

You're quickly (very, very quickly) accelerated into your first total flip. The mazelike track will go on to make a total of

The MGM Don't-Miss List

Rock 'n' Roller Coaster (if your kids are over 7)

Star Tours

The Great Movie Ride

Indiana Jones Epic Stunt Spectacular

Voyage of the Little Mermaid

***Beauty and the Beast* stage show**

**Twilight Zone Tower of Terror
(if your kids are over 7)**

Muppetvision 3-D

Fantasmic!

The MGM Worth-Your-While List

The Magic of Disney Animation tour

***Honey, I Shrunk the Kids* movie set**

Sounds Dangerous starring Drew Carey

Backstage Pass

The parade

Who Wants to Be a Millionaire game

Quick Guide to

Attraction	Location	Height Requirement
Afternoon parade	Hollywood Blvd.	None
Backstage Pass	Mickey Ave.	None
Beauty and the Beast stage show	Sunset Blvd.	None
Disney Channel filming	Mickey Ave.	None
Disney-MGM Backlot Tour	Mickey Ave.	None
Fantasmic!	Sunset Blvd.	None
The Great Movie Ride	Hollywood Blvd.	None
Honey, I Shrunk the Kids movie set	New York Street	None
Indiana Jones Epic Stunt Spectacular	Hollywood Blvd.	None
The Magic of Disney Animation tour	Animation Courtyard	None
The Making of . . .	Mickey Ave.	None
Muppetvision 3-D	New York Street	None
Rock 'n' Roller Coaster	Sunset Blvd.	48 inches
Sounds Dangerous	Hollywood Blvd.	None
Star Tours	Hollywood Blvd.	40 inches
Twilight Zone Tower of Terror	Sunset Blvd.	40 inches
Voyage of the Little Mermaid	Animation Courtyard	None
Who Wants to Be a Millionaire— Play It!	Mickey Ave.	None

Scare Factor
0 = Unlikely to scare any child of any age.
! = Has dark or loud elements; might rattle some toddlers.
!! = A couple of gotcha! moments; should be fine for school-age kids.
!!! = You need to be pretty big and pretty brave to handle this ride.

MGM Attractions

Speed of Line	Duration of Ride/Show	Scare Factor	Age Range
n/a	10 min.	0	All
Fast	25 min.	!	5 and up
Fast	30 min.	0	All
n/a	n/a	0	12 and up
Fast	35 min.	!	5 and up
Fast	25 min.	!!	5 and up
Fast	2.5 min.	!	5 and up
Slow	n/a	0	2 and up
Fast	30 min	!	All
Moderate	35 min.	0	All
Fast	25 min.	!	All
Fast	20 min.	!	2 and up
Moderate	3 min.	!!!	7 and up
Slow	15 min.	!	5 and up
Moderate	10 min.	!!	5 and up
Moderate	10 min.	!!!	6 and up
Slow	20 min.	!	4 and up
Slow	60 min.	0	8 and up

Helpful Hint

Lines get long in the afternoon, so after you ride in the morning, get a FASTPASS if you want to return later in the day.

three inversions along with innumerable twists and turns. At one point you rip through an "O" in the HOLLYWOOD sign.

The coaster is fun and addictive, and even those wary of coasters tend to love this smooth, fast ride.

One comfort: Because the whole ride is inside a building, you never go very high, so it shouldn't overly alarm those with a fear of heights. Rock 'n' Roller is more about speed than plunging.

Hidden Mickey

As you go through the rotunda area before boarding, check out the tile floors. There are not one but two Hidden Mickeys in the tiles.

The Scare Factor

Loud and wild, especially at takeoff where you go from 0 to 60 in 1.2 seconds, the coaster is designed for preteens, teens, and young adults. With a 48-inch height requirement, suffice it to say this will be too much for kids 7 and under.

Helpful Hint

MGM has two intense thrill rides, the Tower of Terror and the Rock'n'Roller Coaster. Don't forget you can use the baby swap system if you have young kids in tow.

The Great Movie Ride

Housed in the Chinese Theater at the end of Hollywood Boulevard, the Great Movie Ride debuted as an instant classic. Disney's largest ride-through attraction, it loads steadily and fairly swiftly, but this 25-minute ride draws large crowds and is best toured either in the morning or in the last hour before the park closes.

Each tram holds approximately 40 riders, and your tour guide provides an amusing spiel as you glide past soundstage sets from *Casablanca, Alien, The Wizard of Oz*, and other great films. The Audio-Animatronics figures of Gene Kelly, Julie Andrews, and Clint Eastwood are among Disney's best.

Things suddenly turn ugly as your car stalls and the movie scenes come to life. Depending on which car you've boarded, you're about to be overrun by either a gangster on the lam or a desperado trying to escape John Wayne. Your tour guide may be

Insider's Secret

Most of the waiting area is inside the Chinese Theater; if you see a line outside, rest assured that there are hundreds more tourists waiting inside, and skip the attraction for the time being.

The Scare Factor

On the Great Movie Ride, you'll encounter the Alien from *Alien*, the Wicked Witch from *The Wizard of Oz*, and any number of no-gooders on your trip. Some of the scenes are startling and intense, possibly scary for kids under 7. But the fact that your tram driver disappears and reappears does underscore the fact that it's all "just pretend."

gunned down or your tram taken hostage, but don't fret too much. In a later scene, drawn from *Indiana Jones and the Temple of Doom*, expect another twist of fortune—just in time to reestablish justice and guarantee a happy ending.

Star Tours

Motion simulation technology and a slightly jostling cabin combine to produce the real feel of flight in Star Tours. With the hapless Captain Rex at the helm, your crew is off for what is supposed to be a routine mission to the Moon of Endor. But if you think this mission is going to be routine, you don't know diddly about Disney. "Don't worry if this is your first flight," Rex comforts visitors as they board, "it's my first one, too." One wrong turn later and you're ripping through the fabric of space at hyperspeed, headed toward combat with the dreaded Death Star.

George Lucas served as creative consultant, and the ride echoes the charming as well as the terrifying elements of his *Star Wars* series. The chatter of R2-D2, C-3PO, and assorted droids makes even the queues enjoyable. Star Tours is the best of both worlds, with visual effects so convincing you'll clutch your arm rails but actual rumbles so mild that only the youngest children are eliminated as potential crew members.

Like the Tower of Terror, this ride takes only 10 minutes start to finish, so the lines move at an agreeable pace. It's still better to ride in the morning if you can.

The Scare Factor

Most kids love this attraction, especially if they've seen the *Star Wars* movies. "Like being inside a video game," my own 10-year-old enthuses. Any child over 5 should be fine. One warning: Although not as intense as the similar Body Wars at Epcot, Star Tours can cause motion sickness.

Sounds Dangerous **Starring Drew Carey**

Drew Carey's spy spoof, *Sounds Dangerous,* uses head-sets to make the noises—which emanate as Drew upends a jar of killer bees, drives a car, has a haircut, and visits the circus—eerily intimate.

For long periods of the show you sit in total darkness so as to accentuate the sound effects, and this unnerves some young kids. At nearly every performance at least one toddler is shriek-ing, which obviously un-dercuts the enjoyment of everyone in the theater, not to mention the spooked child in question. For kids with no fear of the dark, the show is an entertaining introduction to the world of old-time radio, where sound told the story.

> **Helpful Hint**
>
> This theater is the small-est at MGM, so check the size of the line be-fore you queue up. *Sounds Dangerous* is generally a good choice for afternoon.

The Magic of Disney Animation

Visitors can meet a Disney animation artist who will show you how to draw a character, and you also get a walk-through tour of the Disney Animation building—the East Coast home of Walt Disney Feature Animation. A special presentation at the Disney Classics Theater lets you relive moments from Disney films, from *Snow White and the Seven Dwarfs* to *Mulan.* Be-cause there is a fair amount of sitting, this is a good choice for afternoon. You can usually get in with a 10- to 15-minute wait. A must-see for film and animation buffs.

Indiana Jones Epic Stunt Spectacular

This stunt show is loud, lively, and full of laughs. You may think the lines waiting outside are the most spectacular part of the show, but, because the 2,000-seat theater is so huge, people standing as far back as the 50's Prime Time Café are usually seated. Either use FASTPASS or line up about 20 minutes before show time, and be aware that afternoon shows are sometimes a mob scene. If that's the case, try again during one of the last two seatings of the evening.

Audience volunteers are part of the show, and your odds of being tapped improve if you show up early and are near the front of the line. Professional stunt people re-create daring scenes from the *Indiana Jones* series, and this 30-minute show is a great chance to learn how those difficult and dangerous stunts end up on film. The finale is spectacular.

Disney-MGM Studios
Backlot Tour

The Backlot Tour begins with a stop at the special effects water tank, where audience volunteers re-create a naval battle scene. Then you stroll through the props department before being loaded on a tram that scoots you through wardrobe and past huge outdoor sets representing a typical small town and a large city. The highlight of the tram segment is a stop in Catastrophe Canyon, where you'll be caught in a flash flood, an oil explosion, and an earthquake. (If you're sitting on the left side, prepare to get wet.) Later you'll ride behind the Canyon and see how the disasters were created.

The Scare Factor

In Catastrophe Canyon, you'll be shaken and splashed, but the disaster lasts only about 30 seconds, and the tour guide immediately explains how it is all done. Most kids find the Canyon the best part of the Backlot Tour. Fine for anyone.

After you disembark from your tram, you'll be near the *Honey, I Shrunk the Kids* Movie Set and the Studio Catering Co. snack bar.

Honey, I Shrunk the Kids Movie Set

The Movie Set is based on the popular Disney movie of the same name. "Miniaturized" guests scramble through a world of giant LEGOs, 9-foot Cheerios, and spider webs three stories high. It's the perfect place for your kids to blow off steam.

Children 2 to 5 can enjoy the Junior Adventurers area, with its downsized maze and slide, where they can play in safety away from the rougher antics of the older kids. It is strongly recommended that toddlers stay out of the three-story spider web, which requires you to climb all the way through before exiting—a daunting task for little legs. Families with preschoolers must stay alert inside the Movie Set: When a child enters a tunnel or climbs to the top of a slide, it's often difficult to judge exactly where she'll emerge. For that reason, the attraction could be called "Honey, I Lost the Kids!"

Helpful Hint

This attraction is very popular with kids 8 and under. The only complaint? It needs to be about four times larger!

Voyage of the Little Mermaid

Using puppets, animation, and live actors to retell the beloved story of Ariel and Prince Eric, *Voyage of the Little Mermaid* remains one of the most popular shows at MGM. Either come early, use FASTPASS, or prepare for a wait.

The special effects in this 20-minute show are the best Disney has to offer; during the brilliant storm scene, you'll feel like you're really under water, and the interplay between the cartoon characters, puppets, and live actors is ingenious. Toddlers may find certain scenes too real for comfort, but everyone else is certain to be dazzled.

The Scare Factor

Although the show is designed for young kids, and most of them are indeed delighted to see Ariel, Sebastian, and other old friends, *Voyage of the Little Mermaid* does have a couple of frightening elements. The underwater storm scene is dark and loud, and Ursula the Sea Witch is portrayed as a large, undulating puppet. Kids who have seen the movie, however, know enough to expect a happy ending and usually make it through the dark scenes without becoming too upset.

MuppetVision 3-D

Look for the hot air balloon with Kermit's picture, and you'll find the *MuppetVision 3-D* movie. The show combines slapstick with sly wit, and everyone from preschoolers to adults will find something to make them laugh. (The preshow is nearly as clever as the main show, so be sure to watch while you wait.) The 3-D glasses in themselves are a

Helpful Hint

The 3-D effects are more convincing if you sit near the back of the theater.

The Scare Factor

Although *MuppetVision 3-D* tested highly among kids ages 2 to 5, some parents reported that kids under 2 were unnerved by the sheer volume of the finale.

kick, and the 20-minute movie is funny and touching—and loud. A good choice for midmorning, when you've ridden several rides and would like a chance to rest.

Beauty and the Beast Stage Show

This 30-minute show re-creates musical scenes from the film of the same name. Be at the theater at least 10 minutes before show time to guarantee a seat, 20 minutes if you want to be near the stage. It's a good choice for afternoon; the theater is covered and large enough to seat several hundred people at once.

The Theatre of the Stars, modeled on the Hollywood Bowl, is the perfect setting for this Broadway-caliber show. The costuming, choreography, and production are first rate, but the story is told a little out of sequence. However, 99.9 percent of the audience have seen the movie and don't find it too confusing.

Who Wants to Be a Millionaire—Play It!

Theme park guests get to vie for the chance to sit in the "hot seat" and play for points that can be traded in for prizes. The live show runs continuously throughout the day in a studio that is a painstaking replica of the TV show set, complete with lighting and sound effects. Anyone who can answer the questions can play the 25-minute game. If a child makes it to the hot seat, a parent can join her to help.

Helpful Hint

Remember that the full name of this attraction is Who Wants to Be a Millionaire—Play It! So get ready to push those buttons. Every member of the audience gets an equal shot at making it to the hot seat, but even if you don't win the Fastest Fingers Question, you're still not out. Continue to play along—when the contestant in the hot seat falters, the audience member with the highest score takes his place.

Contestants get limited edition Millionaire pins for each question they answer correctly. As you get into questions with higher point values, prizes include caps, polo shirts, CD-ROM versions of the game, and trips. The ultimate million-point prize is a Disney Cruise vacation for four.

Insider's Secret

Just as on the show, the contestant gets three lifelines. "Ask the Audience" and "50-50" work just as you would expect but "Phone a Friend" has become "Phone a Stranger." If a contestant opts to use that lifeline, a red telephone with a 30-foot cord rings outside on Mickey Avenue and the attendant hands it to the nearest adult. That person has 60 seconds to help the contestant answer the question.

Playhouse Disney Featuring
Bear in the Big Blue House

Younger kids will love this stage show, located on the site of the former soundstage restaurant. Children are encouraged to sing, dance, and play along in the Big Blue House with Bear and his pals from other Disney shows.

Insider's Secret

Although the Playhouse Disney show is simple, it's a hit with preschool kids. Check your timesheet or the tip board for show times and be in line at least 30 minutes early.

Fantasmic!

In *Fantasmic!*—featuring lasers, fireworks, lighting effects, and music—Mickey performs his role as the Sorcerer's Apprentice, fighting off a horde of evil Disney characters with a variety of special effects, including the projection of film images on a screen of water. *Fantasmic!* is the perfect way to top off a day at MGM. It may be the best show at any Disney Park.

The Scare Factor

Fantasmic! is intense—every Disney villain you can think of shows up for the cartoon Armageddon— and also loud enough to frighten many preschoolers. The scariest thing is the crowd. Be sure to either link hands and hold on as you exit, or hold your seat and let the bulk of the crowd pass.

Afternoon Parade

A themed parade featuring one of Disney's current releases runs every afternoon. The time and the route are outlined on your map. Stake out curb space 30 minutes in advance during the on-season; because the parade route is short, the crowds can be 8 to 10 people deep, and no vantage point is substantially less crowded than another. Although not as elaborate as those in the Magic Kingdom, the parades are popular, full of clever in-jokes, and extremely well done.

Walt Disney: One Man's Dream

In honor of Disney's 100 Years of Magic Celebration, MGM has opened a walk-through attraction about the life of Walt Disney, and this tribute will remain open indefinitely. You'll see artifacts from the Disney archives, a model of Walt's office, and hear audio clips of Walt himself telling the story of the rise of Disney animation and the opening of the Disney theme parks. A must for Walt fans of all ages.

Meeting the Characters at MGM

MGM is a great place to meet the characters. They appear more frequently than at the Magic Kingdom or Epcot, and there are fewer kids per square foot vying for their attention. Check the tip board or your entertainment schedule for times, get your camera ready, and check out these locations.

- A variety of characters greet visitors as they enter the park, usually around 8:30 or 9 A.M. The same characters return to the entrances around 3 P.M.

- The classic characters can be found on Mickey Avenue; look for their trailers. Mickey now greets visitors in his cushy new digs at the end of Mickey Avenue. The well-monitored line makes sure you have time for a photo, autograph, and hug with the main mouse.

- Breakfast and lunch buffets featuring characters from recent films are offered every day during the on-season and periodically during the off-season. Call 407-WDW-DINE to see who is appearing during your visit.

- The *Toy Story* crowd—Buzz, Woody, and sometimes Jessie—hang out at Al's Toy Barn in the Backlot Area.

- Periodically, the *Star Wars* crew can be found outside the Star Tours ride.

- And the Muppets are sometimes "on location" outside *MuppetVision 3-D*.

Food Choices at MGM

In my opinion, the best restaurant at MGM is the Hollywood Brown Derby, which, in fact, I consider the best restaurant in any Walt Disney World theme park. The Brown Derby offers elegant food, impeccable service, a beautifully urbane setting—

and it is still casual and friendly enough to take the kids. The menu includes great steaks and pasta, a knockout scallop appetizer, and the signature Cobb salad.

In truth, the Brown Derby will most appeal to adults who can appreciate the ambitious menu. Other MGM restaurants offer big doses of fun and may be better choices for families. Kids will love the 50's Prime Time Café, which plunks you in the middle of a cheesy sitcom and serves comfort food like meatloaf, pot roast, milkshakes, and mac and cheese. You sit in replicas of baby-boomer kitchens, the waitress pretends to be your mom, and before the meal is over everyone gets into the act. For example, Mom might literally force the kids to finish their green beans by doing the dreaded "airplane" technique.

Equally campy is the Sci-Fi Dine-In Theater Restaurant, where you eat in cars as if you were in a drive-in movie. The food is more ambitious than you expect—salads, pasta, and sandwiches—and it's fun to watch the hokey sci-fi clips on a giant screen. (And it's so dark in there that babies often go down for a postmeal nap.)

Note: For dining at the Brown Derby, the 50's Prime Time Café, or Sci-Fi Dine-In, it's a good idea to arrange priority seating. Guests at Disney hotels can make the call from their hotel room, but if you're staying off site stop at the reservation booth near the tip board as you enter the park. They'll set you up with a dining time and show you sample menus.

Due to its out-of-the-way location near *Muppet Vision 3-D*, Mama Melrose's is definitely the least crowded and fastest of all the sit-down places. You can often walk in without priority seating here, and the pizzas, pasta, and salads are really very good.

If you just want a quick nosh, the Backlot Express lives up to its name and serves burgers and salads fast. The ABC Commissary has a fairly unusual menu for a fast-food spot—they serve wraps, chicken yakitori, and noodle stir-fries. Starring

Quick Guide to Restaurants

Restaurant	Description
50's Prime Time Café	This restaurant is almost an attraction in itself
Hollywood & Vine Cafeteria of the Stars	Large, attractive art deco cafeteria with character dining
The Hollywood Brown Derby	Restaurant is elegant and lovely
Mama Melrose's Ristorante Italiano	Pizza and a wacky New York ambience
The Sci-Fi Dine-In Theater	Kids give this one high marks

For descriptions of ratings, prices, priority seating, and suitability for kids, see chapter 11.

Helpful Hint

Villains in Vogue is a great place to shop for Halloween costumes, because all the bad guys (and girls) are well represented. Rather go as a princess? Check out the Character Costume Shop near *Voyage of the Little Mermaid*. Is there a wookie in the party? Tatooine Traders, outside of Star Tours, can outfit you as your favorite *Star Wars* character.

Full-Service at MGM

Rating	Price	Priority Seating	Suitability	Details on
★★	$$	Recommended	High	Page 343
★★	$	Suggested	High	Page 345
★★★	$$$	Recommended	Moderate	Page 345
★★	$$	Suggested	Moderate	Page 347
★★	$$	Recommended	High	Page 351

Rolls specializes in pastries and desserts and is a good place to pick up a snack before the afternoon parade. If your party can't agree on what to eat, head for the Sunset Ranch Market near the Tower of Terror. This is the open-air equivalent of a small food court, and you can send the kids in different directions for pizza, hot dogs, turkey legs, ice cream, and fruit, and then all meet back at your table.

Tips for Your Last Hour at MGM

If you're watching *Fantasmic!*, you'll need to enter the stadium at least an hour in advance—90 minutes during the on-season.

That's quite a wait, so you may want to eat dinner while you hold your seat. The stadium serves hot dogs and snacks, or you can buy food from somewhere else in the parks and take it in with you.

If you're not watching *Fantasmic!*, the last hour before closing is a great time to hit those attractions with long waits earlier in the day. The park virtually empties out as everyone heads toward the show, so it's a good chance to ride the Rock 'n' Roller Coaster or any other biggie that was swamped earlier.

Tips for Leaving MGM

Although a terrific show that more than justifies the inconvenience, *Fantasmic!* draws virtually everyone in the park to one spot at closing and thus makes exiting a nightmare.

Those watching from the Mickey section have the best shot at getting out fast and beating the crowds to the shuttle tram or water taxi. If you're located near the water or in one of the sections to the extreme right or left of the stadium, you have little chance of exiting early. Sit tight and wait for the crowd to disperse, then eat or shop your way through the park, allowing most of the people to exit ahead of you.

CHAPTER

8. The Animal Kingdom

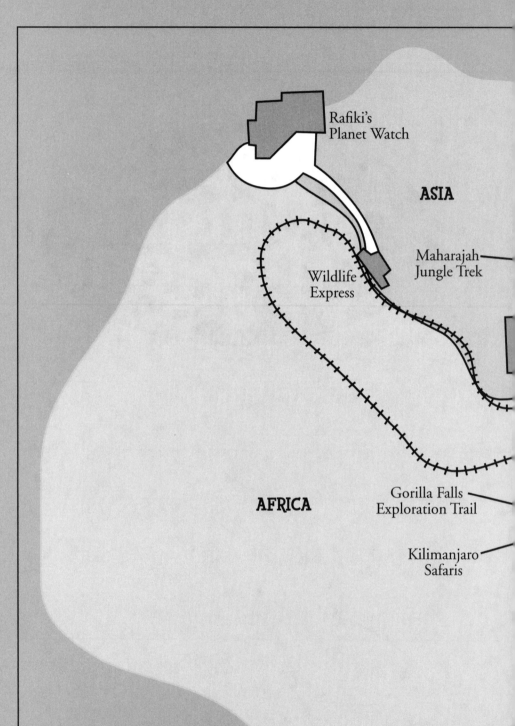

Rafiki's
Planet Watch

ASIA

Maharajah
Jungle Trek

Wildlife
Express

Gorilla Falls
Exploration Trail

AFRICA

Kilimanjaro
Safaris

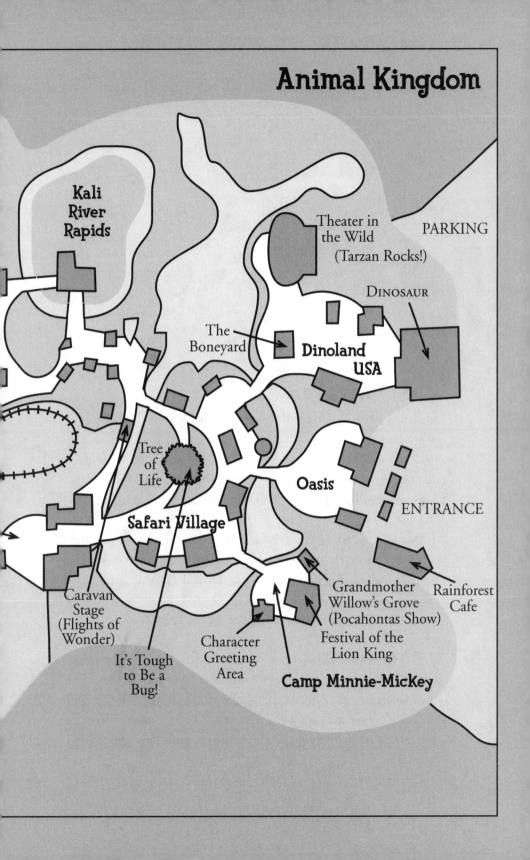

Animal Kingdom

Kali River Rapids

Theater in the Wild (Tarzan Rocks!)

PARKING

DINOSAUR

The Boneyard

Dinoland USA

Tree of Life

Oasis

ENTRANCE

Safari Village

Caravan Stage (Flights of Wonder)

Grandmother Willow's Grove (Pocahontas Show)

Rainforest Cafe

Festival of the Lion King

It's Tough to Be a Bug!

Character Greeting Area

Camp Minnie-Mickey

The Newest Park

Disney's newest park is devoted to animals, both living and mythic. At the center, the 14-story Tree of Life serves as the park icon, much as Spaceship Earth does at Epcot. This park covers more than 500 acres, as compared to 107 for the Magic Kingdom, 157 for MGM, and 300 for Epcot. Most of the space is earmarked for animal habitats, such as the huge 100-acre African savanna. More than 1,000 live animals, representing more than 200 species, can be found in the Animal Kingdom, and the park is also a botanical marvel, with more than 3,000 species of plants represented. "We didn't build the Animal Kingdom," one of the landscapers told me. "We grew it."

The Animal Kingdom consists of the Oasis, Discovery Island, Africa, Asia, Dinoland, and Camp Minnie-Mickey. The big attractions are Kilimanjaro Safaris, Dinosaur, and the 3-D film *It's Tough to Be a Bug!* There are also four stage shows, a water raft ride, and two trails that lead you through animal habitats.

Getting to the Animal Kingdom

The Animal Kingdom parking lot is relatively small; all on-site hotels run direct shuttles, and many off-site hotels do as well. If possible, arrive by bus. If you're coming by car, try to arrive early, before the parking lot is filled.

Getting Around the Animal Kingdom

The only real means of crossing the park is on foot. The layout is basically circular, with the Tree of Life in the center.

Sounds easy enough, but the area around the main entrance can become so crowded that it is nearly impassable in the middle of the day. So if you're trying to move around the park, a better bet is to cut through the Asia section, essentially going behind the Tree of Life. It looks like you're going out of your way (and you are), but the traffic flow works more in your favor.

Tips for Your First Hour in the Animal Kingdom

- At present, on-site resort guests can enter Animal Kingdom one hour early on Monday and Friday. If you want to see maximum animal movement and minimal people movement, set your alarm and go early.

- The Oasis is the entry area, much like Main Street in the Magic Kingdom, and it opens 30 minutes before the stated entry time.

- Head to the Kilimanjaro Safaris. If the wait is less than 30 minutes, ride.

- Enter the Tree of Life, and see the 3-D film *It's Tough to Be a Bug!*

Animal Kingdom Attractions that Offer FASTPASSes

Kilimanjaro Safaris

Kali River Rapids

Primeval Whirl

It's Tough to Be a Bug!

Dinosaur

Animal Kingdom Touring Tips

- Try to hit Kilimanjaro Safaris early. Save shows and interactive exhibits for the afternoon.

- Don't feel you have to see all the live shows, which may be too much sitting for young children. *Festival of the Lion King* is a must-see, but read the descriptions of the others and choose the ones that sound most interesting or age appropriate.

- Because of the relatively small number of attractions, you can tour the Animal Kingdom in four to six hours. This means the park is mobbed between 10 A.M. and 2 P.M. but should begin to clear out somewhat by midafternoon. If you can't be there first thing in the morning, consider arriving about 3 P.M. If you arrive in the afternoon, see the live shows first, saving the biggies like Dinosaur, *It's Tough to Be a Bug!*, and Kilimanjaro Safaris for the last two hours before the park closes. If you don't see everything you'd like to, you can always come back another afternoon.

- Because of their proximity, and because neither park requires a full day to tour, consider combining a visit to the Animal Kingdom with a stop at Blizzard Beach.

Insider's Secret

When the park opens, attendants are usually standing near the Tree of Life, directing guests toward attractions. Because they're on walkie-talkies with the operators of the rides, they can tell you approximate wait times and save you from hotfooting it to an attraction only to find an hour-long wait.

Insider's Secret

In your dash to get to the rides and shows, don't forget that the Animal Kingdom is really all about the animals. The Maharajah Jungle Trek and Gorilla Falls Exploration Trail are major attractions, as well designed as any zoo, but there are other chances to visit the animals as well. You can see such creatures as anteaters and sloths as you enter the park via the Oasis, and there are many small enclaves around the base of the Tree of Life. Stop and check out the kangaroos and lemurs.

Animal Kingdom Attractions

The attractions may be few in number, but they're powerful experiences. Most of them are designed for the whole family to enjoy together.

Discovery Island Attractions

Tree of Life, Featuring It's Tough to Be a Bug!

The Tree of Life is an absolutely amazing edifice, one of the most gorgeous pieces of architecture Disney has ever produced. You'll have plenty of time while you're in line to pick out the dozens of animal carvings seamlessly twisted into the mammoth trunk of the tree.

The 3-D film inside, called *It's Tough to Be a Bug!*, is state-of-the-art and a real highlight for all ages. Like *Honey, I Shrunk the Audience*, the show combines visual and tactile effects, and the cast of buggy characters, including the Termine-ator and an accurately named Stinkbug, are so funny that almost everyone leaves this attraction laughing. The best special effect of all is at the very end; it's a real "gotcha."

Helpful Hint

The Tree of Life is so visually impressive that many visitors entering the park head there first. If you can't see it early in the morning, save it for late afternoon.

The Scare Factor

It's Tough to Be a Bug! is a huge hit with most kids, but there are a couple of scary scenes. At one point, large spider puppets drop down from the ceiling over your heads, and at another the theater goes dark and you hear the sounds of swarming mosquitoes . . . and there's the chance your seat might give you a small electrical zap, indicating you've been stung. The majority of children under 10 seem to find this great fun, but there's usually at least one child crying per audience. If your kids are scared of the dark or bugs, they probably should skip the show.

Africa Attractions

Kilimanjaro Safaris

This is the Animal Kingdom's premier attraction, a ride that simulates an African photo safari. Guests board lorries for a

The Animal Kingdom Don't-Miss List

It's Tough to Be a Bug!

Kilimanjaro Safaris

Dinosaur (if your kids are 7 or older)

Festival of the Lion King

The exploration trails, including Gorilla Falls and Maharajah Jungle Trek

Primeval Whirl

The Animal Kingdom Worth-Your-While List

Kali River Rapids

Flights of Wonder

Pocahontas Show **(for kids 7 and under)**

Tarzan Rocks!

Chester and Hester's Dino-Rama

Triceratop Spin

two-mile ride through the African savanna. Water and plant barriers are so cunningly incorporated that the animals appear to be running free. Your guide helps you tell the impalas from the gazelles, and at times the lorry comes startlingly close to the wildlife. The story line is that you're helping the reserve's game warden look for elephant poachers who have abducted a baby elephant, Little Red.

Disney has gone to great pains to give the animals as much freedom as possible and ample space to roam, which

Quick Guide to

Attraction	Location	Height Requirement
The Boneyard	Dinoland	None
Character Greeting Area	Camp Minnie-Mickey	None
Cretaceous Trail	Dinoland	None
Dinosaur	Dinoland	40 inches
Festival of the Lion King	Camp Minnie-Mickey	None
Flights of Wonder at Caravan Stage	Asia	None
Gorilla Falls Exploration Trail	Africa	None
Grandmother Willow's Grove	Camp Minnie-Mickey	None
Kali River Rapids	Asia	42 inches
Kilimanjaro Safaris	Africa	None
Maharajah Jungle Trek	Asia	None
Primeval Whirl	Dinoland	48 inches
Tarzan Rocks! at Theater in the Wild	Dinoland	None
Tree of Life, featuring *It's Tough to Be a Bug!*	Safari Village	None
Triceratop Spin	Dinoland	None
Wildlife Express to Rafiki's Planet Watch	Africa	None

Scare Factor

0 = Unlikely to scare any child of any age.
! = Has dark or loud elements; might rattle some toddlers.
!! = A couple of gotcha! moments; should be fine for school-age kids.
!!! = You need to be pretty big and pretty brave to handle this ride.

Animal Kingdom Attractions

Speed of Line	Duration of Ride/Show	Scare Factor	Age Range
n/a	n/a	0	All
Moderate	n/a	0	All
Fast	n/a	0	All
Moderate	10 min.	!!!	7 and up
Moderate	25 min.	0	All
Fast	25 min.	0	All
Moderate	n/a	0	All
Fast	12 min.	0	All
Moderate	7 min.	!	4 and up
Moderate	20 min.	!	6 and up
Fast	n/a	0	All
Slow	7 min.	!!	5 and up
Fast	30 min.	0	All
Slow	10 min.	!	All
Slow	10 min.	!	All
Fast	n/a	0	All

means that some safari trips yield more sightings than do others. On our last trip we had great views of the rhino herd and came unbelievably close to one bold giraffe, and the lions reclined so gracefully on their rocks that they might have been a poster for a Disney film. Others have reported seeing more— or less. One rule of thumb is that the animals are more active when it's cooler. In other words, go in the morning if you can, both to see the animals and to cut down on your time in line. This ride is the Dumbo of the Animal Kingdom, posting waits two or three times those of any other attraction.

The Scare Factor
Your Kilimanjaro Safaris vehicle will bump and bounce quite convincingly but kids of all ages love the safari.

Be aware that although Little Red is rescued in the end and the ride ends on a happy note, the poachers have shot the mother of a baby elephant—shades of Bambi—and this may be upsetting to younger children. The imagineers have created this ride not only to be fun and exciting but also to underscore some points about the dangers facing animals in the wild.

Gorilla Falls Exploration Trail
Located just as you leave Kilimanjaro Safaris, this is a self-guided walking trail. The landscaping is gorgeous, you can linger as long as you like, and at one point you pass through the area where Gino the silverback gorilla lives. (The dominant male in a gorilla troop is called the silverback because he is ordinarily older than the other animals and often has gray hairs mixed in with the black.) Gino and his harem are on one side of the trail, and the bachelor gorillas are on the other side.

At different points along the trail, you'll pass everything from mole rats to hippos, but kids seem to especially like the meerkats and warthogs in the Pumbaa and Timon exhibit.

Hidden Mickey

It's Hidden Mickey city at Rafiki's Planet Watch. There are more than 25 concealed in murals, tree trunks, and paintings of animals.

Insider's Secret

Family Fun magazine has set up interactive stations in all the major sections of the Animal Kingdom, much like the Kids' Zones activities in Epcot. At each stop in the "Discovery Club," kids play a game to help them understand more about animals and how they interact with their environment. In camp Minnie-Mickey, for example, they reach into a hollow log and try to identify objects like turtle shells and antlers simply by feeling their shapes. At the first stop, children receive a booklet that has fun games and puzzles to help pass time while waiting in line, and at each subsequent stop they receive a stamp. When all six stamps are collected, they're given an official Rafiki "Friend of the Animals" pin.

Wildlife Express to Rafiki's Planet Watch

This 10-minute train ride gives you a glimpse of the animal care that goes on behind the scenes, even showing you where the animals sleep at night. The ride offers a little rest after a morning of touring, and the trains themselves are nifty looking.

You disembark at Rafiki's Planet Watch, an utterly out-of-the-way exhibit in the farthest-flung

Helpful Hint

Conservation Station is a pretty good hike from where the train lets you out. Complimentary strollers are available at the depot: Borrow one for a few minutes if the kids are tired.

section of the park. In the Affection Section, kids can touch and cuddle small goats and sheep. Low-key, with several interactive exhibits, this is a good choice for the afternoon but skippable if you're on a tight touring schedule.

Dinoland Attractions

Dinosaur

Guests are strapped into "high-speed" motion simulation vehicles and sent back in time to the Cretaceous period to save the iguanodon (a gentle, plant-eating dinosaur) from extinction.

The Scare Factor

The height requirement at Dinosaur has been lowered to 40 inches. Still, the attraction does incorporate atmospheric scariness with a wild-moving ride. Fine for 7 and up, iffy for preschoolers.

It's a truly noble mission, but it ain't easy. On the way, Disney throws everything it has at you: asteroids, meteors, and, oh yeah, a few people-eating dinosaurs. A combination track ride and motion simulation ride, Dinosaur can be rough and wild—but it is also lots of fun.

Theater in the Wild, Featuring Tarzan Rocks!

This large amphitheater is home to some of Disney's most ambitious stage shows. Check your entertainment schedule for show times, and be there about 20 minutes early to ensure a good seat, or arrive 30 minutes early on a busy day. The current show, *Tarzan Rocks!*, features an excellent live band, aerial ballet, dazzling roller-skating stunts, and favorite characters from the film. There's something for any age, preschoolers to teens.

The Boneyard

A great attraction for preschoolers, the Boneyard is a playground designed to simulate an archaeological dig site. Kids can dig for "fossils," excavate bones, and play on mazes, bridges, and slides. The park is visually witty—where else can you find slides made from prehistoric skeletons?—and has funny surprises, such as a footprint that roars when you jump on it.

Visit the Boneyard after you've toured the biggies and the kids are ready to romp for a while. The play area can become hot in the Florida afternoons, however, so remember the sunscreen and water bottles, and don't stay too long.

Helpful Hint

The good news is that kids can lose themselves in the Boneyard and happily play there for an hour or longer. The bad news is that parents can lose their kids as well. The Boneyard is big and sprawling so keep your eyes on young children at all times, especially when they're on the slides. When they enter at the top, sometimes it's hard to tell what chute they're in or where they'll emerge.

Hidden Mickey

In the wooly mammoth dig site, there's a Hidden Mickey formed with two hard hats and a fan.

Chester and Hester's Dino-Rama

The idea of this mini-land is that Chester and Hester, owners of the campy T-shirt and trinket shop near the exit to Dinosaur, have built a dino-themed fair with wacky midway games and rides. Along with the arcade games on the midway, you'll find Triceratop Spin, a circular ride similar to Dumbo—except you fly in dinosaurs, naturally, and the beasts tilt back and forth as you climb or descend.

Primeval Whirl is a coaster-style ride with 13 spinning cars, sharp turns, and a couple of mild drops. It's a kiddie coaster designed for the 10 and under set, but the spins and hairpin turns add up to plenty of thrills. The height requirement for this ride is 48 inches.

The Scare Factor

Triceratop Spin is appropriate for any age. Primeval Whirl is a definite step up in intensity and is best suited for 5- to 10-year-olds. Some younger kids will love it; the ride is outdoors and totally visible, so if you're unsure if your kids can handle it, watch the ride go through a few cycles before you line up.

Helpful Hint

The Boneyard and Chester and Hester's Dino-Rama are good spots for young kids to hang out while their older siblings ride Dinosaur.

Camp Minnie-Mickey Attractions

Character Greeting Area

Camp Minnie-Mickey is the Animal Kingdom equivalent of Toontown—you'll find three separate greeting areas where you can line up to meet the characters, all adorably decked out in safari gear. The greeting areas are especially mobbed just before and after the *Festival of the Lion King* show, so plan to get your photos and autographs at a different time.

Festival of the Lion King

Every Disney park seems to have a sleeper hit—an attraction that ends up being far more popular than the imagineers anticipated—and this is it for the Animal Kingdom.

The 25-minute show features what you might expect—singers, dancers, the characters from the popular movie—but it is also chock-full of surprises in the forms of acrobatic "monkeys," flame swallowers, and "birds" that dramatically take flight. The costuming is incredible, the performers are exceedingly talented, and the finale is guaranteed to give you goose bumps.

The show is currently staged eight times a day. To ensure you'll be seated at all, you need to line up 30 to 40 minutes in advance. The show is a good choice for early afternoon, just after lunch, when you're fairly well rested.

Pocahontas Show
This smaller show, nice for younger kids, features Pocahontas, Grandmother Willow, and live animals. A strong message about conservation and wildlife protection is woven into the story. Show times are indicated on your entertainment schedule. Another good choice for afternoon.

Insider's Secret

Some of the Pocahontas shows are designated as animal training sessions, and these can be especially interesting for kids. The trainers work with small forest animals such as raccoons and skunks to get them used to the presence of crowds and the animals are sometimes taken out among the audience. These sessions are usually held in the morning; times are marked on your theme park map.

Asia Attractions

Caravan Stage, Featuring Flights of Wonder
A lovely display of birds in free flight. You'll see falcons, vultures, hawks, and toucans that demonstrate their unusual talents. The

birds fly very low over the heads of the audience, and the background story of the show is quite funny.

You should get a seat if you show up 10 to 20 minutes early. Again, show times are noted on your entertainment schedule, and stage shows are generally a good choice for afternoon.

Kali River Rapids

Guests will board eight-passenger rafts for a descent down a raging river through rapids and waterfalls. Expect to get very, very wet, quite possibly soaked, depending on where you are sitting in the raft. Bring your trusty poncho, if you have one, stow cameras in the lockers before you board, and be sure to keep your feet up on the center bar. A wet fanny is an inconvenience, but drenched socks and shoes can lead to blisters and ruin your whole trip.

This water ride also illustrates the dangers of clear-cutting jungles; you'll pass through a variety of landscapes during your wet journey, from lush to barren, illustrating how irresponsible harvesting leaves the land vulnerable to erosion.

The Scare Factor

A very mild ride, with one sizable descent on the way. Fine for anyone—unless they're afraid of getting splashed! We're talking major water here. The height requirement is 42 inches.

Maharajah Jungle Trek

Another lovely walking path, this one re-creates the habitats of Asia. You'll encounter Bengal tigers, Komodo dragons, gibbons, and other animals on your trek. You can spend anywhere from 10 minutes to an hour on the path.

Although not billed as a major attraction, the Maharajah Jungle Trek, along with the Gorilla Falls Exploration Trail, is part of what makes the Animal Kingdom so unique. The close proximity to the animals; the painstaking effort to re-create their natural habitats; the use of trees, bushes, and water to replace fencing; and the beauty of the architecture (with lots of hidden Mickeys along the way) make the trail worth an hour of your time. The giant fruit bats are a special treat for kids, but the tigers are the undisputed stars of the show.

Insider's Secret
The Animal Kingdom has fun interactive street entertainment occurring throughout the park. For example, there's DeVine, a moving human topiary, that blends in so well with the vegetation that she's been known to startle some guests.

Helpful Hint
The best places to see the characters in the Animal Kingdom are the character greeting area in Camp Minnie-Mickey and the Discovery Island Character Landing near the entrance to Dinoland.

Food Choices in the Animal Kingdom

Since the Animal Kingdom closes the earliest of all the parks—between 5 and 7 P.M. depending upon the time of year you visit—people rarely eat dinner there. Thus, Disney hasn't concentrated on building sit-down restaurants, figuring most people will just grab fast food at lunch.

The only sit-down restaurant in the park is the Rainforest Café. It's a chain, but it's fun, and they've recently introduced some fairly ambitious new menu items. (To check out what's offered, log on to www.rainforestcafe.com.) The only drawback is that wait times can be long, even if you eat at off hours. Since the Animal Kingdom has relatively few attractions and most families can do the park in less than a day, you might want to just stick to fast food and keep moving.

My favorite of the fast-food places is Tusker House in Africa. There's a pleasant riverside outdoor eating area offering both shade and entertainment in the form of live African music. The most amazing thing about Tusker House is that it serves vegetables—more rare in Disney World than Bugs Bunny T-shirts—that are cooked fresh every 15 minutes. Menu standards include a grilled chicken salad served in a bread bowl with balsamic vinaigrette and a half-rotisserie chicken with mashed potatoes and vegetables. At $7.99 a plate, the latter is the food bargain of Disney World.

Quick Guide to Full-in the Animal

Restaurant	Description
Rainforest Cafe	Great fun!

For descriptions of ratings, prices, priority seating, and suitability for kids, see chapter 11.

Insider's Secret

Dawa Bar, an outdoor dining area adjacent to the
Tusker House, has entertainment such as live music
or acrobats throughout the day. It's a great afternoon resting place.

Flame Tree Barbeque, located near the entrance to Dinoland, is another good choice. You won't be too surprised to
learn that they serve barbeque—and even a North Carolina native like me has to concede that it's pretty good barbecue. But
what sets Flame Tree apart from the other fast-food places is a
truly beautiful outdoor eating area. You have your choice of tables spread around a lagoon with bridges, fountains, and statu-
ary everywhere. Because there are so many lush, shady eating

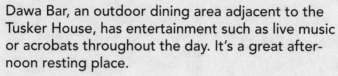

Service Restaurants
Kingdom

Rating	Price	Priority Seating	Suitability	Details on
★★	$$	Not accepted	High	Page 351

areas in the Animal Kingdom, it really does blur the line between fast-food and sit-down dining.

Helpful Hint

A morning character breakfast is held at Restaurantosaurus. Call WDW-DINE for exact times and prices.

Finally, another good spot for a quick bite is the often-overlooked Chakranadi Chicken Shop in Asia. The offerings here are a bit unusual—chicken satay in peanut sauce, ears of corn in hot butter, and potstickers in a spicy Asian broth. Everything is yummy, with more of a kick than you'd expect from theme park fast food, and the Chicken Shop also has—guess what?—a shady patio. (All those trees they planted at the Animal Kingdom are really starting to pay off!) It's the perfect place for land lovers to hang out while the rest of the party rides the nearby Kali River Rapids.

Insider's Secret

Why is there no closing show at the Animal Kingdom? Coming up with a big show to rival *Fantasmic!*, the Magic Kingdom parades, or IllumiNations is a real challenge for the imagineers. Most evening shows require pyrotechnics such as fireworks, and too much noise and light would scare the animals. Ergo, at least for now, no closing show.

Tips for Your Last Hour at the Animal Kingdom

There is currently no big closing show at the Animal Kingdom, so leaving isn't really a problem. Many people finish their touring and leave the park by midafternoon, just as the afternoon wave of guests is coming in.

Tips for Leaving the Animal Kingdom

The parking lot is small, and all on-site hotels run buses.

Blizzard Beach is located near the Animal Kingdom, and they often share shuttles. You may want to bring your bathing suits along and spend the morning at the Animal Kingdom and the afternoon in the water park.

CHAPTER 9

The Disney World Water Parks

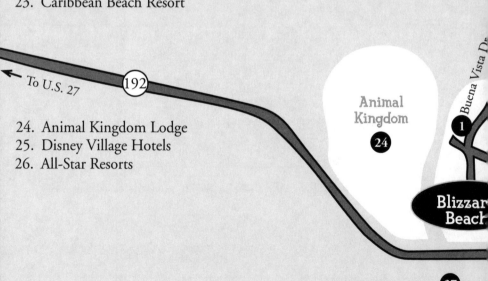

Magic
Kingdom

13

12

11

10

Floridian Way

9

8

To U.S. 27   192

Animal
Kingdom
24

Buena Vista Dr

1

Blizzard
Beach

27

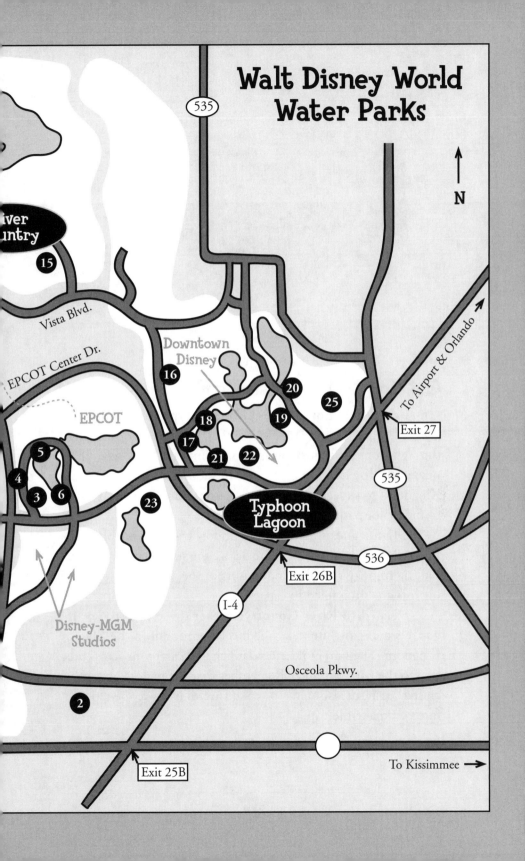

Getting to the Water Parks

On-site visitors should take the bus to Typhoon Lagoon or Blizzard Beach. Getting to Typhoon Lagoon may involve sitting through stops at all three bus pickup points at Downtown Disney; and Blizzard Beach often shares a bus with the Animal Kingdom, so expect a slightly longer commute than you'd have to the major parks.

Off-site guests driving to Typhoon Lagoon and Blizzard Beach should definitely be there before the stated opening time. During midday and afternoon hours in the summer, the parking lots are often filled to capacity.

Headed to River Country? Either drive directly, or if you're staying on site, take the bus or monorail to the Magic Kingdom. The Fort Wilderness launch will carry you across the lake to the park entrance. Remember that the park is presently closed for refurbishment so make sure that it's reopened before you make the trip.

Quiz: Which Water Park Is Right for You?

The most important thing in a water park is
A. The slides.
B. The waves.
C. The pools.

The ages of our kids are
A. Preteens and teens.
B. A mix—they're 11, 8, and 4.
C. Preschoolers and toddlers.

Long lines are
A. To be expected. This is Disney World, after all.
B. Tolerable at the big-deal rides,
but I like to get away from the crowd sometimes.
C. The last thing I want when I'm trying to relax.

When we go to a water park, we
A. Go early and stay all day.
B. Show up in the evening and use the time to unwind.
C. Just drop in for a couple of hours to cool off.

I'd most like to lie by the pool with
A. Who has time to lie by the pool?
B. The latest Tom Clancy book and a piña colada.
C. A big old shade tree and a slice of watermelon.

As a family, we're looking for
A. Excitement.
B. Variety.
C. Relaxation.

Mostly A's? Hit the slopes of Blizzard Beach.

Mostly B's? There's a wave with your name on it at Typhoon Lagoon.

Mostly C's? Wade into River Country.

River Country

Billed as an "ol' swimmin' hole perfect for splashin' and slidin'," River Country was completely overshadowed by the openings of Typhoon Lagoon and Blizzard Beach.

Insider's Secret

River Country is often closed due to weather—the lake water gets cold much faster than the pools at the other water parks. River Country is also closed for refurbishing until spring of 2004. Be sure to confirm that it is open before you travel over.

This small five-acre park never gets as crowded as Typhoon Lagoon and Blizzard Beach, which are 10 times larger. River Country draws far fewer preteens and teens, and the water level in the center of Bay Cove is only about chest deep on an 8-year-old.

Bay Cove, the largest section of River Country, features swing ropes, two water slides, and White Water Rapids, an exhilaratingly bumpy inner-tube ride down a winding 230-foot-long creek. The nearby swimming pool offers two small but steep slides that shoot riders into midair; kids smack the water 8 feet below with such force that they can barely stagger out of the pool and make it up the stony steps to try it again . . . and again.

Helpful Hint

River Country remains a good choice for families with young kids or anyone who doesn't swim very well.

Younger kids will prefer the Ol' Wading Pool, a roped-off sandy-bottomed section of Bay Cove with four small slides cut into a wall of boulders, designed specifically for preschool-ers. Because older kids are kept out of this section and the slides empty into a mere 18 inches of water, parents can relax on the many lounge chairs scattered along the Ol' Wading Pool beach.

Again, the Park Hopper Plus pass lets you in gratis, but in-dividual tickets are available at $15.95 for adults (and children over 9) and $12.50 for kids ages 3 to 9. River Country is a fine place to picnic, and there are a couple of fast-food stands on site.

If you're going by car or taking a shuttle, be aware that the River Country parking lot is quite far from the park. You'll catch a shuttle from the parking lot, drive through Fort Wilder-ness Campground, and be let out near the gates. Those coming from Fort Wilderness or those who have taken the launch from the Magic Kingdom to Fort Wilderness have only a short walk to the River Country entrance.

Helpful Hint

Although Typhoon Lagoon and Blizzard Beach can take up a whole day, a swift-moving 10-year-old can try out every attraction at River Country in two hours flat. For this reason, it's a good water park to drop into when the theme parks are sweltering and everyone needs to unwind for a couple of hours.

River Country Touring Tips

@ Although the oversized swimming pool is heated, making fall and spring swimming a delight, it's obviously impos-sible to heat the bay. River Country is usually closed dur-ing December, January, and February and can be chilly during the spring and fall. Call 407-824-4321 for infor-mation about hours of operation.

@ Families not returning to their hotels in midafternoon can use River Country to break up a day in the Magic Kingdom. Stow your bathing suits in one of the lockers beneath the Main Street Railroad Station in the morning. When the park gets hot and fills up in the afternoon, exit the Magic Kingdom and take the launch marked "Fort Wilderness Campground." (The 15-minute boat ride is so pleasant that it almost constitutes an afternoon getaway in itself.) If you're staying off site, this option is less time-consuming than returning to your hotel pool. After a few hours in the cool waters of River Country, you can hop back on the launch and be in the Magic Kingdom within minutes.

@ Horseback riding is located near the River Country parking lot; if you're planning to try the trail rides during your Disney stay, it makes sense to combine the horseback riding with an afternoon at River Country. Great for younger kids, the pony rides and Fort Wilderness petting farm are located right at the River Country main entrance. The ponies are available from 10 A.M. to 5 P.M., cost $3 to ride, and are incredibly gentle.

Helpful Hint

Remember that you're swimming in a lake, not a pool. The netting does a good job on critter control, but this is not the day to wear your new $90 white swimsuit.

Typhoon Lagoon

Disney has dubbed its 56-acre Typhoon Lagoon "the world's ultimate water park," and the hyperbole is justified. Where else can you slide through caves, picnic with parrots, float through rain forests, and swim (sort of) with sharks?

Typhoon Lagoon occasionally becomes so swamped with swimmers that it closes its gates. On a regular basis during the holiday weeks, the park be- comes so crowded that no one is admitted after 10 A.M., to the great dismay of families who have put on their bathing suits, swabbed themselves with sunscreen, and prepared for a day in the pools.

Helpful Hint

If you're visiting during a holiday or midsummer, plan to arrive at the water parks at opening time—or wait until evening.

For anyone with a Park Hopper Plus pass, entrance to Ty- phoon Lagoon is included. Otherwise admission is $31 for adults (and children over 9) and $25 for children 3 to 9.

Typhoon Lagoon Attractions

Humunga Kowabunga

This ride consists of two water slides that propel riders down a mountain at 30 miles per hour. No kids shorter than 48 inches are allowed. This is the most intense attraction in the park, ca- pable of momentarily taking your breath away.

Helpful Hint

For women and girls, a one-piece suit is your best bet. A young Disney employee informed me that the most desired duty in all of Typhoon Lagoon is to stand at the bottom of Humunga Kowabunga, help- ing riders out of the chute—apparently at least one woman per hour loses her swimsuit top during the descent.

Storm Slides

Three curving slides deposit riders in the pool below. Kids of any age can ride, but it's suggested that they be good swimmers, because although the pool isn't deep, you do enter the water with enough force to temporarily disorient a nervous swimmer. Most kids 7 to 11 (and some who are younger) love these zesty little slides, but if you're unsure if your kids are up to it, wait at the edge of the pool where the slide empties, so you can help them out.

Each of the three slides—the Rudder Buster, Jib Jammer, and Stern Burner—offers a slightly different route, although none is necessarily wilder than the others.

Mayday Falls

A Disney employee helps you load into the giant rubber tubes and gives you a gentle shove. What follows is a fast, giggly journey that more than once makes you feel as if you're about to lose your tube.

Keelhaul Falls

This corkscrew tube ride is full of thrills. Smaller tubes with built-in bottoms are available for small children, and lots of kids as young as 4 reported that they loved this ride.

Gangplank Falls

Weather whitewater rapids in four-passenger rafts. Slower and milder but much bumpier than Mayday or Keelhaul, Gangplank is a good choice for families with kids too young for the other whitewater rides. Gangplank Falls loads slowly, however, and the ride is short, so hit it early in the morning, especially if you think your kids will want to go down more than once.

If the kids are small, sometimes more than four people are allowed into a raft.

Surfing Lagoon

Ride machine-made waves up to 6 feet high in a 2.5-acre lagoon. The waves come at 90-second intervals and are perfectly designed for tubing and bodysurfing. Every other hour the pool is emptied of tubes, and the wave machine is cranked up to allow for bodysurfing. A foghorn blast alerts you when a big 'un is on its way. Although the Surfing Lagoon lets anyone in, don't take small children out too far during the hours designated for bodysurfing—every 90 seconds 400 shrieking teenagers will bear down on your head. A special bonus: Surfing lessons are available in the morning before the park opens. Call 407-824-SURF for details.

Whitecap Cove and Blustery Bay

The Surfing Lagoon has two small, roped-off coves, where smaller waves lap up on toddlers and babies.

Castaway Creek

Castaway Creek is a meandering 2,000-foot stream full of inner tubes. Guests simply wade out, find an empty tube, and climb aboard. It takes about 30 minutes to circle the rain forest, and there is a bit of excitement at one point when riders drift under a waterfall. There are numerous exits along the creek, so anyone who doesn't want to get splashed can hop out before the falls. In general, a very fun, relaxing ride, appropriate for any age or swimming level.

Shark Reef

An unusual attraction, Shark Reef is a saltwater pool where snorkelers swim "among" exotic marine life, including sharks. The sharks are behind Plexiglas, of course, and are not too numerous, so anyone expecting the casting call for *Jaws* will be disappointed.

Helpful Hint
Most of the fun at Shark Reef is in getting to view the brightly colored fish up close, but if your kids are unsure, the underwater viewing area will give them a good feel for what snorkeling is all about.

Take the kids down to the viewing area first, and let them observe the marine life and other snorkelers and then make up their own minds.

Ketchakiddee Creek

This is a water playground sized for preschoolers, with geysers and bubblers in the shape of crocodiles and whales, as well as slides and a small whitewater raft ride. No one taller than 48 inches is allowed to ride, which is a pleasant change from most of the park rules, although parents are encouraged to enter the area and help their kids. Lifeguards are everywhere, and there are lots of chairs nearby for adults.

Mt. Mayday Scenic Trail

This footpath leads almost to the top of Mt. Mayday, where the shipwrecked Miss Tilly is stranded, and offers views of the slides and rides below.

Helpful Hint

Summer afternoons in Florida often mean thunderstorms . . . and even a rumble of distant thunder can lead to water park closings. If you're visiting in the summer and want to make sure you get to try everything, visit water parks first thing in the morning.

Blizzard Beach

When word got out in the travel industry that Disney was opening another water park, there was great speculation as to the theme. Having already designed the ultimate country swimming hole and the ultimate tropical lagoon, what could the imagineers come up with this time?

A melting ski lodge, of course. Blizzard Beach is built on the tongue-in-cheek premise that a freak snowstorm hit Orlando and a group of enterprising businesspeople built Florida's first ski resort. The sun returned in due time, and for a while it looked like all was lost—until someone spied an alligator slipping and sliding down one of the slushy slopes. Thus Blizzard Beach was born. The snow may be gone, but the jumps, sled runs, and slalom courses remain, resulting in a high-camp, high-thrill ski lodge in the palms.

Blizzard Beach centers on "snowcapped" Mt. Gushmore. You can get to the top via ski lift or a series of stairs, but how you get down is up to you. The bold can descend on the Summit Plummet or Slush Gusher, but there are medium-intensity flumes, inner-tube runs, and whitewater rafts as well. The motif extends into every element of the park: There is a chalet-style restaurant, Plexiglas snowmen, and innumerable sight gags like ski marks running off the side of the mountain. The original skiing alligator has returned as the resort mascot, Ice Gator.

Blizzard Beach was built in response to Typhoon Lagoon's popularity and draws huge crowds. Come early in the morning or prepare for monster waits. A Park Hopper Plus pass gets you in free; otherwise, admission is $31 for adults (and children over 9) and $25 for children 3 to 9.

Blizzard Beach Attractions

Summit Plummet
The icon of the park, this slide is 120 feet tall, making it twice as long as Humunga Kowabunga at Typhoon Lagoon. A clever optical illusion makes it seem that riders are shooting out the side of the mountain into midair; the real ride is very nearly as intense, with a 60-degree drop that feels more like 90. Top speeds on Summit Plummet reach 55 miles per hour, a full 10 miles per hour more than on Space Mountain—and you don't even have a seat belt. The height requirement is 48 inches. In short, this flume is not for the faint of heart.

Slush Gusher

This is another big slide, but this time with a couple of bumps to slow you down. Still, a big-deal thrill, akin in intensity to Humunga Kowabunga at Typhoon Lagoon.

Runoff Rapids

You take a separate set of stairs up the back of Mt. Gushmore to reach these three inner-tube rides. You'll have a choice of tubes that seat one, two, or three people. (Remember, the heavier the tube, the faster the descent.) The rapids are great fun, and each path provides a slightly different thrill, so many people try it over and over. But you'll have to carry your own raft up the seven zillion stairs (157, to be exact!); visit early in the morning before your stamina fails.

Snow Stormers

This is a mock slalom run that you descend on your belly while clutching a foam rubber "sled." The three slides are full of twists and runs that splash water back into your face, and if you'd like, you can race the sledders in the other two tubes to the bottom. Snow Stormers is so much fun that, like Runoff Rapids, hardly anyone does it only once.

Toboggan Racers

Eight riders on rubber mats are pitted against one another on a straight descent down the mountain. The heavier the rider, the faster the descent, so the attendant at the top of the slide will give kids a head start over adults. Not quite as wild as Snow Stormers, this ride is a good choice for getting kids used to the feeling of sliding downhill on a rubber sled.

Teamboat Springs

The whole family can join forces here to tackle the whitewater as a group. The round boats, which an attendant will help you board at the top, carry up to six people, and the ride downhill is zippy and fun, with lots of splashes and sharp curves. This is one of the best-loved rides in the park, drawing an enthusiastic thumbs-up from preschoolers to grandparents. Because parents and kids can share a raft, this is another good first ride to test young children's response before moving on to Snow Stormers or Runoff Rapids. It's much longer, wilder, and more fun than Gangplank Falls, the comparable whitewater ride at Typhoon Lagoon.

Downhill Double Dipper

On this individual tube ride, you go through a water curtain and tunnel, emerge into a free fall, and then exit through a long, steep tube. At one point in the ride, you're completely airborne. The Double Dipper is fun and addictive, but if your kids are young, test them on nearby Runoff Rapids first.

Ski Patrol Training Camp

This special section is designed for kids 5 to 9, and they can walk across icebergs, swing from T-bars, and test their mountaineering skills. There are medium-intensity slides as well. It's a welcome addition for families who have children too old for Tike's Peak but not quite up to the major slides.

Tike's Peak

This is the preschool and toddler section, with yet smaller slides and flumes, igloo-style forts, and a wading pool that looks like a broken ice-skating rink. A separate section for toddlers ensures that they won't be trampled by overenthusiastic 5-year-olds. There are chairs and picnic areas nearby for parents.

Chair Lift

The chair lift offers transportation to Summit Plummet, Slush Gusher, and Teamboat Springs and is also a fun ride in itself.

Melt Away Bay

Unlike the huge Surfing Lagoon at Typhoon Lagoon, this swimming area is relatively small and offers mild swells instead of big waves. Fed by "melting snow" waterfalls, the pool area is attractive and surrounded by chairs and shady huts for relaxing.

Cross Country Creek

This lazy creek circles the park. All you have to do is wade in, find an empty tube, and climb aboard. Expect major blasts of cold water as you float through the "ice cave." (There are exits before the cave if this is just a bit too authentic for you.) It takes about 25 minutes to make a full lap, and it's a pleasant experience for any age.

Helpful Hint

Don't bother bringing your own snorkels, rafts, masks, or water wings. Only official Disney equipment is allowed in the pools.

Typhoon Lagoon and Blizzard Beach Touring Tips

- ℮ The water parks draw a rowdy teenage crowd, which means young kids and unsteady swimmers may get dunked and splashed more than they like. If your children are very young, stay in the children's sections (Ketchakiddee Creek in Typhoon Lagoon or Tike's Peak in Blizzard Beach), which are off limits to older kids.

- ℮ Always crowded, the water parks are extra packed on weekends, because they're popular with locals as well as tourists.

- ℮ Many visitors arrive wearing their swimsuits under their shorts and shirts, which saves time. It's a good idea to bring your own towels, because the rental towels are small. There are plenty of lockers, which rent for $5 with a refundable deposit. The locker keys come on rubberized bands that slip over your wrist or ankle so that you can easily keep them with you while in the water.

@ You can "rent" life vests for free, although they do require a driver's license or credit card for deposit. Snorkeling equipment can be picked up for no charge at Hammerhead Fred's near the Shark Reef at Typhoon Lagoon. An instructor runs you through the basics before letting you loose in the saltwater pool.

@ Because you're climbing uphill all day, half the time dragging a tube or mat behind you, the water parks are extremely exhausting. If you spend the day at a water park, plan to spend the evening touring passive attractions, such as films or shows—or make this your parents' night out and leave the kids with a sitter.

@ The water parks are a good place to picnic, although there are also several places to get fast food.

@ The Lost Kids Station at Typhoon Lagoon is across a bridge and so far from the main water areas that lost children are very unlikely to find their way there on their own. At Blizzard Beach it's at Shoeless Joe's rentals, far from the swimming action. Instruct your children, should they look up and find themselves separated from you, to tell one of the Disney employees. (They all wear distinctive name tags.) The Disney people will escort the children to the Lost Kids Station, and you can meet them there. Because both of these parks are full of meandering

Helpful Hint

If your kids have rubberized beach shoes with nonskid bottoms, be sure to throw them in your beach bag. The sidewalks can be slippery, and the pavement can be hot.

paths, with many sets of steps and slides, it's easy to get separated from your party. Set standard meeting places and times for older kids.

@ Families visiting in the summer and who have Park Hopper Plus passes might consider visiting more than one water park—they're very different experiences. Typhoon Lagoon gets the nod for its pool area: The pool there is huge and has those incredible surfing waves. Blizzard Beach has a superior whitewater ride and more big-deal slides. Typhoon Lagoon is more relaxing and visually attractive. Blizzard Beach is the pow! park, focusing on high-speed thrills.

@ Typhoon Lagoon and Blizzard Beach are often closed for refurbishing during January and February. If you're planning a winter trip, call 407-824-4321 to make sure at least one of the parks will be open during the week you plan to visit. (They usually don't close both at once, unless it gets really cold.)

Insider's Secret

Whichever you choose, be sure to visit a water park early in your Disney World visit. Several families reported that they saved this experience until late in their trip and then found that it was the highlight of the whole vacation for their kids. "If we'd known how great it was, we'd have come every day," lamented one father. "As it turns out, we only went to Blizzard Beach once—on the morning of the day we were due to fly out."

CHAPTER

10

The Rest of
the World

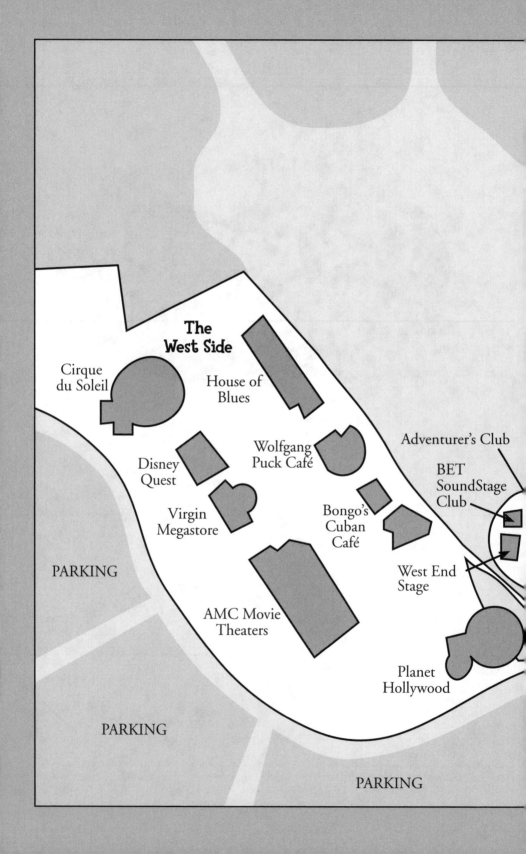

The
West Side

Cirque
du Soleil

House of
Blues

Disney
Quest

Wolfgang
Puck Café

Adventurer's Club

BET
SoundStage
Club

Virgin
Megastore

Bongo's
Cuban
Café

PARKING

West End
Stage

AMC Movie
Theaters

Planet
Hollywood

PARKING

PARKING

Downtown Disney and Pleasure Island

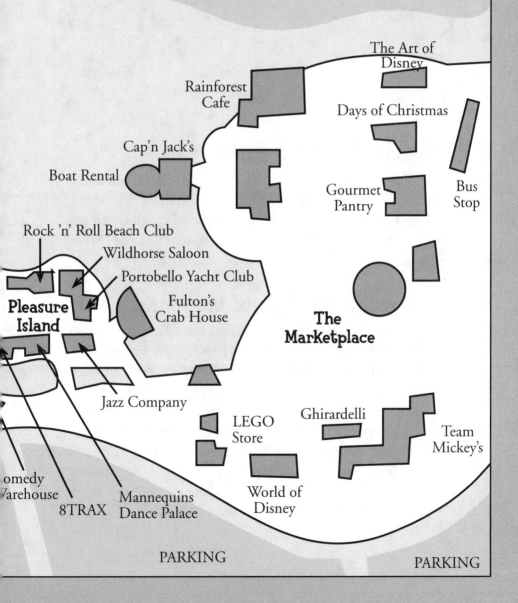

Disney Institute

The Art of Disney

Rainforest Cafe

Days of Christmas

Cap'n Jack's

Boat Rental

Gourmet Pantry

Bus Stop

Rock 'n' Roll Beach Club

Wildhorse Saloon

Portobello Yacht Club

Pleasure Island

Fulton's Crab House

The Marketplace

Jazz Company

Ghirardelli

LEGO Store

Team Mickey's

omedy Warehouse

8TRAX

Mannequins Dance Palace

World of Disney

PARKING

PARKING

Beyond the Major Parks

The major parks get much of the media attention, but many guests report that their best Disney World moments—from racing a Mouse Boat around the Seven Seas Lagoon to settling back at a comedy club—happen in the minor parks of Disney World.

Getting to the Rest of the World

Staying on site? Although the Disney transportation system does a good job of shuttling guests between the on-site hotels and the major theme parks, the system breaks down a bit when it comes to the minor parks. Always consult the transportation guide you're given at check-in for the best route from your particular resort to anywhere on Disney property. If the trip involves more than two transfers and you don't have a car with you, consider taking a cab. They're easy to get from any on-site resort, and the cost of being hauled from one end of Disney property to another is never more than 20 bucks.

Staying off site? If you have your own car, use it. Off-site hotels rarely offer shuttle service to anything other than the major parks. If you don't have a car, call a cab.

Getting to Downtown Disney

Buses run from all on-site hotels to Downtown Disney and make three stops—at the Marketplace, Pleasure Island, and West Side. Those staying at Port Orleans or Disney's Old Key West have boat service directly to the Marketplace, by far the most pleasant way to get there. In addition, on-site and off-site guests can drive directly to Downtown Disney. There is no charge for parking, but the parking lot sometimes fills at night; if so, valet parking ($6) is your best option.

Getting to the Wide World of Sports

Buses are an option, but few run to this out-of-the-way location, and those that do require transfers. Check your transportation guide for the best route from your resort. Some guests report horrific commute times, so if you have your own car, definitely drive. If not, consider a cab.

Getting from One Resort to Another

Your simplest option is to use the theme park that is nearest your home resort as a transfer station. For example, if you're staying at the Yacht Club and have dinner reservations at the Maya Grill in Coronado Springs, take the water taxi over to MGM and catch a Coronado Springs bus from there.

Helpful Hint
If you're not sure of the best way to get somewhere, ask Guest Services at your hotel. Sometimes resorts have cars and drivers or other means to help their guests get around.

Downtown Disney

The enormous entertainment, dining, and shopping complex known as Downtown Disney has three major sections: the Marketplace, Pleasure Island, and West Side. The three sections are linked by walking paths, shuttle buses, and ferry service; not surprisingly, Downtown Disney is packed at night, when the restaurants and clubs are going full force.

Families who would like to try out some of the food, shopping, and entertainment of Downtown Disney without fighting the crowds would be well advised to go in the afternoon. Explore DisneyQuest and the shops, and then eat your

The Don't-Miss List for the Rest of the World

Downtown Disney, for shopping and dining

Cirque du Soleil (expensive but unique)

DisneyQuest (if you have kids over 10)

Pleasure Island (for an adult night out)

Character Breakfasts (if you have kids under 7)

Tours (for all ages)

The Worth-Your-While List for the Rest of the World

Mouse Boats

Miniature Golfing at Winter Summerland or Fantasia Gardens

Wide World of Sports (if you're into athletics)

BoardWalk, for dining and club-hopping

main meal at a truly off time, like 4 P.M. Downtown Disney is a fun way to take a break from theme park touring in the middle of your vacation.

Downtown Disney Marketplace

World of Disney, the largest Disney store on Earth, is a great place to start. You'll find a bit of everything here, so World of Disney is the perfect place for one-stop shopping.

The Days of Christmas shop is another must-see, as is Team Mickey's Athletic Club, which features sporting equipment and clothes. The LEGO Store is just amazing, with a play area out front where

Time-Saving Tip

Warning: Buses stop at all three sections of Downtown Disney, meaning that even a direct shuttle to your resort can be a 30-minute ride, so plan accordingly.

kids can relax and build for a while; there are also stunningly complex LEGO models scattered around the lagoon. If money is no object, stop off at the Art of Disney, where you'll find Disney animation cels and other collectibles. Scrapbook hobbyists will enjoy Disney's Wonderful World of Memories next door, which offers a collection of Disney scrapbook supplies including albums, stickers, pens, and postcards.

Time-Saving Tip

Downtown Disney employs a staggered opening time during the off-season. The Marketplace usually opens at 9 A.M., with Pleasure Island and West Side opening at 11 A.M. If you have any questions about operating hours during the off-season, check with Guest Services at your hotel.

Quick Guide to Full- in the Rest

Restaurant	Description	Location
All Star Café	Loud and raucous	Disney's Wide World of Sports
Bongos Cuban Café	An Americanized version of Cuban dishes	West Side
Fulton's Crab House	Offers a variety of elegant seafood dishes	Pleasure Island
House of Blues	Cajun and Creole cooking along with blues music	West Side
Planet Hollywood	Always fun, film clips run constantly	West Side
Portobello Yacht Club	Northern Italian cuisine	Pleasure Island
Rainforest Cafe	Great fun, but long waits	Marketplace
Wolfgang Puck Café	Terrific pizzas and sushi	West Side

For descriptions of ratings, prices, priority seating, and suitability for kids, see chapter 11.

Service Restaurants of the World

Rating	Price	Priority Seating	Suitability	Details on
★★	$$	Not accepted	Moderate	Page 338
★	$$	Not accepted	Moderate	Page 339
★★	$$$	Recommended	Low	Page 344
★★	$$	Not accepted	High	Page 346
★★	$$	Not accepted	High	Page 350
★★	$$$	Recommended	Moderate	Page 350
★★	$$	Not accepted	High	Page 351
★★★	$$$	Only upstairs	Low	Page 354

The newest store at Downtown Disney is Once Upon a Toy. Just as the name implies, it's a fun stop for the kids who will be wowed by the elaborate toy displays.

The Rainforest Café is great fun because birds and fish (real) and rhinos and giraffes (fake) surround your table while you eat. Check out the incredible bar stools with their flamingo and zebra legs. Long waits are standard at the Rainforest Café, but you can always put your name in and then shop for a while until you're called.

The marketplace has a small playground and sand area, as well as neat splash fountains to keep younger kids entertained. You'll also find the largest—and possibly only?—perikaleidoscope. Or venture down to the dock at the Buena Vista Lagoon to rent one of the zippy Mouse Boats. The cost is $21 per half hour; kids under 12 must ride with an adult. Although the boats appear to be flying, they really don't go very fast, and they're a fun, safe diversion for all ages.

Hidden Mickey

Look closely at the interactive fountains near the entrance to the Marketplace. Does the shape look familiar?

Insider's Secret

Downtown Disney is a great spot for the first night of your vacation. Many families arrive in the afternoon and are understandably reluctant to use up a day on their ticket for only a few hours in the park. Downtown Disney is a great solution—it doesn't require a ticket but it still has plenty of Disney spirit and is a great way to lure everyone into the spirit of the vacation.

Pleasure Island

At the Pleasure Island Nightclub Theme Park, the motto is "It's New Year's Eve every night!" The island comes alive at 7 each evening when its three dance clubs, two comedy clubs, jazz club, and 1970s-style disco open their doors. A different featured band puts on a show each evening, winding down just before midnight, when a street party culminates in the New Year's Eve countdown, complete with champagne, fireworks, and confetti.

Money-Saving Tip
The $20 admission gives you unlimited access to all the clubs. If you have a Park Hopper Plus or Ultimate Park Hopper pass, you're entitled to free admission to Pleasure Island. At present a deal is available that gives you five extra evenings at Pleasure Island for $5—a good deal if you want to go club-hopping every night. If you just want to see the shops and restaurants of Pleasure Island, there is no admission charge until 7 P.M., when the clubs open.

Children under 18 are welcome if accompanied by a parent or guardian (except at Mannequins and the BET Sound Stage). Although Pleasure Island is clearly geared toward adults, some families do bring their kids. This is a wholesome, Disneyesque nightclub environment—that is, there's no raunchy material at the comedy club, drunks are discreetly handled, and security is tight. There's also a fair amount of entertainment right out on the street.

But if you choose Pleasure Island for parents' night out and want to make a real evening of it, get an in-room sitter for

the kids. Most hotel services close down at midnight, and if you
stay for the fireworks and street party, you won't be back until
after that. With an in-room sitter, the kids can go to bed at
their usual hour.

Pleasure Island Touring Plan

- ℮ Arrive about 8 P.M. Take in the Comedy Warehouse first.
  (The dance clubs don't gear up until later.) This 30-
  minute show, a combination of improvisation and Disney
  spoofs, is proof positive that comedians don't have to be
  profane to be funny. And because so much of the material
  is truly improvised, some guests return to the Comedy
  Warehouse several times in the course of the evening to
  see an essentially different routine each time.

- ℮ For something completely different, try the Adventurer's
  Club, a lavish, eccentric hideaway based on British hunt-
  ing clubs of the 1930s. You won't be in the bar for long
  before you realize some of your fellow patrons are actors—
  and the bar stools are sinking and the masks on the walls
  are moving. Every 30 minutes or so, a seemingly sponta-
  neous comedy routine erupts among the actors; the séance
  routines are especially memorable.

- ℮ Next, stop by the new Jazz Company, which features live
  music and draws an interesting crowd. The Jazz Company

Insider's Secret

Unfortunately, many people just walk in, peruse
the bizarre decor of the Adventurer's Club, and
leave before they have a chance to really get into
this particular brand of comedy. Give it time! The
Adventurer's Club is definitely worth an hour of
your evening. There's nothing like this back
home—unless you're from the Congo—and the
club is a favorite among Orlando locals.

has a wide selection of wines, many offered by the glass, and a light menu, so if you plan to spend a lot of time here, you may not need to eat supper first. The tables are small, the music is relatively subdued, and the clientele is more mellow.

◉ At 8Trax, polyester and disco are still king. It's fun to watch the thirty-somethings sitting in their beanbag chairs, valiantly pretending they don't remember the words to old Bee Gees' hits. At other times the club features '80s night.

◉ Divide your remaining hours between the four dance clubs. The Rock 'n' Roll Beach Club offers a live band and an informal, pool-shooting, beer-drinking, resort-style ambience; Mannequins is darker and wilder and features canned music, strobe lighting, and a revolving dance floor. Developed by Black Entertainment Television, the BET club plays jazz, soul, R&B, and hip-hop music.

Helpful Hint
Be sure to be back outside for the street party and countdown to New Year's.

BET also has concerts, featuring headliners as well as local talent. At the newest club, Motion, a DJ plays top-40 dance music.

Downtown Disney West Side

The West Side expansion of restaurants means that people staying on site without a rental car are no longer tied to restaurants of the theme parks. Far more varied dining, with a casual atmosphere suitable for families, is a bus ride away.

Bongos Cuban Café, created by Gloria Estefan, offers an Americanized version of Cuban dishes, a wildly tropical decor, and loud Latin music. Reservations are taken only for parties of 10 or more, so be prepared to put in your name and spend a while exploring the West Side. Dan Aykroyd's House of Blues serves up Cajun and Creole cooking along with some jazz, country, rock 'n' roll, and, yes, blues music. The Gospel Brunch, which offers plenty of food and an absolutely uplifting atmosphere, runs from 10:30 A.M. to 1 P.M. on Sundays and is an especially good choice for families. The price is $30 for adults (and kids over 12), $15 for kids 4 to 12. Tickets can be purchased by calling 407-934-2583 or 407-934-BLUE.

The sophisticated Wolfgang Puck Café serves terrific pizzas and sushi downstairs. Request the upstairs dining room for tonier adult dining.

The giant blue globe of Planet Hollywood holds props from a variety of movies, the bus from the movie *Speed* hovers overhead, and even the menus—printed with high school graduation pictures of stars—are entertaining. Film clips run constantly on giant screens, and the whole atmosphere is heady, loud, and cheerful.

At the West Side, you'll also find two of Disney World's hottest new attractions: DisneyQuest and Cirque du Soleil.

Helpful Hint

The West Side is also home to a variety of shops, a 24-screen AMC theater, and a Virgin Megastore, which sometimes has concerts out front.

DisneyQuest

Most people call DisneyQuest an arcade simply because there isn't a name for this totally new type of play environment. Within DisneyQuest you'll find five levels of traditional arcade games as well as high-tech interactive experiences that basically allow you to enter into a video game. For example, in Virtual Jungle Cruise you board rafts and literally pick up a paddle to help yourself steer through the rapids, and there are also games where you fly to an alien planet to rescue settlers, engage in a virtual sword fight with comic book bad guys, and become the puck in a hockey-style pinball game.

Time-Saving Tip
DisneyQuest can be overwhelmingly crowded in the afternoon and evening. If you want to try out everything, your best bet is to visit on a weekday morning.

The centerpiece attraction, the one everyone talks about, is CyberSpace Mountain. Bill Nye the Science Guy helps you design your own virtual roller coaster. You build in as many flips, spirals, and hills as you'd like; program in the speed of the car; and even get to name the sucker. When you've finished, your coaster is given a scariness rating from 1 to 5, meaning you can either design a gentle, rolling, grade-1 coaster suitable for kids or a flip-you-over, slam-you-down, rip-roaring grade-5 coaster. (If you end up with a coaster too wild or too tame for your taste, you can redesign it.) Then you enter a booth, are strapped into a car, and you ride a virtual re-creation of the route you just designed, complete with flips.

Helpful Hint
Each zone inside of DisneyQuest is large and may encompass several levels. In other words, this is a very easy place to lose your kids so be especially alert. If you're going to let older kids and teens explore on their own, pick a designated time and meeting space to regroup. Maybe you can link up at the restaurant, the Cheesecake Factory, for a snack.

Needless to say, preteens and teens can get hooked on this stuff very fast, and DisneyQuest is primarily designed for them. (Some parents park teens at the arcade while they eat at one of the West Side restaurants.) But there are games for the younger kids as well, and any age can enjoy the Create Zone, where the Animation Academy teaches how to draw a character.

Helpful Hint
Strollers are not allowed inside of DisneyQuest so plan accordingly.

DisneyQuest usually opens about 10:30 A.M. during the on-season and 11:30 A.M. during the off-season, and daytimes are the best time to go because it can become very crowded at night. Disney has tried several ticketing options for Disney-Quest, with the present plan being a single entry price ($31 for adults and kids over 9, $25 for kids 3 to 9), which lets you play as many games as you like for as long as you like—an alarming thought for the parents of an 11-year-old boy. Admission is also included with the Ultimate Park Hopper Pass—and, in fact, the Ultimate Park Hopper is a good deal *only* if you plan to visit DisneyQuest.

Cirque du Soleil

After a week at Disney World, probably the last thing you're itching to do is pay up to $82 for adults and kids over 9, $49 for kids ages 3 to 9, to watch a 90-minute acrobatic show. But the Cirque du Soleil's "La Nouba" positively wowed the families we surveyed.

More than 70 performers stage the show, which runs twice daily, five days a week (usually, 6 and 9 P.M. Thursday through Monday with matinees during the busy season, but call 407-939-7600 to confirm times and prices). Although the flexibility and athleticism of the troupe will amaze you, it's their ability to use props, sets, costumes, and their bodies to set a mood and tell a story that makes the Cirque du Soleil experience so unique. Don't expect any elephants or people being shot out of cannons; these performances are more like theater than traditional circuses. Cirque du Soleil can best be appreciated by kids ages 8 and up.

Helpful Hint

Cirque Du Soleil has now instituted different prices for different seats. The Premium Seating price—$82 for adults and kids over 9, $49 for kids from 3 to 9—is for the centrally located seats.

For more information online, check out www.cirquedu-soleil.com.

Helpful Hint

It can take quite a long bus ride to get to Downtown Disney West Side where Cirque du Soleil is located—even from an on-site hotel. Because resorts often share buses to Downtown Disney, you may have to sit through several stops before you get to the three separate bus stops at Downtown Disney itself. (The West Side stop is the last of the three.) The moral? If you have Cirque tickets, leave your hotel an hour and a half before show time.

BoardWalk and the ESPN Club

Not up for the sprawl of Downtown Disney? At night, the shops, restaurants, and nightclubs in front of the BoardWalk

Inn take on a whole new glitter. A variety of services and enter-tainment—magic acts, comics, face painting, hair braiding, and midway games—take place along the waterfront. Eat dinner at Spoodles, the Flying Fish Café, or one of the BoardWalk's other fun restaurants (arrange priority seating by calling 407-WDW-DINE), and then rent a surrey bike ($18 to $23 for 30 minutes depending on size) for a wild lap around the lagoon.

Insider's Secret

If you're at Disney World during football season, be sure to drop by the ESPN Club. The place is always mobbed with fans from all across the country cheer-ing on their teams (often in team jerseys), and it feels like it's the Super Bowl every Sunday. Seventy televisions make sure you don't miss a single play—TVs even hang inside the stalls in the bathroom!

The ESPN Club is a good stop for sports enthusiasts. The center contains a broadcast and production facility (meaning celebrity athletes are sometimes on hand) and the ultimate sports bar featuring—and I'm quoting—"the best ballpark cui-sine from around the country." This bold claim translates into sandwiches, salads, and burgers, all sized for hearty appetites.

Two clubs are open strictly to adults 21 and older. The At-lantic Dance Club offers dancing to top-40 music. There is no cover charge. Live bands appear on weekends and a DJ plays on weeknights. For details on format and hours call 407-939-2444. Jellyrolls offers dueling pianos and a sing-along bar. (There is usually a $6 cover charge on weekends.) Either club is a good alternative to Pleasure Island if you'd like some live en-tertainment but just don't have the stamina for club-hopping.

The fact that the BoardWalk is not as vast and crowded as Downtown Disney appeals to many visitors; you can have a good meal and some entertainment here without getting back into the mouse race. And at night, with the glowing Yacht and Beach Clubs visible just across the water and the fireworks of Epcot in the distance, the BoardWalk ranks as one of the most beautiful and romantic spots in all of Disney World. Pull up a rocker and let the world go by.

On-site guests can take monorails or buses to any theme park and then transfer to the BoardWalk bus. If you're staying at the Yacht and Beach Clubs, the Swan, or the Dolphin, just walk. If you have a car, you can either park in the BoardWalk lot or pay for the $6 valet parking (it's free if you're staying at a Disney resort), which is emphatically worth it on weekend evenings, when the resort parking lot tends to fill up.

Disney Extras

Disney Institute

The Disney Institute is currently closed and is in the process of becoming Disney's Saratoga Springs and Spa, a Vacation Club time-share and mixed-use facility. About 200 Vacation Club condos will be available for corporate retreats and conventions. The existing spa, performance center, and cinema will remain and a new restaurant, lounge, and pool area with water slide will be added.

Dinner Shows and Character Breakfasts

Dinner Shows

Book all the dinner shows you would like to attend before you leave home by calling 407-WDW-DINE. Reservations are accepted up to two years in advance and are especially crucial for the Hoop-Dee-Doo Musical Revue, which requires a lot of hoop-dee-doo just to get tickets. The on-site dinner shows include the following:

- *Hoop-Dee-Doo Musical Revue.* The Revue plays three times nightly (5, 7:15, and 9:30 P.M.) at Pioneer Hall in Fort Wilderness. You'll dine on ribs and fried chicken while watching a cute and lovably hokey show that encourages lots of audience participation; $49.01 (includes gratuity) for adults and kids over 12, $24.81 for kids 3 to 11, and American Express cardholders get an additional 10 percent off.

- *Disney Spirit of Aloha.* Formerly known as the Polynesian Luau, nothing much has changed except the inclusion of Lilo and Stitch to the entertainment. You'll enjoy authentic island dancing and not-particularly-authentic island food at this outdoor show at the Polynesian Village Resort. The two seatings are at 6:45 and 9:30 P.M. Prices are $49.01 for adults and kids over 12, $24.81 for kids 3 to 11.

If you're staying off site and don't want to return to the Disney World grounds in the evening, or if you've waited too late to book a Disney show, be advised that Orlando is chock-full of family-style dinner shows that can often be booked on the same afternoon.

Character Breakfasts

The character breakfasts take at least a couple of hours and probably should be skipped if you're on a very tight touring schedule—or if you're watching your pocketbook carefully. But families that stay at Disney World for four or five days give the breakfasts very high marks, especially if they schedule them

Time-Saving Tip

Families who schedule their character breakfast on the last day of their visit also note that the breakfast doesn't "mess up the day," because the last morning of the trip is usually broken up by the 11 A.M. checkout time at most Orlando hotels.

near the end of their stay, when the kids have had plenty of time to warm up to the characters.

The food is pedestrian at the character breakfasts, but who cares? Because it takes a while to meet all the characters (usually between five and seven circulate among the diners) and eat, either come early or, if you're able to make a reservation, try to book the first seating of the day. Prices generally run about $15 for adults, $8 for children. The more elaborate Sunday brunches are also more expensive: about $20 for adults, $10 for kids. Priority seating can be arranged up to 120 days in advance; call 407-WDW-DINE before you leave home.

At present Disney is offering the following character meals:

In the Resorts

- Cape May Café, Beach Club Resort, breakfast 7:30–11 A.M. with Beach Club Goofy and friends. Cost is $15.99, $8.99 for ages 3 to 11.

- Chef Mickey's Restaurant, Contemporary Resort, breakfast 7–11:30 A.M. with Mickey, Minnie, and Pluto. Cost is $15.99, $8.99 for ages 3 to 11. Dinner 5–9:30 P.M.; $20.99, $9.99 for ages 3 to 11.

Insider's Secret

Cinderella's Royal Table, the character breakfast held inside the castle in the Magic Kingdom is very popular with young girls and thus difficult to book. You MUST make your reservations at 407-WDW-DINE a full 60 days in advance to have a chance at this popular breakfast; they now require that you leave your credit card number with them, as well. Because the restaurant is small, and priority seatings difficult to come by, I wouldn't make any promises to little Hannah until I had the priority seating safely in hand.

- 1900 Park Fare, Grand Floridian Resort & Spa, breakfast 7:30–11:30 A.M. with Mary Poppins, Alice in Wonderland, the Mad Hatter, and friends. Cost is $16.99, $9.99 for ages 3 to 11. Dinner 5:30–9 P.M. with Cinderella and friends; $21.99, $9.99 for ages 3 to 11.

- 'Ohana's Character Breakfast at 'Ohana, Polynesian Resort, breakfast 7:30–11 A.M. with Mickey and friends. Cost is $15.99, $8.99 for ages 3 to 11.

Insider's Secret

If you can't get priority seating for the Cinderella breakfast, try the Princess-themed breakfast at Akershus in the Norway pavilion at Epcot where you'll meet Belle and other heroines in a castle-ish setting. Although this Epcot breakfast was added to help stem the demand for Cinderella's Royal Table in the Magic Kingdom, fewer people know about it and it's easier to get in. Another option is to try the Cinderella and friends dinner in the 1900 Park Fare restaurant in the Grand Floridian resort.

In the Theme Parks
Magic Kingdom

- Cinderella's Royal Table in Cinderella Castle, "Once Upon a Time" breakfast with Cinderella and friends, daily 8–10 A.M. Cost is $15.99, $8.99 for ages 3 to 11, plus theme park admission.

- The Crystal Palace, Pooh, Eeyore, Piglet, and Tigger, breakfast 8–10:30 A.M. is $15.99, $8.99 for ages 3 to 11; lunch 11:30 A.M.–2:45 P.M. is $16.99, $9.99 for ages 3 to 11; and dinner beginning at 3:45 P.M. until park closing is $20.99, $9.99 for ages 3 to 11, plus theme park admission.

@ Liberty Tree Tavern in Liberty Square, dinner with Minnie, Pluto, and Goofy daily from 4 P.M. until park closing. Cost is $19.99, $9.99 for ages 3 to 11, plus theme park admission.

Epcot

@ The Garden Grill Restaurant in the Land, with Mickey and friends. Family-style lunch 11:30 A.M.–4:30 P.M. costs $16.99, $9.29 for ages 3 to 11; dinner 4:30–8:10 P.M., $20.99, $9.99 for ages 3 to 11, plus theme park admission.

@ The Akershus (Norway), Princess Storybook Breakfast with Belle, Jasmine, Snow White, Sleeping Beauty, and Mary Poppins, daily 8:30–10:30 A.M. Cost is $19.99, $9.99 for 3 to 11, plus theme park admission.

Disney MGM Studios

@ Hollywood & Vine, buffets with Minnie, Goofy, and Pluto, breakfast 8:30–11:15 A.M. is $15.99, $8.99 for ages 3 to 11; lunch 11:30 A.M.–4:30 P.M. is $16.99, $9.29 for ages 3 to 11, plus theme park admission.

Disney's Animal Kingdom

@ Restaurantosaurus in Dinoland U.S.A., Donald's Prehistoric Breakfastosaurus buffet with Mickey, Goofy, Donald, and Pluto, 7:40–10:30 A.M. daily. Cost is $15.99, $8.99 for ages 3 to 11, plus theme park admission.

Helpful Hint

If you like to spend your mornings in the park, plan your character meal for lunch or dinner instead of breakfast. Waiting for all the characters to work the room can take a while but in the afternoon or evening you'll probably welcome the chance to sit and have a leisurely meal.

Jolly Holiday Packages Featuring
Mickey's Very Merry Christmas Party

Disney World is at its most magical during the holidays. Hours are extended, special parades and shows debut, and a meet-the-characters show and party runs on selected evenings. If you fantasize about seeing it snow on Main Street, this is your chance. (We're talking real snow here, not confetti. It's generated from the rooftops of Main Street and blown down on the crowd below.) Tickets for Mickey's Very Merry Christmas Party should be purchased in advance but are also included in a Jolly Holidays Package, a special all-inclusive holiday deal. Call 407-W-DISNEY for details.

It is quite possible to celebrate Christmas at Disney without getting caught in the crush. The decorations go up just after Thanksgiving, and the special shows, packages, and holiday parties begin soon thereafter. A family visiting in early December can see all the special stuff—except, of course, for the Christmas Day parade—without having to face the harrowing holiday crowds.

Helpful Hint

Mickey's Very Merry Christmas Party is great fun, but it is not a good time to try out the rides. The park is so crowded that lines, especially in Fantasyland, are far longer than usual. If you attend, forget the rides and focus on the special parades and shows.

Each hotel has its own themed decorations as well—a nautical tree for the Yacht Club, starfish and seashells at the Beach Club, Native American tepees and animal skulls for the Wilderness Lodge, and the enormous Victorian dazzler at the Grand Floridian. The themed decorations are so drop-dead fabulous that Disney offers Christmas tours of the resorts, which are popular with Orlando locals. So if you're visiting Disney World between Thanksgiving and New Year's Eve, be sure to save some time just to check out the lobbies of the on-site hotels.

Helpful Hint
If school schedules rule out an early December trip, note that the week before Christmas is slightly less hectic than the week between Christmas and New Year's Eve.

Mickey's Not-So-Scary Halloween Party

On selected evenings during the last two weeks of October, the Magic Kingdom hosts Mickey's Not-So-Scary Halloween Party. As the name implies, this celebration is geared toward younger kids, with costume parades where the kids can interact with the characters, go trick-or-treating throughout the park, visit fortune-tellers and face painters, and enjoy a special Halloween Fantasy in the Sky fireworks show. (If you have preteens and teens who are up for a far more gory scene, check out the scary Halloween Nights at Universal Studios.) The Disney party runs from 7 P.M. to midnight, and advance tickets are $26 for adults and $21 for children 3 to 9. Be sure to let the kids wear their Halloween costumes.

Insider's Secret
Mickey's Not-So-Scary Halloween Party on October 31 itself always sells out way in advance, although other dates are easier to book. Reserve tickets at least 60 days in advance by calling (407) W-DISNEY.

Tours for the Kids and Families

Most of the Disney tours require that guests be at least 14 years old to participate, but there are three special programs at the Grand Floridian that are created especially for kids and one tour in the Magic Kingdom that is designed for families with children of all ages.

These programs are not only great fun for the kids, but also a bargain in the sense that the first three are priced between $20 and $25 per child and include lunch and approximately two hours of child care. At present prices, you'd pay $16 for two hours of child care (not to mention there's a four-hour minimum for most services) and about $5 for lunch, so the program is almost a gimmie. Most important, children love these programs so much that they have all gained in popularity since being introduced and are being offered on more days of the week to accommodate the demand. Reserve your child's space in the programs before you leave home, preferably for the same time that you arrange priority seating for your meals.

Disney's Pirate Adventure

This rollicking two-hour boat tour takes kids on a treasure hunt across the Seven Seas Lagoon with stops at the marinas of all the Magic Kingdom resorts. The counselors help kids collect clues and complete a map that ultimately leads them to buried treasure. A good choice for active kids and those in the 5 to 8 age range who seem to most enjoy deciphering the clues in the treasure hunt. Lunch is served on the pontoon boat after the last stop and everyone leaves with a goodie bag of treasure.

The Adventure meets Monday, Wednesday, and Thursday from 10 A.M. until noon and leaves from the Grand Floridian Marina. Kids ages 3 to 10 may participate in this child-only event that costs $24.95. Call 407-WDW-DINE.

Wonderland Tea Party

Kids join two characters (generally Alice in Wonderland and the Mad Hatter, but this isn't guaranteed) for a tea party held at 1900 Park Fare in the Grand Floridian. The table is festively decorated and a full lunch is served, but this is a tea party in reverse, so naturally the children start with dessert. Afterwards, the characters lead them in a variety of games and each child leaves with a souvenir photo of herself with the characters.

The Wonderland Tea Party is served Monday through Friday from 1:15 to 2:30 P.M. at 1900 Park Fare in the Grand Floridian for kids ages 3 to 10 (no moms!) and the cost is $24.95. Call 407-WDW-DINE.

Grand Kid Adventures in Cooking

In order to start things off on an appropriately messy note, the children decorate their aprons and chef hats by dipping their hands into different colors of paint and then pressing them on their aprons to make bright-colored handprints. Then after a clean-up session, the resort chef helps them make a special treat such as chocolate chip muffins, strawberry shortcake, or miniature apple pies. When the food is finished the kids—in full chef regalia—parade to the Grand Floridian lobby and serve their fellow guests, including their parents, samples of what they've baked.

Adventures in Cooking is a child-only event for kids 3 to 10 and is held Tuesday and Friday from 10–11:45 A.M. The cost is $19.95. Call 407-WDW-DINE.

Family Magic Tour in the Magic Kingdom

Everyone gets into the act on this tour; while the activities are geared toward kids from 4 to 10 years of age, parents and both younger and older siblings can come along. The only rule is that you have to be willing to act silly.

Your tour guide meets you and sets up the premise of that day's tour. Perhaps, for example, Peter Pan has stolen Captain

Hook's favorite hook and the captain is so furious that his band of buccaneers is threatening to take over the whole Magic Kingdom. In order to stop him, you must follow the map that takes you all over the Magic Kingdom—hopping, skipping, jumping, and keeping an eye out for the next clue.

At the final stop of the tour you'll meet up with a character or two and have a special closing surprise. For example, if you get Peter Pan out of trouble, maybe he'll thank you by being your personal guide on the Peter Pan's Flight ride. But there are different scenarios that involve meeting different characters, so don't make any specific promises to the kids. The tour is a great option for families who have done the Magic Kingdom several times and are looking for a new and different spin.

The Family Magic Tour is held Monday through Friday from 10 A.M. until noon and is $25 per person, regardless of age. Call 407-WDW-TOUR.

That Sportin' Life: On Water

Most on-site hotels have lovely marinas with a variety of watercraft to meet every age group's needs. The two major recreational lagoons in Disney World are the Seven Seas Lagoon in front of the Magic Kingdom, which serves Fort Wilderness and the Magic Kingdom resorts, and the Buena Vista Lagoon at the Disney Village Marketplace. In addition, the Yacht and Beach Clubs share a lagoon with the Swan and the Dolphin Resorts; the Caribbean Beach Resort, Coronado Springs, and Port Orleans all have their own canals and lagoons with watercraft for rent.

Because rates at Disney World are "adjusted" frequently, it's not a bad idea to confirm rental prices in advance. In the on-season, reservations are a good idea. To make them from your hotel room or for general information on Disney World sports options, call 407-WDW-PLAY.

You do not have to be a guest of an on-site resort to rent the boats, although the marina will ask for either a resort ID or a Disney World ticket, along with a current driver's license for the larger boats. If you're staying off site and don't want to bother commuting to an on-site hotel, try the Downtown Disney Marketplace.

Water options include the following:

Boat Rental

The Disney fleet includes Mouse Boats ($21 for 30 minutes), canopy boats ($26.50 for 30 minutes), sailboats ($19 for an hour), pontoons ($34 for 30 minutes), pedal boats ($7 for 30 minutes), and canoes ($7 for 30 minutes). The most popular are the Mouse Boats, those zippy little two-passenger speedboats you see darting around the Buena Vista and Seven Seas Lagoons. Drivers must be 12 years old (14 at Downtown Disney), although kids of any age will enjoy riding alongside Mom and Dad.

Waterskiing

A boat, a driver, and full equipment can be rented at Fort Wilderness, the Polynesian, the Grand Floridian, and the Contemporary marinas. The cost is $140 an hour for up to five people, and reservations can be made 14 days in advance by calling 407-824-2621.

Fishing

Angling is permitted in the canals around Fort Wilderness. Rent rods and reels at the Bike Barn. You can fish from shore or take a canoe or pontoon boat deeper into the canals. Resort guests can also drop a line at Port Orleans, Riverside.

Want a Bit More Action?

Guided two-hour expeditions leave daily from Port Orleans, and up to five people can be accommodated for $197 ($80 for each additional hour), which includes the boat, the guide, the equipment, and snacks. Trips also depart daily from the Downtown Disney marina. Make reservations up to 14 days in advance by calling 407-WDW-PLAY.

Swimming

All the Disney World hotels have private pools, but the pools at the Swan and the Dolphin are best for serious swimmers because they have special lanes reserved for laps. Several resorts—the Wilderness Lodge, Coronado Springs, the BoardWalk, and Port Orleans—boast elaborately themed pool areas, some of which almost qualify as miniature water parks.

Surfing

Surfing lessons are sometimes offered at Typhoon Lagoon before the park opens. Call 407-WDW-PLAY for details.

That Sportin' Life: On Land

Tennis

Several on-site hotels (the Contemporary, the Grand Floridian, the Yacht and Beach Clubs, the Disney Institute, the Swan, and the Dolphin) have courts that can be reserved 24 hours in advance. Call 407-824-3578 for details. The tennis courts at Fort Wilderness and Disney's Old Key West are free and operate on a first-come, first-served basis.

There is considerable variation in fees. A court costs $15 at the Grand Floridian, the Contemporary, the Swan, and the Dolphin; tennis is $5 at Disney's Old Key West; and at the Yacht and Beach Clubs the court use is free on a first-come, first-served basis, but they allow you to hold a court if you so wish for $10.

If you'd like private lessons or to participate in a clinic, consider staying at the Contemporary, which has lessons for

$60 an hour. You can also get a package that allows the entire family court time for the duration of your stay. The Contemporary also runs clinics that include a videotaped analysis of your play by the club pro. Call 407-824-3578 for details.

Golf

There are five courses on the Disney World grounds, with greens fees running about $150 for Disney World hotel guests, about $175 for those staying off site. With such pricey fees, anyone planning to golf a lot should consider the World Adventure or some other package. (Disney Club members also get price breaks.) Or you can play in the early evening, when twilight fees drop to as low as $60.

The five courses are the Palm and Magnolia, two fairly demanding courses located near the Magic Kingdom; the Lake Buena Vista Course, which is near the Disney Institute Villas; and Osprey Ridge and Eagle Pines, which share the Bonnet Lakes Golf Club.

To reserve a tee time or arrange for participation in a golf clinic, call 407-WDW-GOLF. Disney World guests can make tee-off and lesson reservations up to 30 days in advance; those staying off site can (and should) make reservations seven days in advance.

Miniature Golf

Fantasia Gardens, an 18-hole miniature golf course across the street from the Disney-MGM Studios, is real eye-candy because of the whimsical statues of characters featured in the classic movie *Fantasia*. The course itself is fairly challenging, with caves, tunnels, and moving obstacles. A second course, Fantasia Fairways, is a miniature version of a real golf course, with sand traps, water hazards, and roughs. The holes are up to 100 feet long, but you play them with a putter. It's difficult enough to drive a veteran golfer to curses, and probably not a good choice for kids.

Both courses are different enough from your miniature golf course back home to justify the time and money invested. Prices are $9.75, $7.75 for kids 3 to 9. For more information, call 407-560-3000.

"Would you like to play in snow or sand?" That's the first question you're asked at Disney's Winter Summerland, the miniature golf course located near Blizzard Beach. Your first clue that there's strange weather ahead: Santa, his sleigh pulled by flamingos, has crash-landed on the roof and skidded through a combination snowbank-sandbank into the wackiest campground on earth.

If you opt to play the icy white "greens" of the winter course, you'll find a snow castle, slalom ski runs, a hockey rink where the sticks are obstacles, and a snowman who squirts you when you successfully sink a putt. Holiday music fills the air, but next door on the summer course the Beach Boys serenade you amid sand castles, pools, and barbecues—and an occasional snoring Santa taking a break on the beach. (Those in the know say summer is the more challenging season—must be all those sand traps.)

Helpful Hint

Although the special effects are cute, Fantasia Gardens is a fairly tough course and best reserved for older kids. Winter Summerland is a better choice for the school-age and preschool set.

There are plenty of surprises on the course, and at least three hidden Mickeys. Rates are $9.75, $7.75 for kids 3 to 9. Just pay the guy in the Winterbago.

Running

Jogging trails cut through the grounds of nearly every Disney World hotel. Consult Guest Services for a map of your particular resort. Wilderness Lodge, with its invitingly shady trails, is an especially good choice for runners.

Horseback Riding

Guided trail rides leave the Fort Wilderness grounds five times a day. Disappointingly, children under 9 are forbidden, even though the horses are gentle and the pace is slow. The cost is $31, and reservations can be made up to 14 days in advance. Call 407-824-2621 for reservations and information before you leave home.

Helpful Hint

If younger kids really want to saddle up, short pony rides are offered from 10 A.M. to 5 P.M. during the on-season at the petting farm at Fort Wilderness, for a cost of $3. No reservations are necessary, but if you want to see if the ponies are available on the particular day of your visit, call 407-824-2832.

Health Clubs and Spas

The Contemporary, Grand Floridian, Swan, Dolphin, Yacht and Beach Clubs, BoardWalk, Animal Kingdom Lodge, Coronado Springs, and Disney's Old Key West all have health clubs, and the cost is anywhere from $8 to $15 per visit, with reduced length-of-stay rates—well worth it when you consider that most of the health clubs have whirlpools and saunas, a nice

Insider's Secret

There are full spa facilities at the Grand Floridian and Animal Kingdom Lodge. A massage can be a lifesaver on day four of a seven-day trip.

wrap-up to a day spent walking around the theme parks. Most of the health clubs are for the exclusive use of that particular hotel's guests, but the facilities at the Contemporary, Swan, and Dolphin are open to all on-site guests.

Cycling

Bikes ($7 an hour or $21 a day) or tandems ($8 an hour) can be rented at the Bike Barn in Fort Wilderness, at the Disney Institute Villas, or at Port Orleans, Coronado Springs, Disney's Old Key West, the Wilderness Lodge, and the Caribbean Beach Resort.

Still have questions? You can get general sports information by calling 407-824-2621.

Disney's Wide World of Sports

This multimillion-dollar complex houses competitions, tournaments, and vacation fitness activities with facilities to accommodate 25 different sports. It's the spring-training home of the Atlanta Braves, and the training site for the Harlem Globetrotters. The facility allows Disney to play host to a wide variety of tournaments and sports festivals. To find out who's playing while you're there, call the Sports Line at 407-363-6600.

The Wide World of Sports also offers the Multi Sport Experience, an interactive playground that challenges guests in a variety of sports including football, baseball, basketball, hockey, soccer, and volleyball. The Multi Sport Experience is included in the General Admission to Wide World of Sports and the Ultimate Park Hopper ticket but it is only offered on select days, which are listed at www.disneyworldsports.com. Children under 18 must be accompanied by an adult.

Entrance to the entire Wide World of Sports complex is $10, $7.50 for kids 3 to 9; call 407-363-6000 for details. Afterward, have lunch at the official All Star Café, where big screens show constant sports events, and there is a slew of athletic memorabilia.

CHAPTER

11

Dining
at Disney

Full-Service Restaurants at Disney

You've come to ride, but you also need to eat. The good news is that the variety and quality of the on-site restaurants has vastly improved in the 11 years I've been doing this guide. The bad news is that as the size of the parks and the crowds has increased, so has the hassle factor in getting seated at your favorite restaurant. Read on for tips on how to choose the best spot for your family—and get in with minimal fuss.

They don't take "reservations" at Disney. Just as employees are "cast members," customers are "guests," and rides are "attractions," reservations are called "priority seating." It's the same basic idea, but it doesn't hold the Disney World restaurants to as specific a time frame. Let's say you have priority seating for four people at 7 P.M. When you show up at seven, your table won't be waiting with your name on it, but you will be given the next available table for four. Waits average between 10 and 30 minutes under the system, but it is far better than being a walk-in.

Time-Saving Tip

Priority seating can be arranged 60 days in advance at the Magic Kingdom, with Cinderella's Royal Table now requiring a credit card number as well. Priority seating can be arranged 120 days in advance at Epcot. (Except for Bistro de Paris, which takes reservations only 30 days in advance.) At MGM, you can arrange priority seating 120 days in advance for lunch, 60 days in advance for dinner. At the Animal Kingdom, only one restaurant accepts priority seating and that's for the character breakfast called Donald's Prehistoric Breakfastosaurus. That restaurant accepts priority seating bookings 120 days in advance, as do all other character dining venues. Confusing, huh?

So how do you arrange priority seating? If you're staying at a Disney resort, you can make the arrangements before you leave home by calling 407-WDW-DINE. Most restaurants take priority seating 60 days in advance, while others—most notably the dinner shows and character breakfasts—will let you arrange priority seating 120 days in advance. If you're staying at a Disney hotel but aren't sure what your schedule will be—or which restaurants look the coolest—you can arrange priority seating from your hotel room by pressing the dining button on your phone.

Insider's Secret

Remember that the character breakfast at Cinderella's Royal Table is THE hot ticket in Disney dining. You must make reservations 60 days in advance to have a prayer of getting in.

For guests staying off site, it's a bit trickier because each theme park has its own system. Except for their character breakfasts, the Animal Kingdom takes no priority seating. (This is probably because they have only one full-service restaurant, the Rainforest Café. If you want to eat there, just show up, get a buzzer, and wait.) At the Magic Kingdom, you go directly to the restaurant in question on the day you visit. Go as early in the morning as possible.

In MGM, drop by the reservations booth at the corner of Sunset Boulevard and Hollywood Boulevard as soon as possible after you enter the park. They have menus for all the full-service restaurants for you to look at. At Epcot—which, thanks to all the international eateries throughout the World Showcase, has by far the most dining options—arrange priority seating at the WorldKey Information Center beside Spaceship Earth.

If you're staying off site and would like to dine at a restaurant in a Disney resort, such as the wonderful California Grill in the Contemporary, either let Guest Relations at your own hotel handle it for you or call 407-WDW-DINE.

Definition of Restaurant Ratings

Food Quality
★★★   A big-deal meal
★★   Decent food
★   Okay in a pinch

Price
$$$ Expensive; adult dinner is about $20 and up
$$ Moderate; adult dinner is about $15
$ Inexpensive; adult dinner is about $10

Priority Seating

Not Offered: This restaurant does not accept priority seating, unless you have a party of 10 or more. Your best bet is to show up at an off time, get a buzzer, and shop or explore nearby areas while you wait for your table.

Suggested: This restaurant is rarely crowded, which may mean that the type of food is unfamiliar to most Disney World guests, the restaurant isn't very good, or it's a perfectly fine place that happens to be in an out-of-the-way location. Unless you're dining during peak hours or touring during a crowded time of the year, you'll probably be able to be seated as a walk-in.

Recommended: This restaurant draws average crowds. Unless you're touring in the off-season or dining at off hours, you'll need to arrange priority seating either from the theme parks or, if you're staying at an on-site hotel, from your room.

Necessary: This is a popular restaurant; arrange priority seating before you leave home.

Suitability for Kids

High: Not only is the place informal, with at least a few food choices designed to appeal to kids, but there's also either some sort of entertainment going on or the locale itself is interesting.

Moderate: This restaurant is reasonably casual and family-oriented.

Low: This is one of Disney World's more adult restaurants, with a romantic ambience, sophisticated menu choices, and leisurely service.

Restaurant Descriptions

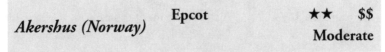

Akershus (Norway)	Epcot	★★ $$ Moderate

There's a buffet, so you get your food fast and have the chance to see things before you make a selection. But most of the food

Quick Guide to Full-

Restaurant	Description	Location
Akershus (Norway)	Lots of fish, picky eaters may rebel	Epcot
All Star Café	All sports, all the time	Disney's Wide World of Sports
Artist Point	Excellent food in a rustic setting	Wilderness Lodge
Biergarten (Germany)	Rousing, noisy atmosphere	Epcot
Big River Grille & Brewing Works	Casual restaurant located on the BoardWalk	BoardWalk
Bistro de Paris (France)	Classic French cuisine, very elegant, very adult	Epcot
Boatwright's Dining Hall	Specializes in tame Cajun cooking	Port Orleans, Riverside
Bongos Cuban Café	Offers an Americanized version of Cuban dishes	West Side
California Grill	One of WDW's absolute best	Contemporary
Cape May Café	Breakfast buffet is very popular	Beach Club Resort
Le Cellier Steakhouse (Canada)	A good spot for beef and salmon—as well as buffalo	Epcot
Chef Mickey's Restaurant	At character breakfast Mickey and crew wander among diners	Contemporary
Les Chefs de France (France)	The ambience of a Paris sidewalk café	Epcot
Cinderella's Royal Table	A chance to meet the princess and her pals	Magic Kingdom
Citricos	Outstanding wine selection	Grand Floridian

Service Restaurants

Rating	Price	Priority Seating	Suitability	Details on
★★	$$	Recommended	Moderate	Page 329
★★	$$	Not accepted	Moderate	Page 338
★★	$$	Recommended	Moderate	Page 338
★	$$	Recommended	High	Page 338
★	$$	Not accepted	Moderate	Page 338
★★★	$$$	Necessary	Low	Page 339
★	$$	Suggested	Moderate	Page 339
★	$$	Not accepted	Moderate	Page 339
★★★	$$$	Necessary	Moderate	Page 339
★★★	$$	Recommended	High	Page 340
★★	$$	Recommended	Low	Page 340
★★	$$	Recommended	High	Page 340
★★★	$$$	Necessary	Moderate	Page 340
★★	$$$	Necessary	High	Page 341
★★★	$$$	Necessary	Low	Page 341

(continued)

Quick Guide to Full-

Restaurant	Description	Location
Concourse Steakhouse	Open, airy, and a bit loud	Contemporary
Coral Café	Themed buffets in the evening	Dolphin
Coral Reef Restaurant	Great view of the Living Seas tank	Epcot
The Crystal Palace	Winnie the Pooh visits guests as they dine	Magic Kingdom
ESPN Club	A great place to watch the game	BoardWalk
50's Prime Time Café	Want to be in a 1950s sitcom?	MGM
Flying Fish Café	One of WDW's absolute best	BoardWalk
Fulton's Crab House	Offers a variety of elegant seafood dishes	Pleasure Island
The Garden Grill Restaurant	American dishes and the Disney characters	Epcot
Grand Floridian Café	Great variety, pleasant ambience	Grand Floridian
Gulliver's Grill at Garden Grove	Whimsical decor, basic food	Swan
Hollywood & Vine Cafeteria of the Stars	Large, attractive art deco cafeteria	MGM
The Hollywood Brown Derby	Elegant and lovely	MGM
House of Blues	Cajun and Creole cooking along with blues music	West Side
Jiko—The Cooking Place	African cooking, open wood-burning stoves	Animal Kingdom Lodge

Service Restaurants

Rating	Price	Priority Seating	Suitability	Details on
★★	$$$	Recommended	Moderate	Page 341
★	$$	For large parties	Moderate	Page 342
★★	$$$	Necessary	High	Page 342
★★	$$	Recommended	High	Page 342
★	$	Not accepted	Moderate	Page 343
★★	$$	Recommended	High	Page 343
★★★	$$$	Necessary	Low	Page 344
★★	$$$	Recommended	Low	Page 344
★★	$$	Recommended	High	Page 344
★★	$$	Suggested	Moderate	Page 344
★★	$$	Suggested	High	Page 345
★★	$	Suggested	High	Page 345
★★★	$$$	Recommended	Moderate	Page 345
★★	$$	Not accepted	High	Page 346
★★★	$$$	Recommended	Moderate	Page 346

(continued)

Quick Guide to Full-

Restaurant	Description	Location
Juan and Only's	Food is plentiful and tasty	Dolphin
Kimonos	The mood is hushed, unrushed, and not for kids	Swan
Kona Café	Pacific Rim food with a tropical emphasis	Polynesian
Liberty Tree Tavern	"Sunday dinner cuisine" and the characters in Revolutionary garb	Magic Kingdom
Mama Melrose's Ristorante Italiano	Pasta with a wacky New York ambience	MGM
Marrakesh (Morocco)	Exotic surroundings and belly dancers	Epcot
Maya Grill	Desserts alone worth the trip	Coronado Springs
Narcoossee's	Some of the best fresh seafood in Disney World	Grand Floridian
Nine Dragons Restaurant (China)	Cuisine representing every region in China	Epcot
1900 Park Fare	Buffet-style, home to some of the best character meals	Grand Floridian
'Ohana	Family-friendly place	Polynesian
L'Originale Alfredo di Roma Ristorante	Most popular restaurant in the World Showcase	Epcot
Palio	Gourmet Italian in a colorful setting	Swan
Planet Hollywood	Always fun, film clips run constantly	West Side
The Plaza Restaurant	Try the sundaes	Magic Kingdom

Service Restaurants

Rating	Price	Priority Seating	Suitability	Details on
★★	$$	Recommended	Moderate	Page 346
★★	$$	For large parties	Low	Page 347
★★	$$	Suggested	Moderate	Page 347
★★	$$	Recommended	High	Page 347
★★	$$	Suggested	Moderate	Page 347
★★	$$	Suggested	Moderate	Page 348
★★	$$	Recommended	Low	Page 348
★★	$$$	Recommended	Low	Page 348
★★	$$	Suggested	Moderate	Page 348
★★	$$	Recommended	High	Page 349
★★	$$	Recommended	High	Page 349
★★	$$$	Necessary	Moderate	Page 349
★★	$$$	Recommended	Moderate	Page 350
★★	$$	Not accepted	High	Page 350
★★	$$	Recommended	High	Page 350

(continued)

Quick Guide to Full-

Restaurant	Description	Location
Portobello Yacht Club	Northern Italian cuisine	Pleasure Island
Rainforest Cafe	Great fun, but long waits	Animal Kingdom/ Disney Marketplace
Rose & Crown Dining Room (UK)	Pub atmosphere and live entertainment	Epcot
San Angel Inn Restaurant (Mexico)	Gorgeous and romantic	Epcot
Sci-Fi Dine-In Theater Restaurant	Way campy—you'll eat in cars	MGM
Shula's	Linebacker-sized steaks in an elegant atmosphere	Dolphin
Shutters	Caribbean fare for the family	Caribbean Beach Resort
Spoodles	Mediterranean cuisine, great tapas	BoardWalk
Teppanyaki Dining Room (Japan)	Chefs slice and dice in the best Benihana tradition	Epcot
Tony's Town Square Restaurant	*Lady and the Tramp* theme and generous servings	Magic Kingdom
Victoria and Albert's	The most elegant of all Walt Disney World restaurants	Grand Floridian
Whispering Canyon Café	Comfort food, family-style service	Wilderness Lodge
Wolfgang Puck Café	Terrific pizzas and sushi	West Side
Yacht Club Galley	A fine choice for breakfast	Yacht Club Resort
Yachtsman Steakhouse	One of the premier steak houses in Disney World	Yacht Club Resort

Service Restaurants

Rating	Price	Priority Seating	Suitability	Details on
★★	$$$	Recommended	Moderate	Page 350
★★	$$	Not accepted	High	Page 351
★★	$$	Recommended	Moderate	Page 351
★★	$$	Recommended	Moderate	Page 351
★★	$$	Recommended	High	Page 351
★★★	$$$	Recommended	Low	Page 352
★★	$	Suggested	Moderate	Page 352
★★	$$	Recommended	Moderate	Page 353
★★	$$$	Necessary	High	Page 353
★★	$$	Recommended	High	Page 353
★★★	$$$	Necessary	Low	Page 354
★★	$$	Suggested	High	Page 354
★★★	$$$	Only upstairs	Low	Page 354
★★	$$	Suggested	Moderate	Page 354
★★	$$$	Necessary	Low	Page 355

is apt to be unfamiliar to the kids, and there's a lot of fish, so picky eaters may rebel. A fine spot for hearty eaters because you can load up at the hot and cold buffet tables. Also a good chance to sample a variety of unusual dishes. The new princess character breakfast is very popular.

All-Star Café	Wide World of Sports Complex	★★ Moderate	$$

This sports bar is the only full-service restaurant at Disney's Wide World of Sports complex. There's lots of sports memorabilia on the walls, as well as TVs blaring sporting events. The mood is loud and raucous, like that of a Planet Hollywood or Hard Rock Café. Expect pizza, sandwiches, pasta, and burgers.

Artist Point	Wilderness Lodge	★★ Moderate	$$

The most upscale of the Wilderness Lodge eateries, Artist Point offers excellent food in a casual—almost rustic—setting. Best known for the maple-glazed salmon, Artist Point features the cuisine, wines, and artwork of the Pacific Northwest.

Biergarten (Germany)	Epcot	★ High	$$

There's plenty of room to move about; a rousing, noisy atmosphere; and entertainment in the form of yodelers and an oompah-pah band. The food, served up buffet style, is nothing special. There are certainly better choices in the World Showcase.

Big River Grille & Brewing Works	BoardWalk	★ Moderate	$$

This casual restaurant is Disney World's only on-site brew pub. It's a good place to sample four new beers and a couple of spe-

cialty ales, but the food—a variety of chicken, ribs, and sal-ads—is pedestrian. Outdoor dining allows you to take in the action of the BoardWalk while you eat.

Bistro de Paris *(France)*	Epcot	★★★	$$$
			Low

The Bistro is quieter, calmer, and more elegant than its sister, Les Chefs de France, which is located below it, down on the street. It is also a tad too civilized for kids under 10. Expect classic French cuisine, a wonderful wine selection, and un-rushed service. An added bonus: Request a table by the window at 9 P.M. and you'll see the fireworks of IllumiNations.

Boatwright's *Dining Hall*	Port Orleans Resort, Riverside	★	$$
			Moderate

This sit-down restaurant at Riverside specializes in very tame Cajun cooking. The catfish, crawfish, and bouillabaisse are de-signed to suit mainstream American palates, and the unwalled rooms mean that it is always noisy.

Bongos Cuban Café	West Side	★	$$
			Moderate

Created by Gloria Estefan, Bongos offers an Americanized ver-sion of Cuban dishes, a wildly tropical decor, and loud Latin music. Reservations are taken only for parties of 10 or more, so be prepared to put in your name and spend a while exploring the West Side.

California Grill	Contemporary Resort	★★★	$$$
			Moderate

This Contemporary Resort restaurant is very popular. One clue to the quality: Disney executives dine here. Not only does the

California Grill offer a marvelous variety of cuisine, with stylish preparation, but the views from the top of the Contemporary are also unparalleled, especially during the Magic Kingdom fireworks. Excellent wine selection.

Cape May Café	Beach Club Resort	★★★	$$ High

A bright and airy eatery in the heart of the Beach Club, Cape May Café has an excellent seafood buffet at dinner, featuring shrimp, scallops, clams, fish, and a couple of landlubber choices like ribs. The breakfast buffet, during which the characters circulate among the diners dressed in adorable old-fashioned bathing attire, is very popular.

Le Cellier Steakhouse (Canada)	Epcot	★★	$$ Low

Nothing much going on here in terms of entertainment or setting, but the steaks and salmon are tasty. Exotic choices such as buffalo or venison are also on the menu, and the desserts are as big as the prairies of Alberta.

Chef Mickey's Restaurant	Contemporary Resort	★★	$$ High

The Contemporary Resort is a fun setting for a character breakfast as Mickey and crew wander among the diners and the monorail whisks by overhead. The evening buffet features pasta, chicken, prime rib, and a variety of salads and vegetables.

Les Chefs de France (France)	Epcot	★★★	$$$ Moderate

Older kids might be wowed by the atmosphere and the chance to order a croquette de boeuf en brioche—surely the classiest

hamburger they'll ever wolf down. A great view of all the World Showcase action.

| *Cinderella's Royal Table* | Magic Kingdom | ★★ | $$$ High |

Located in Cinderella Castle in Fantasyland and nestled high amid the spires of the castle, this restaurant is the most glamorous in the Magic Kingdom. Prime rib is one of the specialties, and the food, even at lunch, is whimsically presented.

Cinderella appears downstairs throughout the day to greet diners and pose for pictures. (Ask what times she is scheduled before you make your reservation.)

The "Once Upon a Time" character breakfast, featuring the Cinderella gang (and sometimes other "princess" characters such as Snow White or Belle), is $15, $8 for kids ages 3 to 11. Priority seating is necessary—and notoriously difficult to obtain.

| *Citricos* | Grand Floridian | ★★★ | $$$ Low |

Citricos offers southern French cuisine in the Grand Floridian. Citricos is known for its outstanding wine list—up to 20 selections are available by the glass, with a specific wine paired with each appetizer and entrée on the menu. A real treat for parents' night out!

| *Concourse Steakhouse* | Contemporary Resort | ★★ | $$$ Moderate |

Located in the cavernous lobby of the Contemporary Resort, the Steakhouse offers all the beef you'd expect, as well as chicken, shrimp, salmon, and pasta. A nice getaway spot for lunch if you're in the Magic Kingdom.

| *Coral Café* | **Dolphin Resort** | ★ | $$ |
| | | | **Moderate** |

A coffee shop by day and a buffeteria by night, the Coral Café is the largest restaurant in the Dolphin Resort. In the evenings, there are often themed buffets such as Italian night or seafood night. Although the service is fast and the food is plentiful, there are better dining choices in the Swan and the Dolphin. Note: Changes in format may be coming.

| *Coral Reef Restaurant* | **Epcot** | ★★ | $$$ |
| | | | **High** |

One whole wall is glass, giving diners a remarkable view of the Living Seas tank. Ask for a lower level for the best view. This restaurant has undergone its share of staff changes and menu revamping over the years and at some times has been better than at others. Last year they brought in a new chef, so maybe the Coral Reef is finally ready to reach its full potential.

| *The Crystal Palace* | **Magic Kingdom** | ★★ | $$ |
| | | | **High** |

Located between Main Street and Adventureland, the Crystal Palace buffets offer a wide variety of food—even that most elusive of all Magic Kingdom foods, vegetables. The characters from Winnie the Pooh visit guests as they dine. Because of the characters, the presence of children's favorites on the buffet, and the hefty dessert bar, the Crystal Palace is a good choice for families. During the crowded season, the restaurant serves three character buffets a day.

The Crystal Palace is especially busy from noon to 2 P.M., so you should aim to go in midafternoon. Priority seating is suggested but not always necessary if you're eating at a really off time, like 4 P.M.

| ESPN Club | BoardWalk | ★ $ |
| | | Moderate |

Anchoring one end of the BoardWalk, the ESPN Club is better known for its TVs, which simultaneously broadcast every sporting event you can imagine, than for its food. Selections include buffalo wings, burgers, nachos, and beer. There's an arcade next door to entertain the kids. It can get packed on weekends when the big games are broadcast.

| 50's Prime Time Café | MGM | ★★ $$ |
| | | High |

With its kitsch decor and ditsy waitresses dressed like June Cleaver, this restaurant is almost an attraction in itself. Meatloaf, macaroni, milkshakes, and other comfort foods are served in a 1950s-style kitchen while dozens of TVs blare clips from classic sitcoms in the background.

"Hi, kids," says your waitress, pulling up a chair to the Formica-topped table. "You didn't leave your bikes in the driveway, did you? Let me see those hands." Assuming that you pass her clean-fingernails inspection, "Mom" will go on to advise you on your food choices. "I'll bring peas with that. Vegetables are good for you."

The camp is lost on young kids, who nonetheless love the no-frills food and the fact that "Mom" brings around crayons and coloring books and then hangs their artwork on the front of a refrigerator with magnets. But it's baby-boomer parents, who were raised on the sitcoms that the restaurant spoofs, who really adore the place. The tacky Tune-In Lounge next door is decorated with exact replicas of the furniture my parents had in their den 40 years ago. Much of MGM is dedicated to nostalgia, but this is nostalgia on a small and extremely enjoyable scale. You can fill up at lunch or dinner for about $10 per person, and the

s'mores—so huge that they cover the pink Fiestaware plate—can be split by the whole family for dessert. (The dessert menu is on a Viewmaster!) Priority seating is advised.

| *Flying Fish Café* | BoardWalk | ★★★ | $$$ Low |

The zany, art deco decor is by Martin Dorf, who also designed the California Grill and Citricos, and the menu changes weekly. The risottos are wonderful, and all the fish dishes excellent, especially the potato-wrapped snapper served with leeks and a cabernet sauvignon reduction. The steaks, charred in herbs on the outside, juicy and tender on the inside, are phenomenal too. One of the best bets in all of Disney World.

| *Fulton's Crab House* | Pleasure Island | ★★ | $$$ Low |

Located on the moored Empress Lilly riverboat, Fulton's offers a variety of elegant seafood dishes.

| *The Garden Grill Restaurant* | Epcot | ★★ | $$ High |

Easily recognizable American dishes, served family style, with some of the food grown in the greenhouses downstairs. The booths are large, so you can stretch out, and the restaurant rotates, allowing diners to observe scenes from the Living with the Land pavilion's boat ride below. Best of all, the characters, dressed in gingham and dungarees, circulate among the diners.

| *Grand Floridian Café* | Grand Floridian | ★★ | $$ Moderate |

If you'd like a good solid meal of traditional favorites, simply served, with a pretty view of the Grand Floridian grounds, the

café is for you. Another good choice for a hearty breakfast and the desserts, especially the Key lime pie, are outstanding.

Gulliver's Grill at Garden Grove	**Swan Resort**	★★	$$ High

This is the largest restaurant in the Swan and, like the Coral Café at the Dolphin next door, it has a bit of a split identity. There's a breakfast buffet in the morning; soups, salads, and sandwiches at lunch. In the evening, Garden Grove becomes Gulliver's Grill, a tribute to Gulliver's Travels. The food is the traditional chicken, steak, and pasta, as well as themed buffets, but the decor is whimsical and fun.

Hollywood & Vine Cafeteria of the Stars	**MGM**	★★	$ High

This large, attractive art deco cafeteria offers a wide variety of chicken. Character breakfasts and lunches are extremely popular—be sure to arrange priority seating in advance.

The Hollywood Brown Derby	**MGM**	★★★	$$$ Moderate

Signature Cobb salad as well as veal, pasta, and fresh seafood are served at the Derby, where, not surprisingly, caricatures of movie stars line the walls. What may surprise you is the quality of the food. This is probably the best WDW restaurant within a theme park. The restaurant itself is elegant and lovely—like stepping back to Hollywood in its heyday, complete with a grand piano. Lunch for an adult will run about $18, dinner $25. Priority seating is advised.

| House of Blues | West Side | ★★ | $$ |
| | | | High |

Dan Aykroyd's House of Blues serves up Cajun and Creole cooking along with some jazz, country, rock 'n' roll, and, yes, blues music. The Gospel Brunch runs from 10:30 A.M. to 1 P.M. on Sundays. The price is $30, $15 for kids 4 to 12; children 3 and under are free. Tickets can be purchased by calling 407-934-2583 or 407-934-BLUE.

| Jiko— The Cooking Place | Animal Kingdom Lodge | ★★★ | $$$ |
| | | | Moderate |

Jiko is the flagship restaurant of the Animal Kingdom Lodge, and the food is contemporary African cuisine with an emphasis on fresh vegetables, grains, and game. Because of the cultural diversity—French, Malaysian, Indian, and English influences abound—African cuisine may be the original fusion cooking. Swahili for "cooking place," Jiko features two wood-burning stoves to simulate the effect of cooking in the open bush. One of the best restaurants on the property and the interesting wine list is exclusively South African.

| Juan and Only's | Dolphin Resort | ★★ | $$ |
| | | | Moderate |

Another Dolphin Resort restaurant, another funky decor—this one designed to invoke a Mexican jail. (Somehow I suspect they're not really this clean or friendly.) Although the Tex-Mex is predictably tame, the food is plentiful and tasty.

| *Kimonos* | Swan Resort | ★★ | $$ |
| | | | Low |

If you love sushi and sashimi, you'll adore the austerely elegant Kimonos in the Swan Resort. The servings are fresh, delicious, and beautifully presented. The mood is hushed, unrushed, and not for kids.

| *Kona Café* | Polynesian Resort | ★★ | $$ |
| | | | Moderate |

The Kona Café offers Pacific Rim food with a tropical emphasis. The fish dishes are especially good, and the desserts are a feast for the eyes and the palate. The banana-stuffed French toast served at breakfast makes parental eyes glaze over with sheer sugary sweetness, but kids love it, and indeed it's one of the most famous breakfasts in all of Disney World.

| *Liberty Tree Tavern* | Magic Kingdom | ★★ | $$ |
| | | | High |

Located in Liberty Square and decorated in a style reminiscent of colonial Williamsburg, the Tavern serves salads, sandwiches, and clam chowder at lunch. The evening menu offers classic American cuisine—a sort of "dinner at Grandma's" with turkey and dressing, pot roast, and mashed potatoes. An evening character dinner, featuring the characters in Revolutionary War–era garb, is $20, $10 for kids 3 to 10. Priority seating is suggested.

| *Mama Melrose's Ristorante Italiano* | MGM | ★★ | $$ |
| | | | Moderate |

This restaurant is tucked away near the *MuppetVision 3-D* plaza and serves "gourmet" brick-oven pizza and a wide variety of

tasty pasta dishes. Expect a rather wacky New York ambience and fairly quick service. The pizzas are a reasonably cheap alternative for lunch; if everyone wants pasta, expect to pay about $12 a head. Occasional specials allow kids to eat free. Priority seating is advised.

Marrakesh *(Morocco)*	Epcot	★★ $$ Moderate

This restaurant offers exotic surroundings, and kids enjoy the belly dancers. The unfamiliarity of the food may pose a problem, but the children's portions are not as spicy as those served to the adults, so if the kids can be persuaded to give it a try, they'll find that roasted chicken tastes pretty much the same the world over.

Maya Grill	Coronado Springs	★★ $$ Low

Unfortunately, the Maya Grill no longer serves the exotic nuevo Latino cuisine that it originally offered. The food is still good but much more pedestrian: pork chops, fish, and chicken.

Narcoossee's	Grand Floridian	★★ $$$ Low

Situated in the white octagonal building on the water at the Grand Floridian, Narcoossee's offers fresh seafood as well as pretty views.

Nine Dragons *Restaurant (China)*	Epcot	★★ $$ Moderate

There isn't much entertainment going on, but the staff is quite happy to accommodate special requests such as, "Can you hold

the sweet and sour sauce on the sweet and sour chicken?" You'll find food from every region of China.

| *1900 Park Fare* | **Grand Floridian** | ★★ | $$ High |

This attractive restaurant, located in the Grand Floridian Resort, is appealing to families because it offers buffets. Ergo, there's a wide variety of choices for picky eaters and you can be assured of getting your food fast. 1900 Park Fare is home to some of the best character meals in all of Walt Disney World. Call 407-WDW-DINE to see which characters will be appearing during your visit. One caveat: Thanks to the pipe organ and all the kiddies, 1900 Park Fare can get very loud.

| *'Ohana* | **Polynesian Resort** | ★★ | $$ High |

A fun family-friendly place in the Polynesian, 'Ohana specializes in skewered meats, tropical fruits and vegetables, and teriyaki- and citrus-based sauces. The food is prepared before your eyes in a large open pit, and there is often some sort of activity, such as hula dancing lessons or limbo contests, to keep kids entertained.

| *L'Originale Alfredo di Roma Ristorante* | Epcot | ★★ | $$$ Moderate |

The Alfredo in question is the gentleman who created fettuccine Alfredo. This is the most popular restaurant in the World Showcase, usually the first to book up despite the fact that the food is pretty much your standard Italian.

| *Palio* | Swan Resort | ★★ | $$$ |
| | | | Moderate |

The Swan is home to this gourmet Italian trattoria. Although the food is upscale (and a bit pricey), the restaurant is informal and cheerful, with brightly colored flags hanging from the rafters. (Which makes sense, because *palio* is Italian for "flag.")

| *Planet Hollywood* | West Side | ★★ | $$ |
| | | | High |

Planet Hollywood is always fun. The giant blue globe parked right beside Pleasure Island holds props from a variety of movies, the bus from the movie *Speed* hovers overhead, and even the menus—printed with high school graduation pictures of stars—are entertaining. No reservations are taken, and the place can get packed at mealtime.

| *The Plaza Restaurant* | Magic Kingdom | ★★ | $$ |
| | | | High |

The Plaza's sandwiches, burgers, and salads are very filling. Try the milkshakes or the staggeringly large sundaes, which are trotted over from the Sealtest Ice Cream Parlor next door. The Plaza is moderately priced and open for lunch and dinner. Priority seating is advised.

| *Portobello Yacht Club* | Pleasure Island | ★★ | $$$ |
| | | | Moderate |

Northern Italian cuisine, including veal, pasta, grilled chicken, and wonderful appetizers. The patio is especially nice in the spring.

| *Rainforest Cafe* | Animal Kingdom/ Downtown Disney Marketplace | ★★ | $$ High |

The Rainforest Cafe is great fun because birds and fish (real) and rhinos and giraffes (fake) surround your table while you eat. Check out the incredible bar stools with their parrot and zebra legs. Long waits are standard at the Rainforest Cafe, but you can always put your name in and then shop for a while until you're called.

| *Rose & Crown Dining Room (UK)* | Epcot | ★★ | $$ Moderate |

This restaurant has a pub atmosphere with live entertainment, charming service, and simply prepared food. The prime rib is probably the best dish on the menu. The inside décor is a bit slapdash but, if you opt to eat outside, you can watch the FriendShips go by on the lagoon.

| *San Angel Inn Restaurant (Mexico)* | Epcot | ★★ | $$ Moderate |

A beautiful location inside the Mayan pyramid of the Mexico pavilion with the Rio del Tiempo murmuring in the background. The service is swift and friendly, and kids can browse among the market stalls of the Mexican pavilion or ride El Rio del Tiempo while waiting for the food. One of the best bets in Epcot.

| *Sci-Fi Dine-In Theater Restaurant* | MGM | ★★ | $$ High |

At least as campy as the 50's Prime Time Café, the Sci-Fi seats diners in vintage cars while incredibly hokey movie clips run on a giant screen and carhops whiz by on roller skates. Standard

fare such as milkshakes and popcorn are on the menu, but more elaborate dinners such as seafood and St. Louis style ribs are also offered. Kids adore the setting and give the Sci-Fi high marks. Be sure to ask about the light-up ice cubes. At the Sci-Fi even the Cokes are happening!

Dark and surprisingly quiet—the kids get so absorbed in the movies that there's little yelling and squealing going on— the Sci-Fi is a good place to refresh and regroup after a morning of vigorous touring. Adults should expect to pay about $12 for lunch or $18 for dinner, and, once again, portions are enormous. Priority seating is advised.

| *Shula's* | **Dolphin** | ★★★ | $$$ |
| | | | Low |

The Dolphin's newest restaurant is an upscale steakhouse brought to you by former Miami Dolphins coach Don Shula. (Quite a nice tie-in!) The restaurant is relaxed and elegantly casual, with subtle use of football memorabilia. You'll need an NFL-sized appetite to finish the 48-ounce Porterhouse or 4-pound lobster. *Note:* This is not, repeat not, a family restaurant. The menu pointedly says: "No children's menu available."

| *Shutters* | **Caribbean Beach** | ★★ | $ |
| | **Resort** | Moderate | |

Located in the Caribbean Beach Resort, Shutters is a Caribbean-themed restaurant, featuring jerk chicken, seafood dumplings with papaya salsa, and French toast bread pudding with roasted bananas and coconut ice cream.

| *Spoodles* | BoardWalk | ★★ | $$ |
| | | Moderate |

The cuisine at this lively and bustling BoardWalk restaurant is Mediterranean, featuring everything from pasta to tapas to couscous. It's fun to try the appetizers, which give you a chance to have just a taste of an unfamiliar dish, so you often end up dining more or less family style. Excellent variety and a favorite of many of our readers.

| *Teppanyaki* | Epcot | ★★ | $$$ |
| *Dining Room (Japan)* | | High |

Located in the Japan pavilion of Epcot's World Showcase, Teppanyaki offers teppan dining at large tables where the chefs slice and dice in the best Benihana tradition. Kids enjoy the presentation, which the chefs often jazz up a bit in their honor, and sometimes ladies circulate among the diners demonstrating origami folding as well.

| *Tony's Town Square* | Magic Kingdom | ★★ | $$ |
| *Restaurant* | | High |

Located in the Main Street Hub, this thoroughly enjoyable restaurant is dedicated to *Lady and the Tramp*, with scenes from the popular film dotting the walls and a statue of the canine romantics in the center. The cuisine, like that of the café where Tramp wooed Lady, is classic Italian, and the portions are generous.

Tony's is moderately priced and open for breakfast, lunch, and dinner. Priority seating is advised.

Victoria and Albert's	Grand Floridian	★★★	$$$
			Low

Extraordinarily elegant cuisine and presentation—with special attention to details such as personalized menus and roses for the ladies. The ultimate spot for parents' night out.

Whispering Canyon Café	Wilderness Lodge	★★	$$
			High

Prepare to saddle up and ride stick ponies to your table at this family-style eatery in the Wilderness Lodge. Buckets of chicken, ribs, beef, and veggies are brought straight to your table. If you'd like home cooking in a casual atmosphere where the kids can run wild, this is a good bet.

Wolfgang Puck Café	West Side	★★★	$$$
			Low

The Wolfgang Puck Café serves terrific pizzas and sushi downstairs. Request the upstairs dining room for tonier adult dining. Visit on an evening when you have a sitter for the kids and are heading over to Pleasure Island.

Yacht Club Galley	Yacht Club Resort	★★	$$
			Moderate

Located right off the main drag in the Yacht Club Resort, the Yacht Club Galley serves up fish, chicken, and beef in a cheerful nautical-themed room. A fine choice for breakfast, where the buffet offers hearty eaters the chance to load up for a day of touring.

| *Yachtsman* | Yacht Club | ★★ | $$$ |
| *Steakhouse* | Resort | | Low |

I'm not sure how a yachtsman gets his hands on so much good beef, but this is one of the premier steakhouses in Disney World. Offering a full selection of hand-cut steaks and chops, with your choice of sauces, the Yachtsman is expensive and low key and has the feel of a comfortable private dining room.

Finding Healthful Food

Restaurants that serve meals meeting the low-fat standards set by the American Heart Association are indicated with a red heart on the theme park map. Chefs at most sit-down restaurants are quite willing to adapt recipes, serving sauces on the side and leaving out forbidden ingredients.

Fruit stands can be found on Main Street and in Liberty Square at the Magic Kingdom, near Echo Lake and on Sunset Boulevard in MGM, and between the China and Germany pavilions at Epcot. They make it easier for families on the move to select grapes or watermelon instead of chips or ice cream and also provide juice instead of the omnipresent theme park soft drink.

Vegetables can be harder to find. Try the Crystal Palace in the Magic Kingdom, the Garden Grill Restaurant at Epcot, and the Hollywood & Vine Cafeteria of the Stars at MGM. The 50's Prime Time Café is also a good choice for home cooking—and as an added bonus your server will actually force the kids to finish their green beans.

The Disney Cruise Line

The Disney Cruise Line Vacation Package

The number of cruise passengers who are bringing the kids along has risen more than 10 percent in the past two years. A coincidence? Probably not. In the summer of 1998, the Disney Cruise Line's first ship, *Disney Magic*, began sailing from Port Canaveral; a second ship, *Disney Wonder*, joined the fleet in 1999. The full seven-day vacation package combines a stay at Disney World with a three- or four-day cruise. (The longer cruise means a shorter stay in Orlando—your call.) In August 2000, *Disney Magic* began offering a seven-day cruise as well.

The Three- and Four-Day Cruises

Ports of call include Nassau and Disney's own private island, Castaway Cay. (The only itinerary difference between three- and four-day cruises is that the longer cruise has a full day at sea.) In Nassau, the shopping is great, but Castaway Cay is the real jewel. You can enjoy a whole day of beach activities—youth counselors lead the kids on a "whale excavation," while older kids join their counselors for a special party on the far side of the island and adults recuperate on a white-sand beach.

The goal is to make the vacation "seamless" by eliminating all the check-ins, long waits, and innumerable hassles associated with many cruise vacations. You're met at the Orlando airport and transported directly to your resort, where you will find waiting all documentation you need for the entire week. The key to your hotel room will be the key to your stateroom on the ship, and you can use it as a charge card both at Disney World and on the ship.

Disney cruises are perfect for the family who needs a bit of everything in the course of a one-week vacation: time for the adults to relax alone, get a massage, and have a meal without the kids as well as time together as a family. Families whose kids vary in ages are especially sold on the cruises because there are so many kids on board and the age categories in the youth program are very tight, making it equally likely that your 3-year-old and 13-year-old will have each found a friend by the end of the first day. Let's face it—nothing is more relaxing than a vacation where everyone is happy.

To order a brochure and video, call 800-511-1333 or contact your travel agent.

Helpful Hint

After you've enjoyed three or four days in Disney World, you simply leave your bags in your room and board a comfortable motor coach for the 90-minute drive to Port Canaveral. When you get to the terminal, no further check-in is needed; simply go directly to your stateroom, and your luggage is delivered within a few hours. The vacation package is designed so that the more relaxing cruise segment follows the rather exhausting theme park segment of the week.

The Seven-Day Cruise

For families who have already visited the theme parks several times or who want a little more time at sea, *Disney Magic* offers a seven-day cruise that visits several ports of call throughout the Caribbean.

The Eastern Itinerary includes stops in St. Marten, St. Thomas, St. John, and Castaway Cay. The Western Itinerary stops in Key West, Cozumel, Grand Cayman, and Castaway Cay. Shore excursions include everything from snorkeling and regatta races to submarine tours and trips to the Mayan ruins.

While on board, you'll have the same perks as the three- and four-day cruises, but because the seven-day trip has three full days at sea, some extras have been added—a new magic-themed stage show, nighttime tropical celebrations, champagne brunches, and high teas.

Approximate Costs

Calculating the exact cost of your cruise depends on a few key factors—the time of year, the size of your family, and the level of cabin or stateroom you choose. It's probably a little too late to do anything about the size of your family, but the other two factors are within your control. Guests booking a suite on the ship will lodge at the Grand Floridian during the Orlando part of their vacation; families in an ocean-view stateroom with veranda will stay at a deluxe resort like the Polynesian or Beach Club; and if you choose an inside stateroom on the ship, while in Orlando you'll stay at one of the midpriced resorts like Port Orleans Resort.

All the staterooms on board are new and nice, designed for families and therefore 25 percent larger than standard cruise ship cabins—so it's really just a matter of how much space you're willing to pay for and how posh a resort you want in Orlando.

Money-Saving Tip

As for time of year, off-season savings are not as great as you might imagine; late August to mid-December is value season, when rates are about 10 percent cheaper. Spring and summer are the regular season; the holiday weeks around Christmas and Easter are slightly more expensive.

For example: A family of four taking the full seven-day vacation during the summer and staying in a deluxe ocean-view stateroom during their cruise and the BoardWalk during the land segment of the vacation should expect to pay about $6,000. If that same family going that same week is willing to book a regular-sized stateroom and stay at Port Orleans, the price drops to the $4,500 range.

The price includes round-trip airfare to Orlando, your lodging on the ship, your lodging in Orlando, theme park tickets, meals and entertainment on the ship, and transportation between the Orlando airport, your Disney World hotel, and Port Canaveral. In short, most things are included except for your meals during the Orlando segment of the trip and any extras, such as a massage or snorkeling instruction, that you elect to add.

Money-Saving Tip

Early-booking discounts can lower the total cost by as much as $700 per vacation, but they are available only during periods when booking is slow. It never hurts to try to get an early-booking discount or at least an upgrade to a better stateroom or resort.

The cost of the seven-day cruise is slightly less than the seven-day land-and-sea package. At present, the seven-day cruise averages about $4,000 for a family of four, but if you want a larger stateroom or are sailing at a popular time, that cost is more likely to be around $5,000. To check out all your options and figure exact costs, call 800-951-3532 or visit the Web site at www.disneycruise.com.

Lodging

Lodging is all about location and size. Your cruise brochure contains sketches of all the different cabins, ranging from a standard inside stateroom—which is designed for three people but can sleep four in a pinch—to a two-bedroom suite, which can easily sleep seven people. The majority of the staterooms are in the deluxe ocean-view category, many of them with verandas, and most are about 200 to 250 square feet. (In fact, almost 75 percent of the cabins are outside staterooms, so if you're planning to save a few bucks by booking an inside stateroom, call early.)

Because you're in your cabin so rarely, cruise veterans recommend focusing more on the resort you'll be staying at in Orlando. Once your travel agent has told you the resorts that are available in the price category you've selected, turn to chapter 2 of this book and decide which one is best for you. Then choose the corresponding stateroom on the ship. If you're taking the seven-day cruise, the size and location of your stateroom is more of a factor, because you will be at sea for three full days.

Dining

Disney makes dining on board very special. For starters, you don't dine in the same restaurant every night. "We figured that a family on vacation wouldn't ordinarily eat at the same restaurant three nights in a row," says Amy Foley of the Disney Cruise Line. "So why would a family on a cruise ship want to eat in the same dining room every night?"

Instead, you experience "rotation dining," trying a different onboard restaurant each evening of your cruise. (Your server and tablemates rotate right along with you.) On *Disney Magic* there is Lumiere's, which is decidedly French and the most elegant of the eateries, based on *Beauty and the Beast.* On the *Wonder*, you'll find upscale seafood at Triton's.

Insider's Secret

Palo, the adults-only restaurant, serves the best food on both ships and is very popular. So popular, in fact, that if you want to book a table, you'll need to go to the restaurant immediately upon boarding the ship to make your reservation. Otherwise you risk being shut out.

On both ships there's Parrot Cay, where the mood and the food are Bahamian and casual, but Animator's Palate is the real show-stopper, an interactive dining experience in which the restaurant transforms into a brilliant palette of color as you dine. As the meal begins, the room is black and white, right down to the framed cartoon sketches on the wall and the servers' somber attire. With each course, color is added—to the artwork, the table settings, and the servers' costumes.

On both *Disney Magic* and *Disney Wonder*, adults have a fourth dining option, Palo, an Italian restaurant perched high atop the ship, offering a sweeping view of the ocean. It offers by far the best food on both ships. The excellent wine-tasting classes are held there as well.

Ports of Call

The three- and four-day cruises spend one day in Nassau, giving guests a chance to shop, sightsee, or play the slot machines. There are shore excursions, aimed toward families, and kids of all ages are apt to enjoy a horse-drawn carriage ride, but, frankly, the Nassau stop exists to placate the adults on board who miss the presence of a casino. Parents of very young children report that—especially if they want to go shopping in the crowded straw market—it was easier to leave the children on board in the kids' program than try to take them along.

The seven-day cruise offers a choice of itineraries, available on alternating weeks. The Western Itinerary calls at Key West, Grand Cayman, Cozumel, and Castaway Cay. The Eastern Itinerary takes in St. Martin, St. Thomas, and Castaway Cay. Shore excursions are offered at every stop, but if you can afford to take in only one, consider introducing the kids to snorkeling. Both Grand Cayman in the Western and St. Thomas in the Eastern offer snorkeling, and both offer a better variety of fish and coral than you'll find on Castaway Cay. (Most kids 8 and older, assuming they're reasonably strong swimmers, can master the mask and tube. Everyone has life jackets, so you can periodically bob and rest.)

Insider's Secret

Disney Cruise Line guests can now reserve shore excursions in advance. Prior to their sailing, guests receive shore excursion information and can call or fax DCL Special Services to sign up for shore excursions any time within 60 days of their sail date. This is a great option, because it eliminates the biggest hassle most families face upon boarding—that is, the mob scene at the shore excursion desk.

Castaway Cay

All the cruises stop at Castaway Cay, a private island where you disembark at the pier (cutting out the time-consuming tender-boarding process often required when a large ship stops at a small island) and stroll onto a pristine beach. Once there, you can rent sailboats or sea kayaks, snorkel, bike, play volleyball, or simply sun yourself. Lunch is cooked right on the island, a party band plays all day, and, in case you left your sunscreen back in the cabin, you can even shop. Castaway Cay is primitive in the same sense that Gilligan's Island was—in other words, not very.

The children's program leads youngsters on scavenger hunts, whale excavations, and sand castle–building contests; older kids are allowed to explore the whole island under the watchful care of the counselors. Teens get to play a version of "Survivor Island." Adults can go to the mile-long quiet beach, sip a piña colada, or have an open-air massage in a private cabana. The setup is perfect for families, allowing a mix of time together and time apart.

Kids' Programs

Disney's Oceaneer Club for kids ages 3 to 8 covers almost an entire deck of the ship, a welcome change from the cramped and depressing quarters many cruise lines designate for youth programs. The Disney characters are often on hand, and the well-trained, unbelievably upbeat counselors lead the youngsters in games, crafts, parties, and costumed plays.

Kids 9 to 12 hang out in Disney's Oceaneer Lab, which has computers, electronic games played on giant video walls, and plenty of games and contests to get the preteen crowd interacting with one another. Teens have their own space, called Common Grounds, designed to resemble a coffee bar.

Helpful Hint
In-room sitting can be arranged if parents of younger kids want to have a late night out without worrying.

Activities run all day long and into the evening, so you can pretty much drop off and pick up the kids whenever you want.

When families first board the ship, counselors meet with parents to explain the program and help kids ease in. Parents are given a pager so that they can be reached at any time.

Insider's Secret
Children, already overwhelmed by the size and newness of the ship, sometimes suffer a bit of separation anxiety at the first drop-off. Try to persuade them to join the activities that first evening, when everyone is new and fast friendships are made. The counselors are trained to look for shy or nervous children and help them make a smooth transition into the group's activities.

There are three pools on board: one, shaped like Mickey, with a pint-sized tube slide for little kids; a second "sports pool" for games and the rowdier activities of older children; and a third "quiet pool" for adults.

Onboard Entertainment

The cornerstone of onboard entertainment is the 975-seat Walt Disney Theater, one of the most technologically advanced theaters in the world and certainly the most remarkable facility of its kind on any cruise ship. Here Disney showcases Broadway-style shows, some of them new and some based on Disney classics. These are must-see productions, especially *Disney Dreams*, which is shown on the final evening.

Studio Sea, a family lounge, provides dance music, family-oriented cabaret acts, and participatory game shows starring the audience. The Mickey Mania trivia game is a real blast. At the top of the ship, check out the ESPN skybox, where sports fans are surrounded by multiple screens broadcasting sports events from around the world. The Buena Vista Theater shows a variety of Disney movies daily.

Insider's Secret

The onboard spa offers a range of services, including some designed exclusively for couples. Even just hanging out in the beautiful sauna and steam area is a great way to kill an afternoon. If you want to book a massage or facial, especially on a day when the ship is at sea, go immediately to the spa after boarding the ship to make an appointment. Otherwise the best times get snatched up.

Adults can congregate in the entertainment districts, dubbed Beat Street on *Disney Magic* and Route 66 on *Disney Wonder*. Expect a comedy club with an improv troupe, a dance club that alternates between rock and country-and-western music, and a sophisticated piano bar.

To learn more about the Disney Cruise Line, check out prices, or book a vacation, visit www.DisneyCruise.com on the Web, or call 888-DCL-2500.

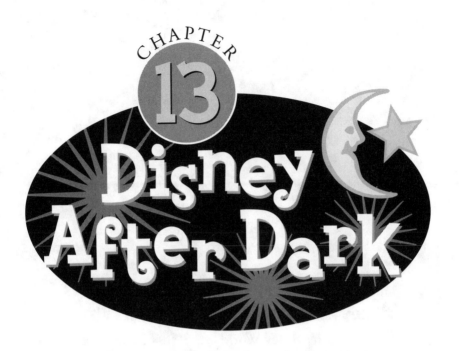

CHAPTER

13

Disney
After Dark

Disney World After Dark with the Kids

Is there life in Disney World after 8 P.M.? Sure there is. The crowds thin, the temperature drops, and many attractions are especially dazzling in the dark. Orlando is a town that naps but never sleeps, where miniature golf courses and McDonald's stay open all night. During peak seasons the major theme parks even stay open until midnight, so it's easy to have fun at night. But needless to say, the particular kind of fun you'll have depends on whether the kids are with you.

Evening Activities for the Whole Family

The Evening Parade in the Magic Kingdom

SpectroMagic, the current incarnation of Disney's ever-popular evening parade, blends lasers, lights, and fireworks for a dazzling display. The parade runs only on selected evenings during the off-season but every night during the on-season. In the busiest weeks, there are two showings; the 11 P.M. parade is rarely as crowded as the 9 P.M. one.

Insider's Secret
The evening light parade is a don't-miss. If you're visiting during the off-season, plan your schedule to ensure that you'll be in the Magic Kingdom on one of the evenings it's slated to run.

Fantasmic!
Likewise, this evening show at MGM is a must-see.

IllumiNations at Epcot
IllumiNations can be viewed from anywhere around the World Showcase Lagoon at Epcot closing time. With fireworks, laser lights, stirring music, and choreographed fountains spurting in three-quarter time, IllumiNations is a definite must-see.

The Electrical Water Pageant
If you're staying on site, the Electrical Water Pageant may actually float by your hotel window, because it is staged on the Seven Seas Lagoon, which connects the Polynesian, Contemporary, Grand Floridian, and Wilderness Lodge resorts. Times vary with the season, but generally you can see the Pageant at 9 P.M. from the Polynesian, 9:20 from the Grand Floridian, 9:45 from Wilderness Lodge, and 10:05 from the Contemporary. (Call Guest Services at your hotel for exact show times.)

If you're not staying on site, simply ride the monorail to the resort of your choice. The Electrical Water Pageant plays every night, even during off-season. Although it's a much shorter and less elaborate show than SpectroMagic or *Fantasmic!*, nothing can beat the effect of multicolored lights twinkling on darkened water.

Arcades

It's no secret that kids flip for arcades, and all on-site hotels and most off-site ones have them. The most state-of-the-art games are at DisneyQuest in Downtown Disney.

Downtown Disney

The Marketplace and Pleasure Island stores stay open past the park closing times. Some families wait to shop until late at night, and the restaurants here serve food past 10 P.M. as well.

Fireworks

A rousing fireworks display is visible from anywhere in the Magic Kingdom at about 10 P.M. during the on-season. The show is short but exciting, and at holiday times a more extensive fireworks extravaganza is presented. (Be there a few minutes early to witness Tinkerbell's Flight.)

The Rides at Night

At Epcot it is easier to ride big-name attractions like Test Track and Mission: Space during the dinner hour when everyone heads to dine in the World Showcase.

In the Magic Kingdom, the Big Thunder Mountain Railroad is much more fun in the dark; Splash Mountain feels like a totally different ride, and Cinderella's Golden Carrousel is especially magical at night.

Helpful Hint

Those attractions with the two-hour lines at noon are far more accessible at night, so it's worth revisiting any ride you passed by earlier in the day.

Likewise, at MGM, you can slip onto the Twilight Zone Tower of Terror or the Rock 'n' Roller Coaster while people troop toward *Fantasmic!*

Night Swimming

Blizzard Beach, Typhoon Lagoon, and River Country all run extended hours in the summer, and the crowds are far thinner after 5 P.M. It stays hot in Orlando well into a summer evening, and, because you don't have to worry about heat exhaustion or sunburn, many families with young kids actually prefer evening swimming. Hotel pools stay open very late as well, some until after midnight.

Miniature Golf

Nighttime is the best time to check out Fantasia Gardens or Winter Summerland.

BoardWalk

Lively and gorgeous at night, the BoardWalk is a hub of family-style activity. After dinner you can rent a surrey bike, try the midway games, or have your face painted or your hair wrapped.

Disney World After Dark Without the Kids: Finding a Sitter

Why would any decent parent seek a sitter while on a family vacation? Consider this scenario: Meaghan's sucking the inside of her mouth. Loud. Mom keeps making everyone stop while she readjusts the strap of her shoe to accommodate the blister she picked up halfway around the World Showcase Lagoon. You spent $168 to get through the Magic Kingdom gates—and Devin spends the entire afternoon feeding quarters into the same arcade game that's in the local mall back home. Dad has been singing the first line—and only the first line—of "Zip-a-Dee-Doo-Dah" since Thursday. You've asked to see the kiddie menus from nine different restaurants in nine different Epcot countries, and you end up at the America pavilion fast-food joint because Kristy won't eat anything but a hot dog. It's 108 degrees, this trip is costing $108 an hour, and that infernal sucking sound is getting on your last nerve. In short, you have third-day-itis—and it's only the second day of your trip.

Helpful Hint

Although it may seem un-American or even sacrilegious to suggest building time apart into the middle of a family vacation, the truth is that everyone will have more fun if you occasionally break up the group for a while. Even the most devoted of families aren't accustomed to being together 24 hours a day—for every meal, every ride, every potty stop. Every minute.

Some of the hotels in Orlando have responded with programs designed to get the kids involved with other kids so that parents can have some peace and privacy. Kristy can eat her hot dog, Meaghan can make sucking noises, and Devin can play Cosmic Invaders 77 straight times without parental glares. The adults can dare to order a meal that will take three hours to enjoy and can linger over their coffee. Everyone returns refreshed and recharged, with some happy stories to tell, and you can start the next day actually glad to be together again.

If you decide to schedule a parents' night out during your trip, you'll soon learn that Orlando offers an array of child care options. Several of the on-site hotels have full-fledged kids'

Insider's Secret

The key point is to make your plans before you leave home, either by selecting a hotel that has a kids' club or by arranging for an in-room sitter. If you suddenly get an urge for fine dining at 4 P.M. on a Saturday in July, it will be hard to find a sitter. But if you've checked out your options in advance, it's a breeze.

clubs, and where else on earth can your child be bedded down by a real-life Mary Poppins? Among the off-site hotels, there is a large range in cost and quality among the child care programs; many of the off-site programs are free to hotel guests (at least during certain hours), which can mean big savings for parents.

In-Room Sitters

You'll need to arrange for an in-room sitter if any of the following conditions apply:

- You have a child under the age of 4. Very few of the organized kids' clubs will accept children younger than 4, and most require that all children be potty-trained. (Under Florida law, children must be 3 and potty-trained to participate in a group care situation without their parents.)

- You plan to be out after midnight. Most kids' clubs close down at midnight, some as early as 10 P.M. Parents headed for Pleasure Island or Church Street Station, where the action doesn't begin to heat up until 10 P.M., need in-room sitting.

- Your kids are exhausted. If you know in advance that you plan to employ an all-out touring schedule, or your children fall apart after 8 P.M., hire an in-room sitter who can put them to bed at their usual time. Most of the kids' clubs at least try to put preschoolers down in sleeping bags by 9 P.M., but this can involve moving them, and possibly waking them, when parents return.

- You have a big family. Even with the add-on per-child rate, you'll come out cheaper with an in-room sitter than you will trying to book five kids into a program.

If you decide you'll need in-room sitting, begin by contacting your hotel. Many hotels are happy to arrange the sitting for you through a licensed and bonded agency, and this saves a bit of hassle. The person at the Guest Services desk is also apt to give you a good recommendation on which service to try; if guests aren't pleased with a sitter or a service, the hotel is undoubtedly the first to hear about it.

Want to make your own plans? For those staying on site, Kids' Night Out provides trained sitters for all the Disney hotels; call 407-827-5444 at least eight hours in advance. The rate is $13.50 an hour, $15.50 an hour for two kids, and there's a four-hour minimum.

At least six independent agencies dispatch sitters to the off-site hotels, but the following two agencies have received especially high marks from our readers:

| ABC Mothers | 407-857-7447 |
| Super Sitters | 407-382-2558 |

These services stay busy during the summer months, so it's not a bad idea to book them before you leave home. Rates are typically about $10 an hour with a four-hour minimum and an extra-child charge of $2 an hour per child. An $8 transportation fee is also common, meaning that in-room sitting for two kids for four hours runs close to $50—not a cheap option, but for many parents it's well worth the cost.

On-Site Kids' Clubs

The following on-site hotels have kids' clubs (all are area code 407):

Animal Kingdom Lodge	938-3000
BoardWalk	939-5100
Polynesian	824-2000
Contemporary	824-1000
Wilderness Lodge	824-3200
Dolphin	934-4000
Yacht and Beach Clubs	934-8000
Grand Floridian	824-3000

The clubs generally run in the evening for kids 4 to 12. The clubhouses are well stocked with Disney-themed toys—as well as computers, video and arcade games, and large-screen TVs. The cost is $8 an hour, and reservations

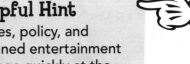

Helpful Hint

Prices, policy, and planned entertainment change quickly at the kids' clubs, so confirm everything when you make your reservations.

are required. (Not much advance notice is needed, but you can make reservations by contacting Guest Services at the appropriate hotel; on-site guests get first crack at the available slots, but if the clubs don't fill up, space is available to off-site visitors.) The clubhouses open between 4 and 5 P.M. and run until midnight, and cookies and milk are served at bedtime. Kids must be toilet-trained—even Mary Poppins has her limits.

The Polynesian offers the most elaborate kids' program, the Neverland Club, with buffet food and entertainment for the youngsters. Cost is $8 per hour; call 407-939-3463 to make reservations. This program is so popular with kids that some families have listed the Neverland Club as one of their children's favorite Disney World attractions.

Dining Without the Kids

Certain on-site restaurants are more enjoyable without children, so once you've found a sitter, reserve a table for two at one of these establishments.

Bistro de Paris	Romance Factor ♥♥♥♥	$$$

Located upstairs from Les Chefs de France and accessible by a back staircase entrance, the Bistro is a lovely secluded spot with excellent French fare. The wine list is one of the best in Epcot, and you find few kids at the Bistro de Paris, making it the perfect getaway when you need a break and some adult time.

Victoria and Albert's   Romance Factor ♥♥♥♥ $$$

For a very special evening, there is one place in Disney World so elegant and so removed from the classic Disney image that you'll never feel sticky fingers creeping over the top of the booth behind you. Kids are never seen at Victoria and Albert's in the Grand Floridian, where harp music plays, candles flicker, and ties and jackets are required for men.

Where Disney has built a reputation on providing pleasure to the masses, this 50-seat restaurant proves there is also room in Disney World for highly individualized service. When Henry Flagler built the railroad that opened Florida to the oil magnates of the late 1800s, Queen Victoria and Prince Albert sat on the British throne. Now, in one of those "only Disney would go to such trouble" details, all hosts and hostesses in the restaurant call themselves Victoria or Albert.

Your menu will have your own name handwritten on the top; waiters describe the selections for the evening, and the chef often circulates among the tables. At the end of a six-course meal, ladies are presented with long-stemmed roses and their menus. This is the most expensive restaurant in Disney World,

Insider's Secret

What's more special than an evening at Victoria and Albert's? An evening at the chef's table. Visitors are seated inside the kitchen where chef Scott Hummel treats them as his private guests. The chef's table is the proverbial "once in a lifetime" gourmet experience, and you need to reserve months in advance. Call 407-WDW-DINE for details.

hands down—the prix fixe dinner is currently $85 per person, $120 with wine—but it's so special that you'll be talking about it for years afterward. On the evening we visited, the salad was a floral arrangement in a crouton vase—until Victoria tapped the side of the crouton, releasing the greens into a fan-shaped pattern on the plate—and the coffee service was more elaborate than a Japanese tea ceremony.

California Grill   Romance Factor ♥♥ $$$

Not only does the California Grill offer a marvelous variety of cuisine, with stylish preparation, but in addition, the views from the top of the Contemporary are unparalleled, especially during the Magic Kingdom fireworks. Here's how to make sure you see the show. Call 407-824-4321 to find out what time the fireworks will be showing on the night you plan to visit. Then call 407-WDW-DINE and arrange priority seating for a half hour earlier. As the fireworks begin, the restaurant dims the lights and pipes in the sound track of the show. Pure magic!

Citricos   Romance Factor ♥♥ $$$

Located in the Grand Floridian, Citricos is one of Disney's finest restaurants, featuring southern French cuisine and an unparalleled wine selection, many available by the glass. The restaurant's commitment to wine is so deep, in fact, that 19 of their servers are certified sommeliers.

The menu is updated frequently to take advantage of fresh ingredients, and the presentations are both visually exciting and delicious. The veal shank is a house specialty, but the scallops are outstanding as well. Citricos has been described in such magazines as *Esquire* and *Wine Spectator* as being one of the rising stars of Disney dining.

Flying Fish Café   **Romance Factor ♥♥ $$$**

Located on the BoardWalk, the Flying Fish is widely considered to be one of the best restaurants in the entire Disney World complex. Signature dishes include snapper wrapped in a potato crust and yellowfin tuna, but the steaks are outstanding too. Decorated in the same style as its sister restaurant, the California Grill, the Flying Fish is bustling and crowded, with the tables quite close together. Priority seating is a must, but eating at the bar is also a good option, because you can watch the chefs as they work.

Insider's Secret

Couples who are dining late and leaving a resort restaurant after the transportation system has begun to close down will find it tricky to get back to their own resort. If you have your own car, drive. If you don't drive, you can use Downtown Disney, whose buses run until 2 A.M., as a transfer station. But a cab is by far your easiest option. The valets at any resort can hail you one, and the cost for a ride from one end of Disney property to another is usually less than $10.

CHAPTER

14

Universal Orlando

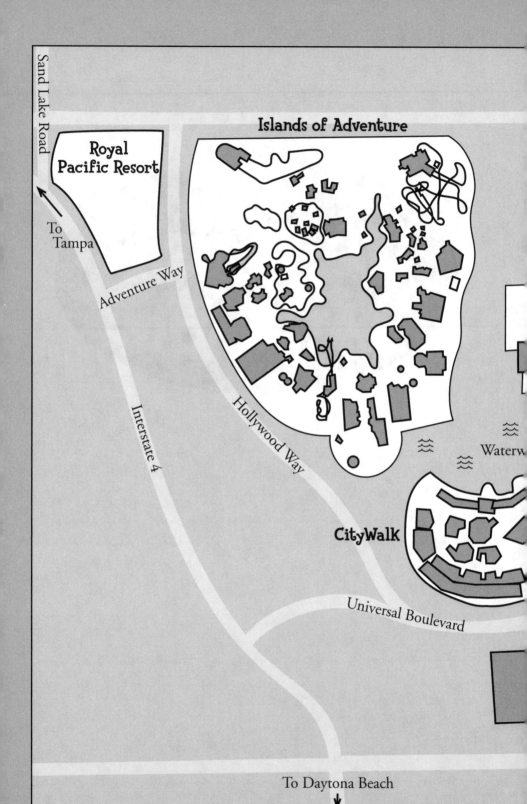

Universal Orlando

Turkey Lake Road

Universal Studios
Florida

Vineland Road

Hard Rock Hotel

Waterway

Major Boulevard

Portofino Bay Hotel

Kirkman Road

ARKING GARAGES

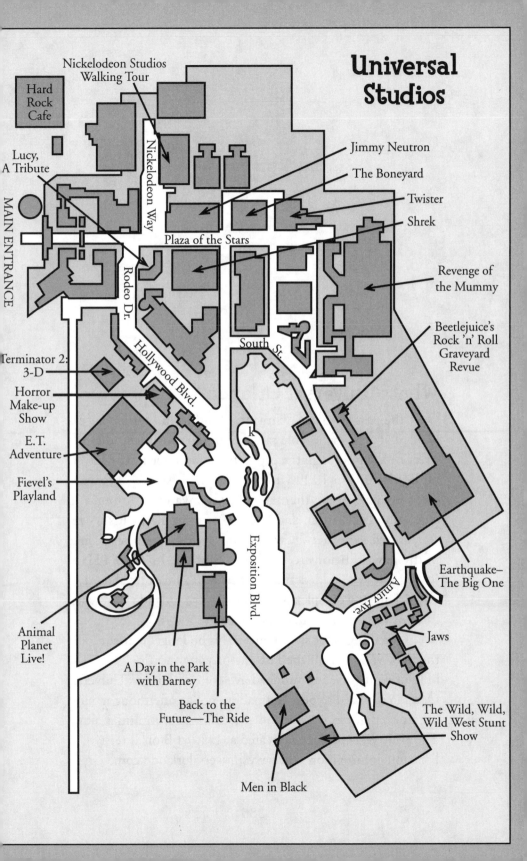

Universal Studios

Hard Rock Cafe

Nickelodeon Studios Walking Tour

Lucy, A Tribute

MAIN ENTRANCE

Nickelodeon Way

Rodeo Dr.

Plaza of the Stars

Jimmy Neutron

The Boneyard

Twister

Shrek

Revenge of the Mummy

Terminator 2: 3-D

Horror Make-up Show

E.T. Adventure

Fievel's Playland

Hollywood Blvd.

South St.

Beetlejuice's Rock 'n' Roll Graveyard Revue

Animal Planet Live!

A Day in the Park with Barney

Back to the Future—The Ride

Exposition Blvd.

Amity Ave.

Earthquake— The Big One

Jaws

The Wild, Wild, Wild West Stunt Show

Men in Black

What's Universal Orlando?

Over the past few years, Universal Studios in Florida has expanded at an unbelievable rate, buying so much land that the street running through the property has been renamed Universal Boulevard. In 1999 Universal opened Islands of Adventure, a totally new theme park; CityWalk, a dining and entertainment district; and Loew's Portofino Bay, a luxury resort, as well as a waterway with boat service connecting all three of the new additions to Universal Studios. In 2000 a Hard Rock Hotel was added and the Royal Pacific came aboard in 2003. This new complex is called Universal Orlando, and when it is finished it will contain a total of five resorts.

One thing is for sure: Universal is no longer content to be the park you visit on the last day of your vacation, after the bulk of your time and money have gone to Disney. Universal Orlando is poised to be a destination, not an afterthought, aiming to keep guests on site and entertained for multiday stays. The Universal complex is located at Exit 74 B off Interstate 4. For more information visit www.universalorlando.com.

At present, Universal is offering several ticket options (tax is included):

- *1-Day, 1-Park Pass*: $51.95, $42.95 for ages 3 to 9—This allows you admission to either Islands of Adventure or Universal Studios.

- *1-Day, 2-Park Pass*: $82, $66.95 for ages 3 to 9—This allows you to park-hop between Islands of Adventure and Universal Studios.

- *2-Day, 2-Park Pass*: $96.95, $83.95 for ages 3 to 9—This allows you admission to both Islands of Adventure and Universal Studios.

- *3-Day, 2-Park Pass*: $111.95, $96.95 for ages 3 to 9—This allows you admission to both Islands of Adventure and Universal Studios.

In addition, Universal offers Flexpass, which allows you admission into other area attractions:

- 4-Park Flexpass: $175.95, $142.95 for ages 3 to 9—This allows you admission to Universal Studios, Islands of Adventure, Wet 'n Wild, and Sea World.

- 5-Park Flexpass: $209.95, $175.95 for ages 3 to 9—This allows you admission to Universal Studios, Islands of

Helpful Hint
Just as many people misuse the terms "Walt Disney World" and "Magic Kingdom" at Disney, Universal's expansion has led to a bit of confusion with the names.

The entire complex—two theme parks, three hotels, and CityWalk—is called "Universal Orlando." "Universal Studios" is the original theme park, with attractions themed around various movies that Universal Studios has presented over the years.

Adventure, Wet 'n Wild, and Sea World, as well as Busch Gardens Tampa Bay.

Tips for Your First Hour at Universal Studios

ℯ The parking garage is in New Jersey (seems that way, anyhow), so arrive at least 30 minutes before the main gate opens. The cost is $8 a car. (Call 407-363-8000 the day before you plan to visit to confirm hours of operation.) After getting your tickets, you'll wait in a small holding area for about 10 minutes. Hanna-Barbera and Nickelodeon characters often circulate among the crowd to pose for pictures and give autographs. So this is your chance to meet SpongeBob SquarePants, the Wild Thornberrys, and the Rugrats.

ℯ Generally, guests are allowed through the main turnstiles about 20 minutes before the official opening time. If a show is filming on the day you're visiting, this will be indicated on a sign as you enter the park. The attendant at the nearby Studio Audience window can tell you how to get tickets.

ℯ After entering the main turnstile, visitors arriving early are allowed part way down Plaza of the Stars and Rodeo Drive, the two major streets in Universal Studios. If you

Time-Saving Tip

Watching a taping is time consuming. If your kids are young and will be skipping many of Universal's scary attractions anyway, you'll have the time. But if your children are older and you'll be trying to cram all the big rides into your day, it's unlikely you'll want to devote two hours to viewing a taping.

want to ride Back to the Future, Jaws, Men in Black, or E.T. Adventure first, go down Rodeo Drive as far as you're allowed. If you'd rather see Jimmy Neutron, *Shrek,* Twister, Revenge of the Mummy, or Earthquake first, go down Plaza of the Stars until the ropes stop you. Families who haven't had breakfast may have time for a pastry at the Beverly Hills Boulangerie before the ropes drop.

Time-Saving Tip
Remember—what's new is always hottest. First, ride Jimmy Neutron, the simulation ride which replaced the Funtastic World of Hanna-Barbera, and then head directly across the street to the new 3-D show *Shrek*.

@ If you're touring in the off-season, not all attractions will open at 9 A.M.; some open at 9, some at 10, with shows starting even later. Your touring will be pretty much dictated by which attractions are open.

Helpful Hint
For updated information, visit www.universal orlando.com.

Universal Studios Touring Tips

@ The same basic plan you used in the Disney theme parks will also apply here. You need to visit major attractions— Revenge of the Mummy, Men in Black, Back to the Future, Twister, E.T. Adventure, Jaws, Earthquake, Jimmy Neutron, and *Shrek*—early in the morning or in the evening. Take in the theater-style attractions in the afternoon.

@ If you miss one of the major continuously loading attractions in the morning, hold off on it until two hours before the park closes. Midday waits of up to 90 minutes are common at popular attractions such as Men in Black or *Terminator 2: 3-D*, but the crowds ease off a bit during the dinner hour.

@ In the off-season, Universal usually employs a "staggered opening" system where some attractions begin operating at 9 A.M., others at 10, and still others at 11. This will dictate your touring schedule, because you can obviously see only what's open—but it's really no problem, because in the off-season you rarely encounter morning waits anyway.

@ If you plan to see Universal in one day, it's unlikely you'll have time for a midafternoon break such as returning to your hotel or visiting a water park. But the numerous theater-style attractions at Universal offer plenty of chances to rest up and let small kids nap. A lot of shows open around noon, and another wave begins around 2 P.M. Ride in the morning and then catch a midday show, have lunch, and see a second show.

Insider's Secret

Universal saves its ultimate perk for guests at its three posh on-site hotels—Portofino Bay, the Hard Rock Hotel, and Royal Pacific. On-site guests can enter the express lines at both Islands of Adventure and Universal Studios just by showing their room key. That translates to virtually no waiting in line. For information on the resorts call 407-224-7117 or check out www.universalorlando.com.

Time-Saving Tip

Universal Studios offers an Express Pass that works like Disney's FASTPASS.

The Express Distribution Centers are located near the ride in question. Go up to the kiosk, insert your admission ticket, and you'll get the admission ticket back along with an Express Pass telling you when to return. When you do, you'll be allowed to enter a much shorter express line.

The express system is a great way to cut down on your wait times for attractions like Men in Black or Back to the Future. The anticipated wait time in the express lines is a mere 15 minutes.

Guests may only receive one Express Pass at a time. You can get another Express Pass after—

- you've used your existing one
- the one-hour time slot on your first pass has expired
- two hours has passed from the time printed at the bottom of the Express Pass

Helpful Hint

Do you want to sleep in? Visit in the off-season when crowds are light and lines are short. You can arrive at the park about 10 A.M. and still comfortably do everything.

❧ Universal clusters most of its kiddie attractions in one section. The Woody Woodpecker Kid Zone, A Day in the Park with Barney, the large play area called Curious George Goes to Town, Fievel's Playland, E.T. Adventure, and *Animal Planet Live!* are all located in the same general area of the park. This means if your children are preschoolers you can park the strollers once and then walk from attraction to attraction, letting them play as long as they want.

@ The theaters that hold *The Gory, Gruesome, Grotesque Horror Makeup Show,* and *Terminator 2: 3-D* are high capacity, so even if the lines in midafternoon look discouraging, odds are you'll still be seated. Consult the entertainment schedule that you receive with your pass, or check the poster board at the attraction entrance for show times, and then put one parent in line about 20 minutes before the show is due to start. The other can take the kids for a drink or bathroom break. If you all opt to wait in line together, be aware that Universal has placed trash cans all through the queue areas of the high-capacity attractions in acknowledgment of the fact that visitors on a tight touring schedule may well be eating or drinking in line.

@ Headed toward Back to the Future, Men in Black, or another intense attraction? Universal employees will help

Helpful Hint
Universal employs only three height restrictions— 40 inches on Back to the Future, 36 inches on the Woody Woodpecker Nuthouse Coaster, and 42 inches on Men in Black. But just because all kids big enough to sit up are allowed on Jaws doesn't mean it's a good idea to take them; consult the ride descriptions for information on the special effects. Other attractions such as E.T. Adventure and Jimmy Neutron provide separate stationary seating for kids under 40 inches, thus allowing families to go through the attraction as a group.

families traveling with a baby or toddler do a "baby swap" so that everyone can ride.

Money-Saving Tip
Try not to let the kids stop to shop in the morning; not only should you keep moving between rides while the park is relatively uncrowded, but you'll notice that the shops are located to encourage the ultimate in impulse buying. Hold off on souvenir purchases until late in the day when you've seen it all.

The Scare Factor at Universal Studios

Most of the shows and tours are family oriented and fine for everyone, but some of the big-name attractions are too frightening for preschoolers. The motion simulation rides, especially Back to the Future, induce queasiness in some people. And be aware that in general the rides and shows are very loud. Twister and *Terminator* can practically jolt the fillings from your teeth.

Universal imposes very few height restrictions and thus gives parents little guidance. Kids must be 36 inches high to ride the Woody Woodpecker Nuthouse Coaster. Kids under 40 inches are banned from Back to the Future and required to use special seating on E.T. Adventure and Jimmy Neutron. Kids must be at least 42 inches tall to ride Men in Black. But beyond these minimal restrictions, parents are the ones who decide who rides what.

Any child old enough to sit on his own can ride Jaws and Earthquake. Universal seems to set the rules based on how physically wild the ride is—and none of the rides listed bounces you around too much. But they're psychologically scary, and a

Helpful Hint

Because the rides are based on movies, how your child reacted to the movie is a good predictor of how well your child will handle the ride.

visit may lead to more bad dreams than even the wildest of roller coasters. Although individual reactions obviously vary from child to child, read the ride descriptions and consult the list that follows to help you decide.

Fine for Anyone

E.T. Adventure

Jimmy Neutron

Animal Planet Live!

Earthquake

Lucy: A Tribute

Wild West Stunt Show

Beetlejuice's Graveyard Revue (unless the child is afraid of loud noises)

Fievel's Playland, including the water ride

A Day in the Park with Barney

Woody Woodpecker's Nuthouse Coaster

Curious George Goes to Town

Nickelodeon Game Lab

Consider Waiting Until Your Kids Are at Least 7 to Try These

Revenge of the Mummy

Back to the Future

Jaws

Shrek

Horror Makeup Show

Terminator 2: 3-D

Twister

Men in Black

The Universal Studios Don't-Miss List

Revenge of the Mummy

Jimmy Neutron

Shrek

E.T. Adventure

Back to the Future

Jaws

Animal Planet Live!

Wild West Stunt Show

Curious George Goes to Town
(if you have kids under 8)

Twister

Terminator 2: 3-D

Men in Black

The Universal Studios Worth-Your-While List

Earthquake

Horror Makeup Show

Nickelodeon Game Lab

A Day in the Park with Barney (if you have preschoolers)

Attractions Especially Popular with Teens and Preteens

Revenge of the Mummy

Back to the Future

Jaws

Jimmy Neutron

Shrek

Horror Makeup Show

Terminator 2: 3-D

Twister

Men in Black

Beetlejuice's Graveyard Revue

CityWalk

Universal Studios Attractions

Jimmy Neutron

This new simulation ride, opened in spring of 2003, replaced the Funtastic World of Hanna-Barbera, but it's actually just a fresh take on the popular simulation ride premise. In addition to Jimmy, the ride will feature plenty of friends from the Nickelodeon lineup, such as the Wild Thornberrys and SpongeBob SquarePants, which will make it an automatic hit with fans of the cartoons.

In the preshow, guests are introduced to Jimmy's latest invention, a spy camera, but then—as is so often the case in the world of theme park rides—something goes dreadfully awry. The audience is loaded into motion-simulation vehicles to help Jimmy defend the earth from an alien attack. The vehicles rise, tilt, and lurch in reaction to what's happening on the large screen in front of you and while the actual movement of the "rockets" isn't much, the special effects combine to make you feel as if you're really hurtling through space. The result is a fun ride and a great introduction to the feeling of flight simulation.

The Scare Factor

The presence of familiar Nickelodeon heroes like Jimmy and SpongeBob will ensure that most kids, even many preschoolers, will be clamoring to ride. The action sequences shouldn't alarm kids raised on Saturday morning cartoons, but the motion simulation may be another matter. If you're prone to queasiness or think it might be too intense for your kids, ask for the stationary seating. If that goes okay, you can always return and ride in the motion simulators on your second time through.

Time-Saving Tip

Like other attractions along the Plaza of the Stars, lines form by 11 A.M. as late-arriving visitors walk through the front gate and simply queue up for the first attractions they see. Visit Jimmy Neutron first thing in the morning, both to avoid the crowds and to use the ride as a gauge for how well your kids will handle the more intense flight simulation ride, Back to the Future.

Time-Saving Tip

As Universal's newest attractions, Jimmy Neutron and *Shrek* will draw longer than average lines and since they are located close together and near the theme park entrance, the crowds may become overwhelming. To reduce your wait time, get an Express Pass for one attraction before lining up for the other. By the time you exit the first attraction, you should be able to use your Express Pass to immediately board the second.

Shrek

Another big change at Universal is the opening of the 3-D show *Shrek*, housed in the former location of the Alfred Hitchcock show. *Shrek*, needless to say, is a much more appealing concept for kids.

In the preshow we'll learn that vile little Lord Farquaad has plans to destroy Shrek from the great beyond. As you enter the main theater, you'll be given 3-D glasses, but what makes this show really special and different from the other 3-D attractions around town is that you're also seated in special chairs that will make the experience tactile as well as visual. What does that mean? You'll not only see and hear the things happening on the screen but you'll feel them and smell them as well. (Mercifully, taste is the one sense not engaged in the show.) It's very high-tech and also a lot of fun.

The Scare Factor

Shrek was not open to the general public as we went to press, so we were unable to gauge the reactions of children. While Lord Farquaad is not exactly the most intimidating movie villain of all time, the special effects are extremely convincing and the whole show is very loud, which may be too much for preschoolers. Kids school age and older should do fine.

Men in Black: Alien Attack

Remember the scene in *Men in Black* where Will Smith tries out for the force? Think you could do better?

The premise is that guests are rookie agents riding through the streets of New York armed with laser guns called "alienators." But unlike the tame targets in Disney's Buzz Lightyear, these aliens can strike back, sending your vehicle into an out-of-control spin.

As you shoot at the 120 Audio-Animatronic aliens, the ride keeps track of your individual score and the collective score of the six people in your vehicle. You're not only fighting off aliens, but also competing against the team of rookies in the car beside you. Here's where it gets cute. Depending on how well you and your vehicle mates do, there are alternate endings to the ride. Will you get a hero's welcome in Times Square or a loser's send-off?

Because you're actually in a video game, it reasons that video game rules apply—the more you play, the better you get. Can you spell addictive? Come early if you want to ride more than once.

The Scare Factor

Most kids take the aliens in Men in Black in stride—especially if they've seen the movie and know what to expect.

Time-Saving Tip

Families with older kids should head for Men in Black directly after trying out Jimmy Neutron and *Shrek*. This attraction draws long lines by midmorning.

Insider's Secret

Hooked on Men in Black? If you're willing to split off from your party, the singles line moves much faster than the general line.

Insider's Secret

Want to max your Men in Black score? Near the end of the ride (when you face the mega-alien in Times Square), you will hear Zed instructing you to push the red button on your control panel NOW. Whoever hits their button at this crucial point gets a whopping 100,000 bonus points. Take that, space aliens!

Helpful Hint

There are lockers outside Men in Black where you can store backpacks and large packages free of charge while you ride. The ride isn't that wild, but space in the training vehicles is very tight, so use the lockers if you're carrying anything bulky.

Back to the Future

Flight simulation technology makes a quantum leap forward—or is it backward?—in Back to the Future. After being briefed by Doc Brown (played by Christopher Lloyd of the movie series) in a preshow video that bad-boy Biff has sabotaged his time travel experiments, you'll be loaded into six-passenger DeLoreans.

What follows is a high-speed chase back through the prehistoric era. The cars bounce around pretty violently, but it's the flight simulation techniques that are the real scream-rippers, far more intense than Disney's Star Tours or Body Wars. Passengers who can bear to glance away from the screen will notice that as many as 12 DeLoreans, arranged in tiers, take

The Scare Factor

At one point in your trip through the prehistoric era, you're even swallowed by a dinosaur, making the ride much too much for most kids under 7, although technically anyone taller than 40 inches is allowed to board. If your child wants to try it, brief him or her that the majority of the effects can be erased simply by closing your eyes—and that's not a bad tip to keep in mind yourself if you're prone to queasiness.

Time-Saving Tip

You can cut down standing in line at major attractions in three ways.

- Use the Express Pass system.
- Stay at a Universal Orlando resort. Guests get Express privileges even without the Express Passes.
- Be willing to split up. The single rider line moves much faster, especially at an attraction like Men in Black.

the trip simultaneously, making Back to the Future a sort of ultimate drive-in movie.

Earthquake

After a preshow hosted by Charlton Heston, visitors travel through two separate theaters where they learn how special effects and stunts were done in the *Earthquake* movie. (The special effects and intricate models of San Francisco are something of a revelation to most kids, because few have seen the original movie, made more than 20 years ago.) In the second preshow, audience volunteers play quake victims, which is great fun for the kids who are chosen.

After the preshow, you are loaded onto your subway for the ride segment itself. Earthquake is a very short ride and less intense than you may have been led to believe from the advertisements. Most kids hold up through the rumbles, fires, floods, and train wrecks just fine, and as one mother wrote, "It's fun to feel it really happen instead of watching it on a screen." It's even more fascinating to watch the water recede, the concrete mend itself, and the broken turnstiles arise when the ride is over!

Helpful Hint

Several Universal attractions, most notably Earthquake and *Shrek,* require visitors to move from theater to theater in the course of the presentation. It keeps the lines outside moving steadily but is tough on families lugging a sleeping child. If your youngster dozes off during one of the preshows of these attractions, it is easier to hold her than attempt to put her down because you'll undoubtedly be moving on within a few minutes.

The Scare Factor

The final segment of Earthquake, where you're trapped in a San Francisco subway station during the quake, is short but intense. Besides the rumbles, a water main will break, electrical fires will break out, and at one point a truck crashes through the pavement above you. It's dramatic, but most preschool kids—especially if they've been briefed about what to expect—aren't too frightened. The noise level will frighten many toddlers.

Twister

After a taped intro by Bill Paxton and Helen Hunt, you're led into the main show area. There a five-story-high tornado will be created right before your eyes. The tornado, along with accompanying fires and explosions, swirls through the building while you watch from two platforms. You'll feel the wind, the rain, and the rumbles, and, yes, the flying cow from the movie comes along for the ride.

The Scare Factor

Twister is a dramatic experience—and extremely loud. The intensity is heightened by the fact that you're trapped in a relatively small space for the duration of the show. The experience is too frightening for preschoolers; most kids over 5 will be okay.

Terminator 2: 3-D

Universal's most high-tech action show combines 3-D effects, live actors, and movie clips. (The best special effect is the way

Quick Guide to

Attraction	Height Requirement
Animal Planet Live!	None
Back to the Future	40 inches
Beetlejuice's Graveyard Revue	None
A Day in the Park with Barney	None
Earthquake	None
E.T. Adventure	None
Fievel's Playland	None
Horror Make-up Show	None
Jaws	None
Jimmy Neutron	None
KidZone	None
Lucy, A Tribute	None
Men in Black	42 inches
Nickelodeon Tour	None
Revenge of the Mummy	n/a
Shrek	None
Terminator 2: 3-D	None
Twister	None
Wild West Stunt Show	None

Scare Factor
0 = Unlikely to scare any child of any age.
! = Has dark or loud elements; might rattle some toddlers.
!! = A couple of gotcha! moments; should be fine for school-age kids.
!!! = You need to be pretty big and pretty brave to handle this ride.

Universal Attractions

Speed of Line	Duration of Ride/Show	Scare Factor	Age Range
Fast	20 min.	0	All
Moderate	7 min.	!!	7 and up
Fast	20 min.	!	5 and up
Fast	15 min.	0	All
Moderate	20 min.	!	5 and up
Slow	15 min.	!	All
Moderate	n.a.	0	All
Fast	20 min.	!!	7 and up
Moderate	10 min.	!!	7 and up
Moderate	15 min.	!	5 and up
Moderate	n.a.	!	7 and up
Fast	n.a.	0	All
Fast	25 min.	!!	7 and up
Moderate	45 min.	0	All
n.a.	15 min.	!!!	7 and up
Moderate	30 min.	!!	7 and up
Slow	25 min.	!!!	7 and up
Moderate	15 min.	!!	5 and up
Fast	20 min.	!	All

the live actors seem to emerge from the movie screen onto the stage and then later run back "into" the movie.) The show is fast and dramatic—just like the film series it's based on—and the ending is explosive.

Terminator 2: 3-D, because of the size of the theater, is relatively easy to get into and best saved for the afternoon.

The Scare Factor

Although not as violent as the film series, the show has some startling effects that may be too much for kids under 7. Again, it is extremely loud.

E.T. Adventure

The charming ride begins with a brief preshow featuring Steven Spielberg and E.T., after which you file through a holding area and—somewhat mysteriously at the time—are required to give your name in exchange for a small plastic "interplanetary passport." Then you move on to the queue area, which winds through the deep, dark woods and is so evocative that it even smells and sounds like a forest. (Universal in general does a bang-up job of setting the moods in the queue areas: E.T. is designed to make you feel small and childlike.)

After handing "passports" to the attendant, children under 40 inches tall or anyone elderly, heavy, pregnant, or otherwise unsteady are loaded into flying gondolas. Others get to ride bicycles, and the lead bike in each group has E.T. in the front basket. You rise up and fly over the forest in an effective simulation of the escape scene in the *E.T.* movie. After narrowly missing being captured by the police, you manage to return E.T. to his home planet, a magical place populated by dozens of cuddly aliens.

The ride closes on a fun note, because as you sail past E.T. for the final time, he bids you farewell by name. When you give your name to the attendant before you enter the queue area, it is computer coded onto the plastic passport. As you give up the passport and are loaded into your group of bicycles, the cards are fed into the computer. The ride thus "knows" who's riding in that particular batch of bicycles, which enables E.T. to say, "Good-bye, Jordan; Good-bye, Leigh; Good-bye, Kim . . . ," and so on as your family flies past.

Helpful Hint

Unfortunately, this "personal good-bye" system frequently malfunctions, so I wouldn't mention it to the kids at all. That way, if it works, everyone is extra delighted, and if it doesn't, the ride is still an upbeat experience.

Jaws

As the people of Amity Beach learned, that darn shark just won't stay away. Jaws carries you via boat through a big outdoor set. The shark rises from the water several times quite suddenly, the unseen boat before you "gets it" in a gruesome way, and there are also grenade launches, explosions, and a fuel spill. There's tremendous splashing—especially on the left side of the boat—and most of the boat captains throw themselves totally into the experience by shrieking, shouting, and firing guns on cue. It all adds up to one action-packed boat ride. Interestingly

The Scare Factor

Kids 7 to 11 give Jaws a strong thumbs-up, and the ride is popular with many kids under 7. The fact that you're outdoors in the daylight dilutes the intensity. The really brave should wait until evening, when the "shark in the dark" effects are much scarier.

enough, Universal invested $50 million on the ride, which is more than six times what Steven Spielberg spent on the original 1975 movie.

The Gory, Gruesome, Grotesque Horror Makeup Show

A witty pair of young actors illustrate certain makeup effects onstage, but you'll also see clips from *The Mummy, The Fly*, and an astounding man-to-beast transformation scene from the little-known *An American Werewolf in London*. A hapless audience volunteer (an adult) is brought on stage to play victim.

The Scare Factor

Although the movie clips and general gore level are too intense for preschoolers, most kids over 7 can stomach the show. Better than adults, frankly. The show has a PG-13 rating because of the blood and a couple of mildly risqué jokes.

Animal Planet Live!

This is an appealing show for all age groups, but younger kids will be especially drawn to the animal stars. Kid volunteers are taken from the audience. Show times are printed on your map. Because of the large size of the theater, this is a great choice for the afternoon.

Wild West Stunt Show

Funny, fast-moving, and full of surprises, this show ranks at the top of the list with kids 7 to 11 and rates highly with kids under 7 as well. The shoot-'em-ups, fistfights, and explosions are played strictly for laughs, and sometimes the comedy tends to overshadow how dangerous these stunts really are. A good choice for the whole family, and as with *Animal Planet Live!*, it's fairly easy to get into even in the crowded parts of the afternoon.

Fievel's Playland

Fievel's Playland is a cleverly designed play area filled with western-style props, including a harmonica that plays notes as kids slide down it; a giant, talking Tiger the cat; canteens to squirt; cowboy hats to bounce in; spider webs to climb; and a separate ball pit and slide area for toddlers.

Time-Saving Tip

Fievel's Playland often opens an hour or two after the general park. If you ride the big-deal rides and then show up at the playground at the opening time indicated on your map, you'll be able to try the water ride without much of a wait.

The centerpiece of the playground is a 200-foot water ride in which kids and parents are loaded into two-person rafts and swept through a "sewer." The ride is zippier than it looks, will get you soaking wet, and is so addictive that most kids clamor to get back on again immediately. The water ride is very popular and loads slowly, so by afternoon the waits are prohibitive. If you come in the morning, it is possible to ride several times with minimal waits, but by afternoon one ride is all you can reasonably expect.

A Day in the Park with Barney

Designed to appeal to Universal's youngest guests, A Day in the Park with Barney is actually an enclosed parklike setting with pop-art-colored flowers and trees. Barney appears several times a day in a song-and-dance show, and there is also an interactive indoor play area designed for toddlers. This play area is far cooler and calmer than Fievel's next door, and the nearby shop and food stand are never crowded.

Helpful Hint

Universal has located all the attractions for very young children close together; if you have preschoolers, hang an immediate right on Rodeo Drive after you enter the park and follow the signs to E.T. Adventure. *Animal Planet Live!*, A Day in the Park with Barney, E.T. Adventure, Curious George Goes to Town, KidZone, and Fievel's Playland are all located within close proximity to one another, so a family with kids who are all under 7 can set up base here and enjoy more attractions in sequence.

KidZone

The centerpiece of this latest addition to the kids' play area is a small roller coaster called the Nuthouse Coaster. Somewhat like Goofy's Barnstormer at Disney, the ride is zippier than you'd guess and kids have to be 36 inches tall to ride. Watch it make a couple of runs before you line up with your 3-year-old.

Curious George Goes to Town

Perhaps a better name would have been Curious George Goes to the Car Wash. This large interactive play area is a simulated city that includes climbing areas, ball pits, and lots of chances to get very, very wet. There are fountains in the center and water cannons up above; many parents let their kids wear bathing suits under their shorts so they can strip down and really get into the spirit of the place. A great way to cool off in the summer, but if you're going in the off-season, either save it for the warmest part of the afternoon or keep walking.

On the other hand, if you're up for a maximum splash, a clanging bell over the Fire Department or City Water Tower indicates that a big wave of water is under way. On a hot summer day, this may be the highlight of the park for young kids.

Helpful Hint
At Curious George Goes to Town, you can attempt to follow the footprints in order to stay dry as you maze your way through the town—but what kid is going to do that? The footprints do cut down a bit on parental drenching.

Helpful Hint
In chilly weather the water is shut off, and Curious George Goes to Town becomes a play area. The water ride in Fievel's Playground is also closed on cold days.

Beetlejuice's Graveyard Revue

A rock 'n' roll dance show starring Dracula, the Wolfman, the Phantom of the Opera, and Frankenstein and his Bride, the Revue is popular with the 7-to-11 age group and teens—although the show is so goofy and upbeat that younger kids certainly won't be frightened by the ghouls.

This is a high-tech show featuring pulsating lights, fog machines, synchronized dancing, and wry renditions of rock classics. Because the theater is huge and this 20-minute show plays several times throughout the day, getting in isn't too tough—work it into your schedule whenever it happens to suit you.

Lucy, A Tribute

Fans of *I Love Lucy* should take a few minutes to walk through this exhibit, which houses memorabilia from the famous TV show, including scale models of the Tropicana and the Ricardos' apartment, clothes and jewelry worn on the show, personal pictures and letters from Lucy and Desi's home life, and the numerous Emmys that Lucille Ball won throughout the years. The "California Here We Come Game" is a treat for hard-core trivia buffs. By answering questions about episodes of *I Love Lucy*, game participants get to travel with the Mertzes and Ricardos on their first trip to California. They lost me somewhere in the desert, but perhaps you'll do better.

Nickelodeon Game Lab

Young kids love Game Lab, where audience volunteers play games and one lucky kid is slopped and glopped in the best Nickelodeon tradition. Show times are marked on your map; if you're visiting on a busy afternoon, you might want to get an Express Pass to guarantee yourself a seat.

Insider's Secret

Even if you don't plan to take in the Game Lab or a filming, drop by the Nick Studios entrance and check out the Green Slime Geyser, which periodically erupts and spews into the air an unearthly colored substance about the consistency of pudding.

If you're visiting on a day when one of the Nick shows is filming, you can also volunteer to be in the studio audience. Check the production board as you enter the park to see what's planned.

Insider's Secret

The Blues Brothers Show, featuring not only Jake and Elroy but also a talented singer named Mabel and a gifted sax player, is one of the most popular shows in the park. It plays in the New York section, and show times are marked on your map.

Revenge of the Mummy

In 2004, Universal will open a brand new thrill ride in the space where Kongfrontation used to be. "Revenge of the Mummy" is billed as a "psychological thrill ride," combining a high-speed roller coaster, space age robotics, and "live" pyrotechnic effects.

The ride will begin in authenticated Egyptian sets, and as guests move through the shadowy catacombs they'll encounter a series of visual, visceral, and motion-based effects. There will be a strong story line—based on the popular *Mummy* film series, of course—as well as the movement of a scream-worthy roller coaster.

Thus the ride is a bit of a hybrid between the atmospheric Universal Studios rides and the wild coasters of Islands of Ad-

The Scare Factor

The ride is still under construction and no height requirement has been set as we go to press. Based on the ride description, it's safe to say that Mummy will scare the willies out of preschoolers and some school-age kids as well.

venture. While you're dodging state-of-the-art special effects and the vengeful curses of ghosts, the ride's magnetic propulsion launch system will be thrusting you forward, backward,

Insider's Secret

When "Revenge of the Mummy" opens, it will be (literally) the hottest ride at Universal and will have lines to match. Be sure to use Express Pass and visit as early in the day as possible.

and forward again. The effects culminate with a "ceiling of flame," an overhead fire that hovers only inches above riders' heads, and a skeleton warrior who, in the midst of battle, leaps into your vehicle. Yowza!

CHAPTER

15

Islands of
Adventure

Islands of Adventure

Jurassic Park River Adventure

Dueling Dragons

Jurassic Park

Jurassic Park Discovery Center

Camp Jurassic

Pteranodon Flyers

Dudley Do-Right's Ripsaw Falls

Triceratops Encounter

Sindbad's Village

The Eighth Voyage of Sindbad

Mythos Restaurant

The Lost Continent

Me Ship, The Olive

Toon Lagoon

Popeye & Bluto's Bilge-Rat Barges

Comic Strip Lane

If I Ran the Zoo

Poseidon's Fury

Green Eggs & Ham

Pandemonium Theater

Island Skipper Tours

Seuss Landing

The Amazing Adventures of Spider-Man

Doctor Doom's Fearfall

Marvel Super Hero Island

Caro-Seuss-el

One Fish, Two Fish, Red Fish, Blue Fish

Incredible Hulk Coaster

Port of Entry

The Cat in the Hat

Opened next to Universal Studios in the summer of 1999, Islands of Adventure is the cornerstone of Universal's massive expansion. Now there are two theme parks as well as CityWalk, the sumptuously elegant Portofino Bay Resort, lively Hard Rock Hotel, and exotic Royal Pacific all connected by bridges and waterways.

Islands of Adventure

Parents of younger kids will appreciate the fact that at Islands of Adventure the rides designed for younger kids are every bit as engaging and technologically complex as the fastest coasters. Many theme parks—and even Disney is somewhat guilty of this—pour their creativity and money into the teen and adult attractions, leaving the preschool set with rides where cardboard cutouts swing toward them on door hinges. But at Islands of Adventure, especially in the Seuss Landing section, Universal has created a world that is not only fun but also marvelous to look at and cleverly designed.

A one-day ticket is $51.95, $42.95 for children 3 to 9. For multiday passes, including Universal Studios, turn to chapter 14. Check for any changes by calling 407-363-8000, or go online at www.universalorlando.com.

Tips for Your First Hour at Islands of Adventure

Older kids who are up to a high-intensity experience should veer left on leaving Port of Entry and immediately board the Amazing Adventures of Spider-Man. From there you can move on to the Incredible Hulk Coaster and Dr. Doom's Fearfall, both of which are also on Marvel Super Hero Island.

Younger kids? Turn to the right and immediately enter Seuss Landing. Let the kids build up steam on

Helpful Hint

No matter what your age or risk tolerance, ride in the morning and save the shows for the afternoon.

these gentle rides and then, if they've mustered up the courage for bigger thrills, try the pint-sized roller coaster, Flying Unicorn, located on the Lost Continent.

Islands of Adventure Touring Tips

Given its circular layout, touring Islands of Adventure is relatively easy. And the park is small enough to allow you to make several laps of the circuit without wearing yourself out too badly.

- ℮ Arrive early, especially if your focus is the coasters and the more intense rides. These can draw long crowds late in the day.

- In your initial lap of the park, focus on the rides, especially name attractions that are likely to draw crowds by midday.

- Stop for lunch.

- Begin your second lap of the park, this time focusing on shows and attractions like Triceratops Encounter, which can be toured in a fairly leisurely manner. If you have young kids, use this lap to also hit the interactive play areas: If I Ran the Zoo; Camp Jurassic; and Me Ship, the *Olive*. Midday is also a good time to try the water rides—getting soaked at noon is more fun than getting soaked at 9 A.M.

- Exit the park and have dinner at CityWalk.

- If stamina permits, reenter the park for your third and final lap. Revisit favorites, see shows, or try any attraction that had prohibitive lines earlier in the day.

Time-Saving Tip

Islands of Adventure has instituted the Express system, which works just like Disney's FASTPASS. You insert your admission ticket in the machine at the Express Distribution Center located near the ride in question. You'll get the admission ticket back, along with an Express Pass telling you when to return. When you do, you'll be allowed to enter a much shorter line. It's a great system, capable of cutting your wait time at major attractions to 15 minutes or less.

The only drawback is that guests may receive only one Express Pass at a time. You can get your next pass after—

- you've used your existing pass or the one-hour time slot on the express pass has expired.
- two hours have passed from the transaction time printed on the bottom of the Express Pass.

Helpful Hint

The tip board at the end of Port of Entry keeps you cued into the approximate wait times of various attractions in Islands of Adventure. In addition, time boards announcing rides with little or no wait are scattered throughout the park.

Helpful Hint

Because you can only get one Express Pass at a time, use them judiciously, as for a ride like Dueling Dragons or Spider-Man, which can draw long lines. On uncrowded days you may not need them at all.

Insider's Secret

Universal really knows how to make it worth your while to stay on site. Guests at the Portofino Bay Hotel and Hard Rock Hotel receive Express Pass privileges to almost all the rides and shows in both Universal Studios and Islands of Adventure. Talk about perks!

Height Requirements for Islands of Adventure

Dueling Dragons	54 inches
Jurassic Park River Adventure	42 inches
Dudley Do-Right's Ripsaw Falls	44 inches
Incredible Hulk Coaster	54 inches
The Amazing Adventures of Spider-Man	40 inches
Popeye and Bluto's Bilge-Rat Barges	42 inches
Dr. Doom's Fearfall	52 inches
Pteranodon Flyers	36 inches
Flying Unicorns	36 inches

Islands of Adventure Don't-Miss List

IF YOUR KIDS ARE 7 AND UNDER

One Fish, Two Fish, Red Fish, Blue Fish

Caro-Seuss-el

If I Ran the Zoo

The Cat in the Hat

Camp Jurassic

Popeye and Bluto's Bilge-Rat Barges

Me Ship, the *Olive*

Dudley Do-Right's Ripsaw Falls (for kids over 5)

The Amazing Adventures of Spider-Man
(for kids 6 or 7)

Flying Unicorn

IF YOUR KIDS ARE 8 TO 11

The Amazing Adventures of Spider-Man

Dudley Do-Right's Ripsaw Falls

Popeye and Bluto's Bilge-Rat Barges

Jurassic Park River Adventure

Poseidon's Fury

Dr. Doom's Fearfall

Incredible Hulk Coaster (if they're bold enough)

Dueling Dragons (ditto)

IF YOUR KIDS ARE OVER 12

The Amazing Adventures of Spider-Man

Dr. Doom's Fearfall

Incredible Hulk Coaster

Dudley Do-Right's Ripsaw Falls

Popeye and Bluto's Bilge-Rat Barges

Jurassic Park River Adventure

Dueling Dragons

Poseidon's Fury

Islands of Adventure Worth-Your-While List

IF YOUR KIDS ARE UNDER 7
Discovery Center
Eighth Voyage of Sinbad **(for kids over 5)**
Pteranodon Flyers

IF YOUR KIDS ARE 8 TO 11
Anything in Seuss Landing that catches their fancy
Eighth Voyage of Sindbad
Storm Force

IF YOUR KIDS ARE OVER 12
Anything in Jurassic Park that catches their fancy
Eighth Voyage of Sinbad
Anything in Seuss Landing that catches their fancy
CityWalk

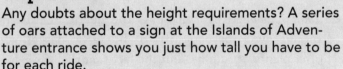

Helpful Hint
Any doubts about the height requirements? A series of oars attached to a sign at the Islands of Adventure entrance shows you just how tall you have to be for each ride.

The Scare Factor at Islands of Adventure

Make no mistake: The rides here are big-deal squealers, and you don't want to guess wrong about what is age appropriate.

The Scare Factor for Kids Under 7

@ *Seuss Landing*: Everything is okay for kids.

@ *The Lost Continent*: Dueling Dragons is an extremely intense coaster, not suitable for preschoolers. *The Eighth Voyage of Sinbad* is generally comic, but the final scene, in which a villainess is set on fire and dropped to her doom, may be too much for some children. *Poseidon's Fury* can be quite loud and intense, but should be fine for any child who doesn't have a fear of the dark. The Flying Unicorn is a kiddie ride with attitude—longer and faster than Goofy's Barnstormer in the Magic Kingdom or the Woody Woodpecker Nuthouse Coaster at Universal Studios. There's a 36-inch requirement. Most kids love the coaster and want to go again and again, but watch it make a couple of runs before you line up.

@ *Jurassic Park*: Camp Jurassic is a great play area and, unless they're afraid of heights, most kids will enjoy the Pteranodon Flyers. The Discovery Center and Triceratops Encounter are a bit educational and geared toward older kids, but they won't frighten anyone. The last drop on the River Adventure makes it too intense for your average preschooler.

@ *Toon Lagoon*: Kids who pass the height requirement should love Popeye and Bluto's Bilge-Rat Barges, which offer plenty of action—but the fact that the whole family is aboard dilutes the scare factor. The last drop series on Dudley Do-Right's Ripsaw Falls eliminates some young riders. Watch the descent from dry land a couple of times, and then make your call.

@ *Marvel Super Hero Island*: Many 6- and 7-year-olds will love the Amazing Adventures of Spider-Man, which bounces you around a lot, but the most dramatic effects are visual. As long as you don't get motion sickness or have a fear of the dark, Storm Force is fine for all ages. The Incredible Hulk Coaster and Dr. Doom's Fearfall? Just keep on walking.

The Scare Factor for Kids 8 to 11

ⓔ *Seuss Landing*: Nothing's scary here—unless the kids are scared of not looking cool.

ⓔ *The Lost Continent*: Older kids in this age group may like Dueling Dragons, assuming they've been on lots of coasters and don't spook easily. The *Sinbad* and *Poseidon* shows should both be good choices for school-age kids.

ⓔ *Jurassic Park*: Kids this age will still enjoy Camp Jurassic, the Pteranodon Flyers, the Discovery Center, and Triceratops Encounter—but the River Adventure will definitely be their favorite. Unless they have a fear of heights—and dropping from heights—it's a good choice for this age group.

ⓔ *Toon Lagoon*: They'll love everything here, including the numerous chances to get wet.

ⓔ *Marvel Super Hero Island*: The Amazing Adventures of Spider-Man is a must-see, and many kids this age will like Dr. Doom's Fearfall and the Incredible Hulk Coaster as well. Both rides are fully outdoors, so watch them a while before you make your call. Unless you get motion sickness, Storm Force is fine for all ages.

The Scare Factor for Kids 12 and Older

The most intense rides are the Incredible Hulk Coaster and Dueling Dragons. On the next tier down, at least in terms of sheer scariness, are Dr. Doom's Fearfall, Jurassic Park River Adventure, Spider-Man, and Dudley Do-Right's Ripsaw Falls.

Islands of Adventure Attractions

Port of Entry

As the name implies, you'll enter through this section, which resembles a wild and colorful Middle Eastern marketplace. Take a glance at the wacky bicycles and other forms of transportation lining the street as you pass. Check out Confisco's Grill, where you'll find character dining—featuring such favorites as Spider-Man, Dudley Do-Right, and the Cat in the Hat—for the same money as an ordinary lunch.

 Helpful Hint

All the common entry stuff—stroller rental, cash machines, ticket booths, and so on—can be found at Port of Entry, as well as several places to eat. This is worth remembering when you get into the park, where the food stands can become very crowded at midday; you may want to return here for lunch.

Seuss Landing

You'll find nothing but pastel colors and curved lines in this world, which looks uncannily like the illustrations in the actual Dr. Seuss books.

Kids are bound to love One Fish, Two Fish, Red Fish, Blue Fish, a very innovative Dumbo-style ride where you board brightly colored fish who fly in a circle. Your fish has a joystick that controls the height of the flight, and throughout the ride you're given directions such as "Red fish, fly high." If you opt to obey the instructions—that is, go "with the book," you stay at least somewhat dry. But if you disobey and go "against the book," a bad fish will squirt water on you. The Universal people assure me that this teaches kids to follow directions—I suspect it really shows them how much fun it can be to rebel—but either way, it's a terrific ride.

You'll also find the Caro-Seuss-el, composed of colorful, moveable versions of the creatures from the Seuss books. You go around and up and down like a classic carousel, but you can also make your beasties blink, flick their tails, or turn their heads. In the Cat and the Hat ride, you're transported on couches through scenes in the book as Things 1 and 2 create mayhem, and the poor goldfish tries to keep everything orderly. Clever and colorful, the Cat puts Disney's kiddie rides to shame.

> **Helpful Hint**
> The lively setting of Circus McGurkus Café Stoo-pendous makes it a great stop for lunch with young kids.

Seuss Landing is the ultimate eye-candy, looking uncannily like the famous children's books. Save time for the interactive play area called If I Ran the Zoo, which offers kids plenty of chances to jump, climb, play tic-tac-toe with a Gak, and, of course, squirt and be squirted.

The Lost Continent

Myths and legends come to life in this mysterious land, home to one of the Islands of Adventure headliners, the Dueling Dragons double roller coaster. Two suspension-style coasters (that is, riders dangle beneath the track) operate at once, coming so close in their mock battle that at three different times the coasters are within 12 inches of each other, giving riders the distinct impression they're going to crash. If Dueling Dragons is a bit too much, younger kids will enjoy the Flying Unicorn, a simple roller coaster that's a kiddie version of a thrill ride—and a good place for them to hang out while older siblings are riding the dragons.

Quick Guide to

Attraction	Location	Height Requirement
The Amazing Adventures of Spider-Man	Super Hero Island	40 inches
Camp Jurassic	Jurassic Park	None
Caro-Seuss-el	Seuss Landing	None
The Cat in the Hat	Seuss Landing	None
Discovery Center	Jurassic Park	None
Dr. Doom's Fearfall	Super Hero Island	52 inches
Dudley Do-Right's Ripsaw Falls	Toon Lagoon	44 inches
Dueling Dragons	Lost Continent	54 inches
Eighth Voyage of Sinbad	Lost Continent	None
The Flying Unicorn	Lost Continent	36 inches
If I Ran the Zoo	Seuss Landing	None
Incredible Hulk Coaster	Super Hero Island	54 inches
Me Ship, the *Olive*	Toon Lagoon	None
One Fish, Two Fish Red Fish, Blue Fish	Seuss Landing	None
Popeye and Bluto's Bilge-Rat Barges	Toon Lagoon	42 inches
Poseidon's Fury	Lost Continent	None
Pteranodon Flyers	Jurassic Park	36 inches
River Adventure	Jurassic Park	42 inches
Storm Force Accelatron	Super Hero Island	None
Triceratops Encounter	Jurassic Park	None

Scare Factor

0 = Unlikely to scare any child of any age.
! = Has dark or loud elements; might rattle some toddlers.
!! = A couple of gotcha! moments; should be fine for school-age kids.
!!! = You need to be pretty big and pretty brave to handle this ride.

Islands of Adventure Attractions

Speed of Line	Duration of Ride/Show	Scare Factor	Age Range
Moderate	15 min.	!!	6 and up
n/a	n/a	0	All
Slow	3 min.	0	All
Moderate	6 min.	0	All
n/a	n/a	0	All
Slow	2 min.	!!	6 and up
Moderate	8 min.	!!	6 and up
Moderate	7 min.	!!!	6 and up
n/a	25 min.	!!	8 and up
Moderate	1 minute	!!	All
n/a	n/a	0	All
Moderate	4 min.	!!!	8 and up
n/a	n/a	0	All
Slow	4 min.	0	All
Moderate	12 min.	!	4 and up
n/a	25 min.	!!	6 and up
Slow	6 min.	!	4 and up
Slow	n/a	!!	6 and up
Slow	3 minutes	!!	All
Slow	20 min.	!	All

Insider's Secret

The red "Fire" Dragon goes a bit faster, but blue "Ice" Dragon has more side-to-side movement. Either is enough to scare you silly, especially if you're sitting in an outside seat, but our readers agree that Fire is a bit more intense.

Helpful Hint

If you want to ride both the Fire and Ice Dragons, you don't have to walk all the way out through the winding queue area and reenter the ride. As you exit one coaster, just tell the attendant that you want to ride the other and he will direct you to a shorter line.

The Eighth Voyage of Sindbad, a funny, fast-paced stunt show with a finale that may be a bit too scary for preschoolers, is a good choice for afternoon. *Poseidon's Fury* is a high-tech show with wonderful special effects. At one point guests walk through a spiraling wall of water. Mythos, the park's most elegant restaurant, is also on the Lost Continent.

Insider's Secret

For a truly nice meal, step inside Mythos in the Lost Continent. The restaurant is beautiful, the service is top notch, and the food is far beyond what you'd expect to find in a theme park. The Tastings of Chocolate ($7) is one of the best desserts you'll find anywhere.

Jurassic Park

The centerpiece of the Jurassic Park section is the River Adventure, a boat ride that takes you through the land of the dinosaurs—five-story-high Animatronic dinosaurs, that is. After a T. Rex decides you'd be a good snack, you escape via an 85-foot downhill plunge—the longest, fastest, and steepest water descent ever built on a theme park ride.

If this sounds a bit much, consider the Pteranodon Flyers, gentle beasts that soar above the interactive play area of Camp Jurassic with riders dangling below. But go early or prepare for an extraordinarily long wait for what is, in essence, a simple kiddie ride.

Time-Saving Tip

Pteranodon Flyers is the true dinosaur of Islands of Adventure. Despite the fact that the ride only lasts 80 seconds and that only kids between 36 and 56 inches tall (and adults riding with them) are allowed to ride, this ride draws horrible lines. Waits of 60 minutes are not uncommon on a day when the rest of the park is uncrowded. Try to get the kids to skip it.

In the Triceratops Encounter, guests will come close to an Animatronic dinosaur who seems to breathe, blink, sneeze, and respond to stimuli such as camera flashes. (*Note*: The ads imply that everyone gets to play with the dino; in reality, one or two kids are pulled from the crowd and allowed to touch and interact.) In the Discovery Center kids can watch an Animatronic baby raptor "hatch" from an egg, and there are some clever interactive games as well.

Camp Jurassic is a wild, wonderful play area, but because it's multilevel, with winding paths, it's easy to lose your kids. If they're under age 7, you'll need to stay with them step by step. Watch out for the water cannons.

Toon Lagoon

Another section geared toward younger kids—although older ones will love it too—Toon Lagoon is designed to get you dripping wet.

The idea is that this is where cartoon characters live when they're not in the Sunday funnies. The major attraction is a log flume ride, Dudley Do-Right's Ripsaw Falls, which culminates in a 75-foot drop that makes it look as if you're falling into a shack filled with TNT. (To give you some idea of the kind of thrill we're talking about here, Splash Mountain drops 52 feet.) Popeye and Bluto's Bilge-Rat Barges is a whitewater raft ride suitable for the whole family. Much wilder than Disney's Kali River Rapids, Popeye and Bluto's Barges will splash you silly.

Helpful Hint

Younger kids will like the play area on Popeye's boat, the *Olive*, where they can fire water guns at the passing occupants of the whitewater rafts.

Other attractions include a cartoon show, which is held in the large Pandemonium Theater and is thus another good choice for afternoon.

Helpful Hint

Take your shoes and socks off while riding Popeye, and stow them in the central cargo hold. The bottom of the boat gets flooded during the ride and you don't want to spend the whole day with squishy shoes.

Marvel Super Hero Island

This is the land where superheroes battle supervillains—and theme park riders test their mettle. The following attractions are extremely intense and certainly not for young children or anyone who's just finished a big platter of green eggs and ham.

On most coasters you slowly climb the first hill, building up speed and courage; on the Incredible Hulk Coaster, you're propelled by a "cannon shot" and immediately flip over and go weightless. About two-thirds of the ride takes place over water, where you make seven different inversions at speeds of 40 miles per hour, and on two occasions you go into a subterranean trench filled with mist and fog.

> **Insider's Secret**
> Although the ride is wild, it's smooth, and some people who don't like to be jerked around swear that the Incredible Hulk Coaster is the most user-friendly coaster in the park.

Next door, Dr. Doom's Fearfall—the story is that Dr. Doom has created a machine that can suck the fear out of you, and he plans to use this accumulated fear to take over the world—shoots riders 180 feet into the air. They dangle for a few seconds, sitting in chairs with nothing under their feet, and then plunge. The first five seconds are the scariest part of the ride; if you survive the initial ascent, the remainder isn't too frightening.

These attractions aren't even the centerpiece of Marvel Super Hero Island. That distinction goes to the Amazing Adventures of Spider-Man, the most state-of-the-art ride at Islands of Adventure. Housed in a 1.5-acre set, Spider-Man combines actual ride movement with 3-D and motion simulation effects—ending in a simulated 400-foot drop. It's as if Universal took the most dramatic parts of Jaws, Back to the Future, and *Terminator 2: 3-D* and combined them into one powerful ride. Spider-Man is the sort of ride you can go on five times in a row and see something new every time.

Helpful Hint

The Amazing Adventures of Spider-Man gets my vote for the best attraction in Orlando. The special effects will convince you that you've battled su-pervillains, rescued the Statue of Liberty, and been lifted, thrown, and caught in Spider-Man's net. But the actual movements of the ride are relatively mild, meaning kids of all ages, older people, and even those with a fear of heights can ride.

The newest addition to Marvel Super Hero Island is Storm Force Accelatron, which is designed to give younger siblings something to do while the older kids tackle the major coasters. A spinning ride (imagine the Mad Tea Party), Storm Force Accelatron is a tribute to X-Men superheroine Storm.

Insider's Secret

Only use the Express Pass on the Amazing Adven-tures of Spider-Man if you've already ridden once and know the story. The Express Pass does speed things up, but it cuts you out of the preshow—which is not only amusing but also sets up the premise of the ride. If you never see the preshow, you'll spend the whole ride wondering, "Why are all those pieces of the Statue of Liberty lying around?"

Money-Saving Tip

AAA cardholders get 10 percent discounts at many full-service restaurants and shops in the park, which is especially nice if you're dining at an upscale place like Mythos. Look for the AAA sign as you enter.

Time-Saving Tip

You can cut down on lines at major Island of Adventures attractions in three ways:

- Use the Express system.
- Stay at a Universal Orlando resort. Guests get Express privileges even without the Express Pass.
- Be willing to split up. The single rider line moves much faster and this is a good option for older kids who like to ride the coasters over and over.

Tips for Your Last Hour at Islands of Adventure

As of this writing, Islands of Adventure has no big closing extravaganza. That, of course, is subject to change. Evening is a good time to revisit favorites, but if you plan to eat at CityWalk on your way out, leave before closing so you won't be caught in the glut of people who hit the gates when the park shuts down.

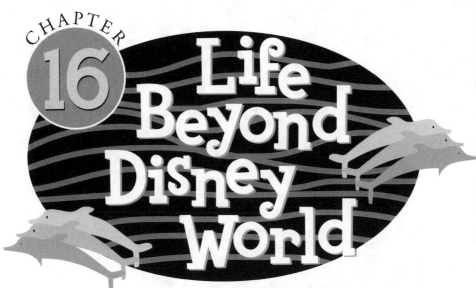

CHAPTER 16

Life Beyond Disney World

Sea World and Other Orlando Attractions

Sea World

Sea World is best known as the home of Shamu and the killer whales. Sea World is a low-stress experience, much less frenzied than the other Orlando parks. Easily seen in six or seven hours, it is laid out so that the crowds pretty much flow from one scheduled show to another, working in the smaller attractions on the way.

Sea World is so beautifully landscaped that you often can't see one stadium from the other, and the sense of space is a welcome change after a week spent at Disney. But the openness also means that children up to age 5 will benefit from a stroller.

Sea World admission is $51.95, $42.95 for ages 3 to 9, but numerous discount coupons can be found floating around Orlando, and the park is also included in the Flexpass plan. The park opens at 9 A.M. and can be comfortably toured in a single day. Call 407-351-3600 for more information. Online information can be found at www.shamu.com.

Journey to Atlantis

On the Journey to Atlantis, guests are transported back to the lost city of Atlantis, on an attraction that combines the excitement of a high-speed water ride and a coaster. Ride designers call this hybrid a water coaster, and it's a thrilling, splashy ride.

Riders board Greek fishing boats and are lured by sirens into the depths of the lost city. The tiny boats twist, dodge, and dive at near-highway speeds through the water. You will see the first drop, which comes out at the front of the building. But Allura pulls you back in for a second, unseen, 60-foot, S-shaped drop. The height requirement is 42 inches.

Kraken

Kraken is the fastest, tallest, and longest roller coaster in Orlando, and that's high praise in a town that takes its fun seriously.

Opened in 2000—which makes it a new attraction by theme park standards—Kraken reaches speeds of 65 mph, and has seven loops and three different points where it plunges underground into misty tunnels. We're talking major league thrills here. Needless to say, most kids under 8 should not ride. The height requirement is 54 inches.

When I first read about Kraken, I suspected the name referred to the sounds your back and neck made as you rode. Not so. The motion of Kraken is as smooth as silk. (The name actually refers to the great underwater dragon-monster of ancient Norse mythology.)

Shows

For years, Sea World's claim to fame has been its shows—especially those that feature the dolphins, the sea lions and otters, and the park icon, Shamu. Although the themes are regularly updated to keep the shows fresh, these three classics are funny, fascinating, and very worthwhile. See them if you do nothing else. All the shows take place in enormous open-air theaters, so touring Sea World is as simple as consulting your map for show times and being at the theater about 15 minutes early (30 minutes on a crowded day). Clever preshows make the wait not only bearable, but also fun.

Insider's Secret

Be forewarned that if you opt to sit in the "splash zone"—the first 10 rows of the stadium—Shamu's good-bye wave will leave you drenched straight through to your underwear. Kids enjoy the blast of saltwater, but if you're touring off-season or catching a nighttime show, it may be wiser to sit farther back and laugh at the unwary tourists down by the tank.

Other shows are updated on a rotating basis. There is generally a waterskiing show, an acrobatics show, and a Polynesian laser light show. Pets Ahoy! features the comic talents of a group of dogs, cats, potbelly pigs, and other animals that were rescued from animal shelters. Work these shows in as your schedule permits; they're well done but not as essential as the Sea World classics that feature dolphins, whales, and sea lions.

Standing Exhibits

Sea World is also known for its fascinating standing exhibits, such as the Penguin Encounter, where you can observe the tuxedoed charmers both above and below the ice floe—and witness their startling transformation from awkward walkers to sleek swimmers. Check your entertainment schedule for feeding time, when the trainers slip about on the iceberg with buckets of fish and the penguins waddle determinedly behind them. The birds ingest the fish in one amazing gulp, and you can stand on the top observation level and watch for as long as you like.

If your kids are too cool to like cute, try the Terrors of the Deep exhibit, where you'll encounter sharks, moray eels, and barracudas at close quarters.

The California sea lions are at the Pacific Point Preserve. In Key West at Sea World, you'll find Florida's own endangered species, the manatee, as well as sea turtles, dolphins, stingrays, and other species indigenous to the Florida Keys. There are also underwater viewing tanks where you can observe many of the animals up close. These continuous-viewing exhibits do not have special show times and can be visited at your leisure as you circle the park. It's especially fun to buy food and feed the animals.

At Wild Arctic, an exhibit dedicated to polar bears, you can opt to ascend to the top of the exhibit to view the bears either via a motion-simulation helicopter "ride" or by walking. (Kids must be 42 inches tall to take the motion-simulation ride.) The best animal viewing is in the underwater tanks. (*Note*: This attraction is a bit of a snooze in comparison to the Disney and Universal motion-simulation rides—if time is too short, opt to walk instead of ride. You'll see just as much.)

The Budweiser Clydesdales are also part of the Sea World family, and children thrill at the chance to meet these huge but gentle creatures. The nearby Anheuser-Busch Hospitality Center is a quiet, cool oasis from the rest of the park; beer samples are given out to adults, and the deli inside is never as crowded as other Sea World restaurants.

Preschoolers and Toddlers

Small children at Sea World welcome the numerous chances to get close to the beasties. My 4-year-old son loved feeding the harmless-looking but actually quite vicious seals and the vicious-looking but actually quite harmless stingrays. For $3 you can get three small fish and toss them to the seals, sea lions, or dolphins; the dolphins and stingrays are also in shallow tanks so that children can reach over and touch them as they glide by.

Insider's Secret

Running a hand along the flank of a dolphin or flinging a fish into the whiskered mouth of a furiously barking sea lion is a real kick for a young child, and the experience will probably stay with her long after the shows and tours have faded from memory. Don't spend so much time dashing from show to show that you forget to stop and savor the small moments of animal interaction.

Another kick for kids is Shamu's Happy Harbor, a play area that is not only happy but huge, with an elaborate web of climbing nets, a ship heavy-laden with water-firing muskets, a splashy climb-through area, a variety of ball pits to sink into, and padded pyramids to climb. After a few hours spent in shows and exhibits, stop by and just let the kids play for a while. There's a shaded area with seats below the climbing pits where parents can relax.

A separate play area for smaller kids ensures that they don't get tangled up in the webs, whacked by an older kid on a tire swing, or, worst of all, confused in the mazes and exit far from where Mom and Dad are waiting. Because several of the play areas involve water, some parents let kids wear their bathing suits under their shorts. It provides a nice in-park break on a summer day of touring. There's a midway and arcade next door, so older kids can hang out while the younger ones play.

Insider's Secret

If the opening bars of *Jaws* never fails to get your pulse rumbling, you may enjoy the Sharks Deep Dive program at Sea World. Guests 10 and up can participate in the two-hour program which begins with a presentation on basic shark info, including the "myths about these misunderstood animals." (In other words, sharks are our friends.) Then guests don wetsuits and either scuba dive or snorkel in a shark cage through a 125-foot long habitat with more than 50 sharks. The dive isn't too long and the sharks in question are indeed among the more harmless species, but it can still be a real thrill for preteens and teens.

The Sharks Deep Dive program costs $150 per person to scuba dive or $125 to snorkel and includes two-day park admission and a T-shirt. Call 800-406-2244 to reserve a spot in advance or visit the tour counter inside Sea World.

If all this is just a little too much excitement, you can still get a great view of the sharks by dining at the Sharks Underwater Grill, a new full-service restaurant located adjacent to the exhibit. You enter through an "underwater grotto" and are seated on the other side of a large see-through tank. The same 50 sharks, as well as colorful arrays of tropical fish, swim by while you dine on Florida/Caribbean specialties.

Educational Tours

If you're feeling guilty about taking the kids out of school, Sea World offers educational tours. (Quick—can you tell the difference between a sea lion and a seal?) Tours focusing on sharks,

Helpful Hint

Appropriately, the crowd at Sea World moves in waves. The shows are timed so that you can move around the park in a circular fashion, taking in one show after another.

This also means however that if you want to visit standing exhibits, feed the animals, or play in Shamu's Happy Harbor, some times are far more crowded than other. For example, Shamu's Happy Harbor is virtually empty while the nearby Shamu show is going on, but the minute the show is over a flood of people stream out and head for the playground.

The moral? If you have young kids and would like to be able to play or interact with the animals in a calm, unrushed manner, make note of when the shows are in session and visit the standing exhibits then.

polar bears, and Sea World's animal rescue and rehabilitation programs are available. They're reasonably priced ($10 for adults, $9 for kids), and reservations are not necessary. There's a well-marked booth where you can buy your tickets on your way into the park. Kids 13 and up can become a "Trainer for a Day" and actually swim with the animals. The cost is $389 but the child gets lots of extra attention.

Camp Sea World

Sea World offers a variety of camps ranging from one-day classes to weeklong adventure camps. For information on all your options, call 800-406-2244 to order brochures or visit the Web page at www.seaworld.org.

Helpful Hint

Camp Sea World activities are popular, so advance reservations are a must. The wonderful brochure not only outlines the available classes for every age group but also gets you so fired up that you want to register for everything.

Discovery Cove

Discovery Cove, which opened adjacent to Sea World in 2000, is the only park that offers its guests a chance to actually have up-close encounters with dolphins and other sea life. Visitors swim and play with bottlenose dolphins, then snorkel through clouds of fish in a coral reef lagoon. Or just enjoy the tropical island ambience of beach chairs, hammocks, swaying palm trees, cooing birds, and hardly any people.

That's right. The most unique thing about Discovery Cove is what it doesn't have. Crowds. This is a reservation-only park that admits a limited number of people per day (1,000 to be exact), but everyone is so spread out that it seems like you have a private beach. With such a low number of guests, you truly have personal attention from the staff, which includes expert trainers (many drafted from Sea World, Discovery Cove's sister park).

Guests check in at a concierge desk (!) and from there a guide takes them on a walking tour of the park, explaining all the activities. A swim in the dolphin lagoon is the undeniable highlight of the day, but reserved for guests 6 and older. The trainers are on hand to teach you all about dolphin behaviors, and the setting can't be beat. Guests are taken into the water in groups of eight, so you have plenty of one-on-one interaction with the dolphin and the chance to hold on to his dorsal fin and take a wild ride across the bay.

The saltwater coral lagoon offers a variety of experiences, including the chance to snorkel among brightly colored fish. (Since the water is calm, clear, and warm and the fish are held captive in the pool, this is a great first snorkeling experience for young kids. They're bound to see something.) In the ray lagoon, you can play with the debarbed stingrays, which grow up to four feet in diameter. Or you can swim among barracuda and sharks housed behind Plexiglas, coming within inches of the predators with no danger.

The freshwater tropical river meanders its way through the park, passing beaches and lagoons. River swimmers pass through several different environments, ranging from a tropical fishing village to an underwater cave. Pass beneath a waterfall, and you'll find yourself inside an immense aviary that houses 300 colorful birds from all over the world.

Helpful Hint
Bring beach shoes. The pools are quite rocky.

When you've experienced all the activities, there's no better way to end the day than by snoozing in your hammock on a white-sand beach. It's honestly hard to remember that you're in Orlando.

So what do you pay for this bliss? $199 per person plus tax. If you're willing to forgo the swim with the dolphins, the price is $109, but you'll be missing a major thrill. (Since kids under 6 aren't allowed to participate in the dolphin swim, the price is automatically $109 for them.) The price covers wetsuits, beach umbrellas, lounges, towels, locker, swim and snorkel gear, and lunch. The price also includes admission to Sea World next door. For details and reservations (remember, they're a must), call 877-4-DISCOVERY, or check out www.discoverycove.com.

Gatorland

Gatorland, surely the most Floridian of all the Florida theme parks, is best known for its Gator Jumparoo, where the beasties jump up to five feet out of the water to retrieve chickens from the hands of their trainers. *The Gator Wrestlin' Show, Jungle Crocs of the World*, and *Snakes of Florida* are also hits with kids.

This campy little place, which you enter through a giant blue gator mouth, also has a small zoo, a kids' interactive area, a water playground, and a train ride. The park can be easily toured in three or four hours. Children might like a souvenir photo of them holding either an alligator or a boa constrictor. And although Sea World certainly doesn't serve dolphin, Gatorland suffers no qualms about biting the hand that feeds it. You can pick up a few cans of Gator Chowder at the gift shop— surely a unique thank-you gift for the neighbors back home who are watering the plants while you're away.

Gatorland admission is $17.93, $8.48 for ages 3 to 12; one child under 3 is free with each paying adult. Call 800-393-JAWS or 407-855-5496, or visit the Web site, www.gatorland.com.

Wet 'n Wild

The atmosphere doesn't stack up to the Huck Finn feel of River Country or the tropical splendor of Typhoon Lagoon, but for families staying off site, Wet 'n Wild is a great place to cool off without getting back into the mouse race.

The Fuji Flyer toboggan ride, the twisting tubes of the Mach 5, and a spiraling descent through the Black Hole are not for the faint of heart. Wet 'n Wild's wildest attraction, the Bomb Bay, sends riders on a six-second free-fall down a 76-foot slide and is, like many of the other big-deal attractions, strictly off limits to children shorter than 48 inches. These rides are enough to knock the breath out of even a strong swimmer; some kids who make the height requirements still aren't up to the intensity of the attractions, so if you have doubts, steer your 8-year-old toward the smaller slides and flumes.

Small children and others who are chickens of the sea can slide along in a Bubba Tub or float down the Lazy River in a big rubber tube. Wet 'n Wild also offers a $1.5-million children's water playground, billed as a "safe, fun environment for kids 1 to 10." Preschoolers and unsteady swimmers have their own wave pool, a miniature raging rapids, and fiberglass flumes designed for riders under 48 inches tall. It's perfect for families whose children range in ages and who need a place that can be both Wet 'n Wild and Wet 'n Mild.

Admission is $32.81, $26.45 for ages 3 to 9. Discounts, which often cut admission price in half, take effect at 3 P.M. during the off-season and 5 P.M. in summer, when the park stays open until 11 P.M. Crowds become far more manageable as the sun goes down, and summer evenings offer live entertainment, poolside karaoke, and the laid-back party atmosphere of a beach club. Or consider the Flexpass, which lets you take in Universal Orlando, Sea World, and Wet 'n Wild. Wet 'n Wild is located on International Drive, which is Exit 74A off Interstate 4. Call 800-992-WILD or 407-351-WILD for details.

Index